Women's Rights and Women's Lives in France 1944–1968

Women's Rights and Women's Lives in France 1944–1968 explores key aspects of the everyday lives of women between the Liberation of France and the events of May '68. At the end of the war, French women believed that a new era was beginning and that equality had been won. The redefined postwar public sphere required women's participation for the new democracy, and women's labour power for reconstruction, but equally important was the belief in women's role as mothers. Over the next two decades, the tensions between competing visions of women's 'proper place' dominated discourses of womanhood as well as policy decisions, and had concrete implication for women's lives. Working from a wide range of sources, including women's magazines, prescriptive literature, documentation from political parties, government reports, parliamentary debates and personal memoirs, Claire Duchen follows the debates concerning womanhood, women's rights and women's lives through the 1944–68 period and grounds them in the changing social reality of postwar France.

Claire Duchen is Senior Lecturer in French at the University of Sussex. She has also taught at the University of Bath and at Oxford Brookes University. She is the author of *Feminism in France from May '68 to Mitterrand* and editor of *French Connections: Voices from the Women's Movement in France*.

Women's Rights and Women's Lives in France 1944–1968

Claire Duchen

London and New York

First published 1994
by Routledge
11 New Fetter Lane, London EC4P 4EE

Simultaneously published in the USA and Canada
by Routledge
29 West 35th Street, New York, NY 10001

© 1994 Claire Duchen

Phototypeset in Times by
Intype, London

Printed and bound in Great Britain by
T. J. Press (Padstow) Ltd, Padstow, Cornwall

British Library Cataloguing in Publication Data

A catalogue record for this book is available from the British Library

Library of Congress Cataloging in Publication Data

Duchen, Claire.
    Women's rights and women's lives in France, 1944–1968/Claire Duchen.
    p.   cm.
    Includes bibliographical references and index.
    1. Women–France–Social conditions. 2. Women's rights–France–History.
    3. France–History–1945 I. Title.
    HQ1613.D82   1994
    305.42′0944–dc20   93–30843

ISBN 0–415–00933–2 (hbk)
ISBN 0–415–00934–0 (pbk)

*To my father Leo
and the memory of my mother Myra*

Contents

Acknowledgements

I have had financial assistance from a number of sources. I am grateful for the small personal grants from the British Academy in 1986 and 1990, supplemented by grants from the Staff Research Fund at Oxford Polytechnic in 1986 and 1988 which allowed me to spend summers researching in Paris. A sabbatical term from Oxford Polytechnic in 1988 allowed me to stay in Paris for five months and a further sabbatical term from the University of Bath in 1990 let me stay at home to write. I owe particular thanks to Tony Harding and Mark Bannister at Oxford Polytechnic and Jolyon Howorth and the School Research Committee at Bath University for their support.

For personal and intellectual support, I wish first to thank Siân Reynolds (without whom . . .), Mariette Sineau, Christine Zmroczek and the Explorations in Feminism collective. I would not have been able to spend time in Paris without the help of (and apartments provided by) Rosi Braidotti, Martine Menès, and Laura Frader; the time spent there would have been less fun without Elizabeth Fallaize, Janet Horne, Judith Miller and Kate Turley.

In 1988 I interviewed women, active in the 1950s and 1960s, who gave generously of their time and experience. I would particularly like to thank Colette Audry, Benoîte Groult, Simone Iff, Marcelle Kraemer-Bach, Yolande Léautey, Michelle Perrot and Marie-Andrée Lagroua Weill-Hallé. I regret that my thanks to Colette Audry and Marcelle Kraemer-Bach can no longer be given in person. On this side of the Channel, I would like to thank Claire L'Enfant at Routledge for her infinite patience and her sound editorial advice, and Jill O'Brien at the University of Bath. I must finally thank Ben Mandelson and my family for their support.

Earlier drafts of parts of chapters 1–3 have been published as follows:

'1944–1946: Women's Liberation?' in *Women in 20th Century French History and Culture. Papers in Memory of Andrea Cady.* D. Berry and A. Hargreaves (eds). European Research Centre, Loughborough University, 1993.

Women and Politics in France 1944–1958. Studies in European Culture and Society. European Research Centre, Loughborough University, 1991.

'Occupation housewife: the domestic ideal in 1950s France' in *French Cultural Studies* Vol. II, No. 1, 1991.

The author and publishers would like to thank Loughborough University and Alpha Academic for permission to reproduce this material.

Acronyms used in the text

Political parties and organisations

FGDS	Fédération de la Gauche Démocrate et Socialiste (Federation of the Democratic and Socialist Left – non-Communist Left)
MRP	Mouvement Républicain Populaire (Popular Republican Movement – Christian Democrat)
PCF	Parti Communiste Français (Communist Party)
PRL	Parti Républicain de la Liberté (Republican Party of Liberty – conservative)
RGR	Rassemblement des Gauches Républicaines (Rally of the Republican Left – centrist)
RPF	Rassemblement du Peuple Français (Rally of the French People – Gaullist)
SFIO	Section Française de l'Internationale Ouvrière (French Section of the International Socialist movement – Socialist Party)
CDL	Comités Départementaux de Libération (Departmental Liberation Committees – local committees set up to oversee the passage from Occupation to peace)
CNR	Conseil National de la Résistance (National Resistance Council – council which drew up plans for organising the French state after the war)

Trade Union Confederations

CGT	Confédération Générale du Travail (General Confederation of Labour – Communist)
CFTC	Confédération Française des Travailleurs Chrétiens (French Confederation of Christian Workers)

CGT-FO	Known as Force Ouvrière (Workers' Strength – movement that broke from the CGT in 1948)
CFDT	Confédération Française Démocratique du Travail (Democratic French Confederation of Labour – born out of the CTFC in 1964)

Women's organisations

MDF	Mouvement Démocratique Féminin (Democratic Women's Movement – associated with non-Communist Left)
MFPF	Mouvement Français pour le Planning Familial (French Family Planning Movement)
MLF	Mouvement de Libération des Femmes (Women's Liberation Movement)
UFCS	Union Féminine Civique et Sociale (Women's Civic and Social Union – Catholic, conservative women's organisation)
UFF	Union des Femmes Françaises (Union of French Women – Communist-dominated women's organisation)

Other acronyms

CAF	Caisses d'Allocations Familiales (Family Allowance Fund) – CAF refers to both the fund and the dispensing body, or offices, and
UNCAF	Union Nationale des Caisses d'Allocation Familiales (National Union of Family Allowance Benefit Offices)
UNAF	Union Nationale des Associations Familiales (National Union of Family Associations – a conservative family lobby)
TF	Travailleuse Familiale (home help)
JACF	Jeunesse Agricole Catholique Féminine (Women's section of the Young Catholic Farmers Movement)
JOCF	Jeunesse Ouvrière Catholique Féminine (Women's section of the Young Catholic Workers' Movement)
ENA	Ecole Nationale d'Administration (National Administration School)
IFOP	Institut Français de l'Opinion Publique (French Institute of Public Opinion)

INED   Institut National des Etudes Démographiques (National Institute of Demographic Studies)

INSEE   Institut National de la Statistique et des Etudes Economiques (National Institute of Statistics and Economic Studies)

Introduction

This book traces the experience of women in France from the end of the Second World War to the events of May '68. Women are remarkably absent from historical accounts of the Fourth Republic (1946–58) and even from accounts of the early years of the Fifth, founded in 1958. The general histories dealing with the postwar period concentrate on the international issues that dominated French political life (wars of decolonisation, the Cold War, the construction of Europe); on postwar reconstruction and the economic modernisation of the 'Thirty glorious years';[1] on the unstable political system of the Fourth Republic; and on de Gaulle and the Gaullist Fifth Republic. Women's lives remained essentially off-stage, both because they were excluded from power and because commentators, analysts and historians simply did not notice gender or think it was important as a social category.

The primary aim of this book is thus to produce an account of those years that puts women onto the map of postwar France, that seeks to discover the nature of the debates directly concerning women that were current, and that explores the terms in which the debates were framed and grounds them in the social reality of the time.

At the beginning of this project, my question seemed straight-forward: where were the women? In the kitchen, seemed to be the answer. The few famous female faces were either those who incarnated the triumph of (royal) domesticity (Grace Kelly after her marriage) or who flouted it and shocked by their transgressions (Simone de Beauvoir, Brigitte Bardot, Françoise Sagan). The decade of the 1950s has been described to me as dominated less by political instability and wars of decolonisation than by Moulinex and the baby boom. Reluctant to believe this, I wanted to find out 'what really happened'.

A number of questions and issues run through an exploration of what it meant to be a woman in France during the 1944–68 period: how did the experience of war affect women's postwar lives? What did the French political world envisage for women? What impact did the welfare state have on the domestic sphere? What were the ideals of femininity promoted at the time? What was the relation between discourses of womanhood and women's lives? What changed for women during the twenty-four years under discussion? And who (or what) was responsible for these changes?

There is particular emphasis in the book on the earliest postwar years, a time when everything seemed possible and indeed real change *was* possible. The tremendous hopes of 1944–5, women's belief that the law would ensure that they would become equal citizens, equal partners at work and even (maybe) at home, were gradually disappointed. I wanted to follow through the expectations of the earliest years and understand how and why the new Republic failed in its theoretical commitments to women.

At the end of the war, the future of France was mapped out, a new democracy designed, a new economy planned and a new society imagined. The redefined postwar public sphere required women's participation for the new democracy, and women's labour power for reconstruction. It was considered equally imperative that women's contribution to production should be reproduction. A certain ambiguity was inscribed in the new Constitution which did not differentiate between men and women in some clauses (those proclaiming equal political rights, equal rights at work), but did in others (those concerned with the family and motherhood).[2] Women were thus addressed as an aggregate of roles and functions – mother, worker, citizen – as if these roles were distinct entities with no connection to each other.[3] The connections were of course many and complex, and the ambiguity of the Constitution had concrete implications for women's lives. The equal rights clauses remained largely paper statements; the meanings wrapped up in the word 'mother' or 'worker' sometimes conflicted; the image of woman-as-mother had a powerful impact on the insertion of women into public life.

In the earliest postwar years, motherhood (in the context of the profound inequality between the sexes in the family sanctioned by the Civil Code) was considered to be the key issue concerning women, in the eyes of the state. At a time when labour power and reproductive power were both in demand, ways to reconcile domestic and professional obligations were not sought. The French government concentrated on encouraging women to be mothers and did little to entice them into the labour market. The postwar ideal of femininity revolved around the home, which was heavily promoted as the place where women could be happy and fulfilled. Housewifery was said to be a science, an art, a profession as worthy as any other; motherhood was the crowning achievement of a woman's career, her 'métier de femme'.

I chose to concentrate on 1944–68 for two main reasons. First, the women I interviewed for this book remember their lives as being 'traditional' in the 1950s and 1960s, and describe those decades as a time in which 'nothing happened'. Bounded by the disruptions of war on one side and social upheaval on the other, the intervening years easily appear uneventful. Advances in women's rights legislation, the birth of the women's liberation movement, rapid changes in employment patterns and lifestyle were features of the 1970s rather than of the 1950s and 1960s. A chronology of legislative changes directly concerning women shows a gap between the 1946 decree on equal pay for equal work and the 1965 reform of the marriage law. I wanted most particularly to look at a period during which it is commonly said that 'nothing happened'. I ask: what, exactly, is it that happens, when 'nothing happens'?

The second reason was linked to the fact that it was a period during which it is said that there was no feminism. One of the main aims of the book is precisely to locate feminism in France between these dates. My own previous work concentrated on the post-'68 women's liberation movement (Mouvement de Libération des Femmes, MLF),[4] taking May '68 as its starting point. But starting points are always, in a sense, false beginnings, and I wanted to see how the terrain for post-'68 feminism had been prepared by the women who had gone before and who had been forgotten by the women who proclaimed in 1970 that it was 'libération des femmes: année zéro' (women's liberation: the beginning').[5]

It quickly became clear that the apparently silent decade of the 1950s was by no means a period of inactivity, of quiescence, of acceptance of the state's version of womanhood. During the 1950s, there certainly were organisations and groups and individuals discussing women's rights, analysing women's 'condition', and campaigning around specific issues. Throughout the postwar decades, the Ligue Française pour le Droit des Femmes (League of Women's Rights) monitored equal rights practice and the lack of it, pointing out discrimination and protesting, urging women to action. From the mid-1950s, a movement in favour of legalising contraception provided the spearhead of progressive thinking about women's lives; from the mid-1950s onwards, women politicians attempted to force revision of the Civil Code onto the political agenda. There were women's sections in political parties and trade unions, discussion groups, women's professional associations, groups of women graduates, groups of progressive educators. There was *Le deuxième sexe* by Simone de Beauvoir. However, this did not add up to a groundswell of opposition to the ideal of domesticity: issues of women's rights, analyses of women's 'condition', remained disparate discourses – they were not posited as a general challenge to women's oppression, and they addressed very specific audiences, who either did not know of each other or who disagreed over the most basic questions.

The 1960s are represented as years when women won new freedoms and this was clearly true (although credit for them was usually taken by someone else). In the 1960s, discussion of women's rights issues shifted ground, became more public. Reform of the law on contraception was taken up by François Mitterrand in his 1965 presidential campaign; family planning clinics were opening up throughout France in spite of the fact that contraception was not yet legalised; books were appearing which spoke of the changing role of women; Betty Friedan's *The Feminine Mystique* was translated; in July 1965, the marriage laws were reformed, altering women's status within the family; in 1967, the Loi Neuwirth finally reformed the 1920 law on contraception.

By the mid-1960s, too, the government 'pronatalism' (policy of encouraging a rising birthrate) of the immediate postwar decade had faltered, the family lobby had lost its pre-eminence, and the vision of the happy housewife-mother of three clearly did not correspond to the reality of women's lives. The birth rate had begun to drop; married women and mothers were staying at work or returning to paid employment with only a short period out for childcare. Increased levels of education had led to different expectations, and by the mid-1960s the impact of women's altering position in the labour market was finally felt in the domestic sphere. The ideal of the woman at home, 'la femme au foyer', was increasingly out of step with reality and, at least in the press, underwent a gradual transformation: from the mother at home always at the disposal of her children, the ideal woman became superwoman, able to juggle responsibilities inside and outside the home and offering her child quality time – a concept usually associated with more recent decades but already to be found in the 1960s. Housewifery was no longer proposed as a profession as worthy as any other. The home and family constituted part of a woman's life, but were no longer expected to provide her ultimate fulfilment.

The closing section of the book looks at May '68 and asks how to locate the events of May in the postwar history of women's rights and feminism in France. All the women I interviewed during my research, active in women's rights campaigns before 1968, perceived May '68 as the moment when consciousness was raised; many of them participated or at least sympathised with the students. But the women of pre-May women's rights campaigns were not the May activists. Indeed, May marked a youth-led rejection of what the activists perceived as the bourgeois capitalist Gaullist technocratic consumerist state – everything to which the postwar French world aspired, and of which most of the pre-'68 women's rights activists wanted to be a part.

May '68 was a double-edged experience for the women participants, and their experience of alternative left-wing groups was not entirely positive. Following May '68, women activists decided instead to abandon their mixed groups, create their own agenda and fight their own revolution, developing a style, a practice and an analysis that drew on the May Movement as well as on previous struggles, but that was completely their own.

When looking at women's experience during the twenty-four years between the end of the war and May '68, a profound ambiguity is evident, surrounding women's relation to the state, to the labour market, to the family – an ambiguity provided by the tensions contained within competing notions of women's place, women's role, women's destiny. Discourses on womanhood each participated in contexts with a purpose that only incidentally included women: they fitted a Communist, Catholic, or Republican political agenda; they addressed women as voters, readers, consumers or producers; they were concerned with family, health, education or demography. The discourses were not always connected to what women wanted, or to what they did, but this did not reduce their impact on women's lives.

I have worked mainly from written sources to try to build a picture of women's lives and debates on womanhood in France between 1944 and 1968. None of the sources can be left unquestioned: statistics conflict, and hide as much as they reveal; empirical studies carried out on different aspects of women's lives (time-budget studies, attitudinal surveys), asked value-laden questions, used small samples and sometimes drew unconvincing conclusions.[6]

Each type of source – party political publications and other organisational material, prescriptive literature, women's magazines, autobiographies and memoirs, government statistics, sociological studies and political science commentary – has its own imagined audience, its own objectives. Newspapers will focus on the apparently newsworthy or the quirky: women's suffrage is unexciting, but a picture of nuns going to vote is worth printing. Women's magazines avoid subjects which cause conflict, thereby skilfully avoiding mention of the outside world as far as possible and creating a cosy picture of female complicity based on household concerns. Women writing their memoirs recreate their own lives in their own way. Party political publications will show the party line, but will not necessarily tell us about the attitudes and behaviour of the rank and file. Confronted with these interpretative problems, I have had to revise my notions about the intention of the historical project, abandon the (maybe naive but nonetheless compelling) search for 'what really happened', accept conjecture and contradiction, the multiplicity of narratives and truths.

No book can aspire to provide a comprehensive picture of women's experience throughout France, in all social classes and in all professional and domestic situations. Nor can 'women' simply be treated as a homogeneous group. I have had to select issues: some have been touched on only slightly, others have reluctantly been left out. This is an introductory work, which hopes to open areas for further research.[7] Working out the relative or actual significance of any part of it has not been easy, and any errors of fact or interpretation are my sole responsibility.

1 Liberation

> We were liberated. In the streets, children sang, 'We won't see them again, it's all over, they're finished.' And I said to myself again and again: it's all over, it's all over. . . . Day and night, with our friends, talking, drinking, strolling, laughing, we celebrated our deliverance.[1]

The liberation of France began with the Allied landings in June 1944 and continued for many months. Indeed, it is impossible to say exactly when it ended, for 'Liberation' meant many different things: the military operations of the Allied forces which signalled the end of the German occupation of France; the end of the war in Europe and in the world; the return of prisoners of war, deportees and others who had been absent from France, and their reintegration into French society; the re-establishment of a democratic form of government, marking the end of the Vichy régime (the 'état français') and the end of the provisional government of General de Gaulle. The years of the Liberation could therefore be said to have lasted until the beginning of 1947, when the new Fourth Republic was finally in place.

The military liberation of Paris was accomplished in August 1944. War correspondent Catherine Gavin wrote that the earliest signs of the approaching liberation – the 'unobtrusive movements of troops and trucks which started the German retreat from Paris' – were first seen by housewives, queuing for bread in the early morning.[2] By late August, in spite of the continued presence of snipers, the streets of Paris were full of excitement and joy. A young boy recorded the day of 25 August 1944 in his diary:

> Arm in arm, we walked towards the Place de la Nation, along with hundreds of other people. The atmosphere was extraordinary!

People sang, called out to each other, laughed, kissed each other! A huge people's celebration was going on around us when we got to the St Antoine area. A crowd of cyclists was heading for the Bastille and it was quite a spectacle to see all those girls, their skirts flying in the wind, pedalling and singing, escorted by groups of young men running alongside them.... Near the Pont de Sully, an accordion player outside a café was playing popular tunes, and several couples danced on the pavement, in an impromptu party.[3]

In her book on the liberation of Paris, historian and journalist Edith Thomas described the excitement that followed the news. Thomas wrote: 'At the Arc de Triomphe, people have placed red, white and blue flowers on the tomb of the Unknown Soldier. It is completely hidden by flowers, but there are still more coming: red, white and blue, red, white and blue.'[4]

The American historian Willis Thornton wrote:

Paris was exuberant and rejoicing. The lights were on despite blackout regulations ... accordion and gramophone music wafted along the summer night air, and from street corners arose from time to time the *Marseillaise*. Some tried to dance in the streets despite the broken glass, and there were reunions by the thousand. [5]

Emotional reunions sometimes took place very publicly: in the diary kept with her sister Benoîte, novelist Flora Groult wrote:

I witnessed a scene which brought tears to my eyes: a young boy on one of [General] Leclerc's tanks suddenly saw his father at the end of the street and cried out to the watching crowd in a hoarse voice: 'It's my father.' They rushed towards each other with the awkward, moving gestures of those who haven't seen each other for a very long time and who put all their tenderness and their emotion in the first touch.[6]

Women greeted the liberators enthusiastically and patriotically: 'Parisian women had put all their good taste and ingenuity into using the three colours: red jacket, blue skirt, white flowers; blue suit, white handbag, red shoes; red belt on a white and blue dress.'[7]

Catherine Gavin pointed out how the gaiety of the surface covered continued shortages:

Their [the girls'] sun-tanned legs were bare, for it was still warm, and they wore sandals with wooden platform soles and short, very full skirts; their hair was dressed *à la pompadour* above their laughing painted faces. . . . Male eyes, justifiably charmed by the Parisiennes, failed to see that the pretty bright dresses would turn to blotting paper under a shower of rain, that the slim heels wore sticking-plaster where the springless shoes had chafed, that the perfumed hair was lustreless because of the long shortage of fats. Only beauty and gaiety were described in the first reports from liberated Paris.[8]

Accounts of the Liberation, whether historical, fictional or personal, emphasise the presence of American soldiers. They brought chocolate, nylons and chewing-gum, and also brought some frivolity and fun to France after four years of deprivation. It was considered legitimate to go out with American soldiers, in obvious contrast to the years of Occupation when, as Hanna Diamond says, for young women who wanted to have a good time, 'having fun meant spending time with the Germans'.[9] Simone de Beauvoir wrote of the American soldiers:

> they strolled along casually, and often looked drunk; they sang and whistled as they rolled unsteadily along the pavements and on the metro platforms; they stumbled as they danced in bars and their roars of laughter revealed their teeth white as children's. . . . For me, the casual comings and goings of the Americans incarnated freedom.[10]

Benoîte Groult, in her autobiographical novel *Les trois-quarts du temps*, also evoked the atmosphere of the Liberation days. Her heroine Louise, a former English teacher, signs up at the French–Allied reception centre as a volunteer interpreter. Her role is to escort such American, Canadian or Australian liberators as were interested to museums and national monuments – to introduce them to French culture. The girls who sign up want, above all, to eat:

> [All the restaurants] offered the same treasures to hungry bellies: as much concentrated milk as you could drink, steaks that were worth twenty food coupons, pastries as heavy as the Taj-Mahal, dripping with cream, and other goods that had existed only as fantasy for five years. . . . The hostesses viewed the Americans with their eyes in their stomachs. Each soldier, however ugly, was worth his weight in chocolate, protein, glucose, and like Pavlov's dogs, each girl began to salivate at the sight of a uniform.[11]

The Groult sisters had themselves been cultural escorts to American and Canadian soldiers around Paris, speaking fluent English as they did. Writing about how well they were eating, Benoîte said that her mother was 'ready to write a "thank you" note to President Roosevelt, because the arrival of his troops meant that I put on 5 kilos in weight'.[12]

Appetite for food was matched by appetite for sex. Groult wrote that, somehow, the usual rules did not apply in those days and young middle-class women who would never usually dream of such behaviour found it completely normal to sleep with American soldiers:

> But Americans weren't men, they were liberators! She [Louise] would have found it indecent to make love so quickly with a Frenchman. But Americans weren't Frenchmen, they were fighters who had to be rewarded for coming to our land, so far from home, to a possible death.[13]

In the unusually relaxed and tolerant atmosphere of the Liberation days, Americans were taken home by young French women for a bath or a meal. They were welcomed and in turn were generous, offering gifts of soap or bacon, often unaware that these items had become luxuries for the families who had taken them in. Flora Groult, this time, wrote:

> This afternoon, I was visiting Mother and I looked out of the window: I caught sight of a lovely-looking American, as if I'd designed him myself, with short blond hair and forget-me-not blue eyes. He was trying to make himself understood by a group of French people who didn't speak English. Moved by a sense of duty (hmm ...) I went down to help him. Mamma mia! He was so handsome! ... He was looking for a place to eat, so I invited him to dinner.... We sat down to eat and, without thinking, he ate one of our last eggs. Could he have guessed ... that we only had four left? ... After dinner we accompanied 'our' American back in his jeep. Wonderful to be in a jeep. He will come back to see us: he promised. He was so handsome, my first liberator![14]

The euphoria and frivolity of the Parisian Liberation, while a welcome relief, did not last long: the rest of France was not freed at the same time, and areas through which the German retreat took place could not yet celebrate. Added to this was the fact that the Allied landings caused an unforeseen amount of damage, more in some places than had resulted from the German invasion: the speed with which France had fallen in June 1940 meant that there had not been German bombing on a massive scale. Four years of Occupation with the French economy completely geared towards the German war effort, plus the damage caused by the Liberation and the German retreat, had left France in ruins.

France was devastated. In 1944, agricultural production was, on average, under half of its 1938 level,[15] affected by the continued absence of about 500,000 young agricultural workers still prisoner in Germany, by the lack of fertiliser and the non-replacement of essential machinery.[16] Industrial production had also suffered, with raw materials lacking and, in particular, coal shortages creating dreadful hardship over the winter of 1944–5, when for the first time since the beginning of the war 'non-priority' consumers in Paris received no coal ration at all.[17] Furthermore, in 1944, roughly two million Frenchmen and women were still in Germany, either as prisoners of war, as political or racial deportees, as volunteer workers or through the forced labour scheme (Service de Travail Obligatoire, STO) or having joined or been forced into the German army, the Wehrmacht or the Waffen SS.[18] Overwhelming tasks faced the new government in every sphere of public life, from providing France with a new political framework and rebuilding the industrial and agricultural infrastructure to dealing with the immediate human problems of the day which mostly concerned provision of food, fighting the black market, finding housing for the homeless, and organising the return of prisoners of war and deportees.

What were these years of Liberation like for women? During the Occupation, women had been as implicated as men in both Resistance and collaboration;[19] households had been disrupted and women had shouldered new responsibilities; lives had been disturbed, perhaps irrevocably. Women had been imprisoned, deported, shot, like men. Like men, women had sought simply to survive.

War is often represented as disorder and disruption of gender roles.[20] Absent men are replaced in the labour market by women; women make financial decisions, become *de facto* heads of household (even if this is not acknowledged by the state). Women gain independence, whether they want to or not. During the Occupation, the distinction between the private and domestic world of women and the public world of men had been broken down both by the activities of women in public life and by the intrusion of politics into the home: the domestic had been politicised by the Occupation as, for instance, the act of cooking became subversive if the meal was for a member of the Resistance.[21] The domestic had also become a more public affair: queuing, scavenging for firewood or for water, sharing the scarce cooking facilities and the limited food. Activities that usually took place in the privacy of the home now took place out in the open. The home itself had sometimes been transformed into a hybrid community, no longer composed of a single family unit, but of people thrown together out of necessity.

Peacetime implies a return to order, which in turn implies a return to habitual modes of gendered behaviour, considered to be both timeless and natural. For women, this means a return to perceptions of their role as based primarily in the home, as housewife and mother. Yet the Liberation was not quite peacetime and life was certainly not 'normal'. French women, like women elsewhere, welcomed these aspects of the return to peace with mixed feelings; the re-establishment of homes and lives was as difficult for women as it was for men, and a return to a previous life, desired or not, was not always possible.

THE PURGES

At the Liberation, both men and women were called to account for their wartime behaviour, and their actions were either applauded or punished. Liberation mythology has tended to simplify the immediate past and divide the French population into good and evil, Resisters and collaborators. Recent research has begun to uncover the myths and unravel the complexities of behaviour during the war years and at the Liberation, from the perspective of women's lives.[22] As far as the Resistance was concerned, there were some heroines: the (dead) Communist Danielle Casanova was practically canonised, and the name of Berthy Albrecht was as well known as that of Jean Moulin. On the whole, however, women's participation in the Resistance was understated and undervalued if it was acknowledged at all. A blatant example of this was the awarding of the prestigious Croix de la Libération to 1,030 men, five towns, eighteen combat units and six women (four of these being posthumous awards).[23] Women seemed to accept that they played a less obviously dangerous and combative role, which was therefore perceived as less important in the Resistance than the more 'heroic' role of men. Many women did not see their Resistance activities as 'political' and neither sought nor expected any attention to be paid to them. Marie-Madeleine Fourcade, the only woman leader of a Resistance network, was horrified to discover that at the end of the war no provision was made for wives of former Resisters. She described widows living in huts, living on scraps of food and handouts, helped only by the charitable organisations set up to help deportees and Resisters. She fought for these women to be granted a specific status which would mean that they could receive pensions. Interestingly enough, Fourcade states that these women 'had taken the same risks, shared Resistance work with their men' but even she does not suggest that they should be considered as Resisters in the same way as the men.[24]

In the immediate postwar years, when many male Resisters wrote their memoirs, women were reticent, and it is only recently that they have begun to speak about themselves and to claim due recognition.

Women collaborators received more immediate attention. A purge of Vichy or Nazi collaborators was one of the first and most urgent tasks of the new France, for both symbolic and political reasons. Exact figures of those who were on the receiving end of different punishments are difficult to establish. It is now generally agreed among historians of the purges that roughly 10,000 French people were executed, of whom 9,000 were victims of execution without trial.[25] Numbers of those imprisoned were far higher and even more suffered the punishment of 'dégradation nationale' (national degradation) or 'indignité nationale' (national un-worthiness), which could mean a range of measures, including depri-vation of civil rights.[26]

Local case studies requiring meticulous research are now making it possible to piece together the actions of courts set up in different areas to try collaborators. One such study, of the court at Orléans, puts the male/female ratio of those accused of collaboration at 60/40.[27] Among the women whose cases were heard by this court were Germans and a Belgian as well as Frenchwomen. Most of them were housewives (although translators and office workers who worked for the Germans in Orléans seemed to figure prominently) and most of them (55 per cent) were arrested for having denounced Resisters, Jews, boys hiding from the STO in Germany, or members of the banned Parti Communiste Français (PCF, French Communist Party). Women were sometimes arrested because of the activities of their husband and not because of any suspected collaboration of their own. The motive for denunciation was thought to be more often personal vengeance than any sense of patriotic duty.

Myths of a vengeful 'bloodbath' at the Liberation were rife and accounts of the purges that took place stress the 'sex and sadism' of the revenge: both Robert Aron and Herbert Lottman tell popular but unverified horror stories, as of the father who was forced to watch the rape of his virgin daughter, or the women who had their breasts sliced off.[28] While these particular stories may be apocryphal, there is no doubt that Resisters were not always the morally impeccable heroes and heroines of Resistance mythology. It is also quite certain that women collaborators were subject, like men, to imprisonment or other forms of punishment. Women who had been members of the Milice (the Militia, the paramilitary police force) or who were accused of denouncing Resisters were more likely to be brought to court than the women who were accused of so-called 'sexual collaboration'.[29] Women were accused of sexual collaboration ('la collaboration horizontale') more than of any other form of collaboration, and their most common – if unofficial – form of punishment was public humiliation. Some of the women were very young indeed: in Calvados, Henri Amouroux reports that fifty-four female minors were punished by tribunals.[30] Racism came into play too: Amouroux tells of the particular attention paid to women who had been mistresses of the North Africans recruited by the Gestapo.

Margaret and Patrice Higonnet have pointed out that: 'War strengthens the sense that women are property, as well as symbols of national victory. Women who consort with the enemy are stigmatized, humiliated, even executed, while soldiers' romantic interludes in enemy territory are idealized.'[31] Some of the most powerful images of women at the Liberation remain those of women who were punished publicly for allegedly sleeping with German soldiers. Photographs show women, heads shaved, swastikas painted on their chests and backs, paraded naked through the streets, surrounded by jeering crowds. Emmanuel d'Astier de la Vigerie's account of the liberation of Paris quotes the diary of Huguette Robert, described as a 'bourgeoise de la rue de Varenne' who witnessed the following scene from her window:

> A cortège of four shaven women... is moving towards the rue du Bac, more and more people are joining the crowd. One of the women tries to escape. She is caught, people hit her, hurl insults at her, the crowd is inhuman. The poor woman is stripped... on her knees, in front of 102 rue du Bac. A member of the Resistance points his machine gun at her, to kill her. People force her to say she is sorry, she is kneeling there, half-naked, on her knees. It is said that she killed three Frenchmen, that she shot them from her window. What can be done in front of a half-mad crowd? are they going to kill her? No – a French officer arrives and says that she must be taken to prison and tried. The poor woman is still on her knees, half-naked, saying 'I

won't do it any more, I'm sorry': she doesn't have tears in her eyes, she is in shock. She doesn't seem afraid but is quite wild, beside herself. All this is horrible. I have seen people who seem quite inoffensive turn into beasts ready to kill. I am horrified.[32]

Most scholarly accounts of the purges include brief mention of this particular form of punishment, but do not comment further. Information about the women whose heads were shaved, 'les femmes tondues', is mostly gleaned from anecdotes. Herbert Lottman, one of the few writers on the period who gives more than a paragraph to this question, notes that the shaving of women's heads 'seems to have been the first act of purging nearly everywhere; it accompanies arrests, shootings, sometimes replaces them'.[33] He points out that there was no national directive to shave the heads of female collaborators, but the practice was universally tolerated, even encouraged on the grounds that, without actually spilling blood, it provided a 'useful' outlet for the anger and desire for vengeance that so many felt.[34] He goes on to remark, though, that the victims of this act, qualified as 'medieval sadism' by Sartre,[35] sometimes never recovered. Even those who were subsequently quite successfully reintegrated into their village or town life bore the stigma. Rumour and animosity live on: even today, women are pointed out as having been among the 'femmes tondues'. The shaving of women's heads seems to be a remarkably symbolic act, yet serious accounts of the Liberation rarely do more than mention this, the only gender-specific form of punishment, in a few words. Attempts to justify or condone it are weak, to say the least; attention to the subject seems to indicate prurient interest; and so it is passed over as quickly as possible.[36]

It has been suggested that this particular form of punishment indicated hatred of women as much as, if not more than, hatred of Nazism.[37]

Janine, a member of the Resistance at Clermont-Ferrand, will never forget the woman who, accused of being the mistress of a German officer, was paraded through the town, her lover's boots jammed onto her hands which were tied up over her head ... on her shorn head, they had drawn a swastika. Through shaving the heads of these women, a phenomenon which recurs through time ... were the men at the Liberation seeking only to punish Nazism? The shaving of women's heads was an attack on all women.[38]

This contribution to a conference on the Liberation in Toulouse met with hostility from the other participants, who seemed simply to refuse to acknowledge the existence of a gendered dimension to the purges.[39]

It is interesting to contrast this form of punishment and the attitude of both participants and historians towards women's sexual collaboration with the experience and the analysis of the French prisoners of war in Germany. Yves Durand's important book on the captivity of French soldiers contains a significant section concerning prisoners and their relationships with German women. [40] According to Durand, the attachments formed between them were 'only human':

> It is only human that men in their prime, exiled for years and in contact with women in the country where their captivity forces them to live, sometimes in practically intimate contact, developed relationships with them, in spite of the obstacles and dangers that this represented.[41]

This description even makes the prisoners sound fearless, defying the dictates of the enemy, even while in captivity. Yet Durand claims that the men were primarily interested in the women 'as women and not as lovers' (although he does not explain what he means by this distinction); he also reports that the prisoners enjoyed the reputation of Frenchmen in general as being good lovers. The positive, indulgent view of healthy rampant male sexuality colours the historian's interpretation, just as hostility towards female sexuality affected the fate of women who had been sexually active with German men during the war and had thereby transgressed not only codes of patriotism and sexual morality but also codes of feminine behaviour.[42]

Relationships between French prisoners of war and German women were officially punishable, on a sliding scale according to the marital and social status of the woman in question and according to the offence – speaking to a woman, kissing her or sleeping with her – culminating, in the most extreme cases, in the death penalty. On the German side, a married German woman caught sleeping with a French prisoner of war would be severely punished for potentially spoiling the purity of the race. Durand reports that in one camp, a woman discovered would have her head shaved and would be forced to carry a board saying 'I am the mistress of a French prisoner'. Most cases, however, were never discovered: prisoners worked on isolated farms and the liaisons were generally tolerated. Durand even says that one prisoner was (unofficially) admired for impregnating both mother and daughter.[43] The sexual double standard held during the war and caused no comment from later historians.

FOOD

In daily life, there was not much difference between war and peace: the main preoccupation of the majority of the French population was still the same as it had been for the four years of the Occupation: finding food, keeping warm. Food was a national obsession: words such as 'calorie' and 'protein', unknown before the war, had become a familiar part of daily conversations.[44] Food shortages were the most obvious and most immediate problem of daily life. On a train journey in Spain, Simone de Beauvoir was struck by the contrast with France:

> On station platforms, young women were walking, laughing, chatting, wearing silk stockings; in the towns we passed, I could see shop windows piled high with food. When we stopped, people selling fruit, sweets, ham, came up to the train; the station buffet groaned with food. I remembered the station at Nantes where we had been so hungry, so exhausted ... I felt a furious kind of solidarity with French wretchedness.[45]

The French population had naively assumed that shortages had primarily been the result of German occupiers eating food that they should have had themselves, and that, with the Germans gone, rationing would immediately come to an end. In fact, the deprivation suffered during the Occupation intensified in the winter of 1944–5, which was the coldest since 1940. Heating was a major problem and there was not enough coal. Families in Lyon were theoretically entitled to 450 kilos of coal for the month of December 1944. They received 25 kilos, less than 1 kilo a day.[46] Paris had no coal that winter for the first time and it was reported that three babies died of cold in a Paris hospital.[47] Rationing also became harder to bear psychologically, as the population had expectations of instant improvement once the military liberation had been accomplished. De Gaulle said, 'In 1944, the French were wretched, now they are discontented. This is progress.'[48] A shrewd comment maybe, but for most of the French population, it may not have felt like progress. According to Catherine Gavin, housewives were particularly critical of de Gaulle, who, for all his fine speeches, did not seem to have any understanding about the daily tribulations of ordinary life, dominated, as before, by the ration card.[49] De Gaulle seemed far removed from daily life: he made only one speech in which he spoke of the food supply and his attitude towards this crucial problem was considered disdainful, while his perception of his own role was somewhat lofty: he had not come back in order to 'distribute macaroni rations', he apparently said.[50]

Ration cards, symbol of the German Occupation and French humiliation, were torn up when Leclerc's liberating army marched in, but this optimism was premature, and rationing for some products was almost immediately reintroduced.[51] Basic products were still rationed until 1949, coffee until 1950. Rations were even reduced after the war: bread rations, for instance, were reduced from 350g per adult per day to 300g and then to 250g. Meat was rationed at 160g per week, plus 90g of cold meats when they were available. It was pointed out in the Consultative Assembly that since the Liberation, the category J2 (6–13-year-olds) and the elderly had not received any milk rations, whereas during the Occupation the children at least had had their milk.[52] Rations varied from region to region and, in some parts of France such as Bordeaux, were well below the nationally prescribed minimum. In the Consultative Assembly, Communist delegate Georges Marrane reported in March 1945 that the Paris region had had no delivery of butter for two months, and no meat for two weeks.[53] In Nice, it was reported that there had been no butter since the Liberation, and that queues for food and fuel were getting longer, and power cuts worse than they had been during the Occupation.[54] In Rouen in May 1945, the month's rations for adults included 5g of margarine, one egg and 10g of charcuterie, measuring 5 centimetres long by 1 centimetre wide. One butcher displayed a piece of salami of the correct size in the middle of a large platter next to a magnifying glass.[55] In other parts of France (such as Strasbourg), people were better fed – either because they lived in an active agricultural area or because of German stocks, abandoned during the retreat – and refused to reduce their ration to national limits.[56] Charles-Louis Foulon notes that fear of famine meant that there was no solidarity from the rural population for the urban populations who suffered the most, and the inequality of suffering merely raised the levels of urban discontent.[57]

Accounts of the immediate postwar years put daily calorie consumption at anywhere from 1,000 to 1,300 per day per adult in 1945,[58] and it was estimated that about 75 per cent of the population was suffering from some form of malnutrition. American journalist

Janet Flanner, reporting from Paris in 1945, said that there was no plaster of Paris available in hospitals to set broken bones but that, according to French doctors, malnutrition meant that people's bones were 'almost too soft to break'.[59] The Minister of Food had to organise proper distribution of foodstuffs and, most urgently, destroy the black market which still flourished, although in a less organised way than during the war.[60] He clearly failed in both these tasks. For instance, butter prices in 1944–5 could be as much as 1,000F a kilo, or half the monthly salary of the average office worker;[61] the legal price of a litre of milk was 4.60F but on the black market anything from 12 to 30F could be demanded.[62] After the Liberation, many families were in fact worse off than before, as the networks of support and distribution set up during the war (by government, municipalities, Resistance organisations) had broken down and there was no organisation to turn to. Official government reports from various parts of France tell of regular demonstrations by housewives protesting at food shortages and sometimes seizing and distributing products themselves.[63] In the Consultative Assembly, Communist delegate Mathilde Péri spoke in the name of the housewives of France. She told of a delegation of women from the Seine-et-Oise area who went to Paris to see the Minister of Food Paul Ramadier (sometimes known as 'Ramadier-Ramadan' because of the shortages). The women were demanding action against the black market, but left his office 'with the clear impression that nothing would be done'.[64] Radical-Socialist delegate Marianne Verger took up the same theme of governmental inadequacy the next day in the Assembly. She suggested that placing women in the organisations concerned with collecting and distributing rations was one way to ensure a sensible and fair system.[65]

Distribution of food was badly hindered by the state of transport in France. Up to 1944, rail traffic still operated, albeit with restrictions. But, as Pierre Gérard, head of the French railways (SNCF) during part of the Occupation, stated, 'from the beginning of May 1944, the rail service was completely chaotic in France. Trains left as and when they could.'[66] Destruction of roads, of 1,900 bridges and viaducts, 27 railway tunnels, 3,000 kilometres of railway lines, four-fifths of France's barges and 5,200 kilometres of navigable waterways, two-thirds of its goods trains and over 14,000 of its 17,000 prewar trains did not make either personal travel or transportation of goods easier.[67] The flooding caused by the rains of October and November 1944 made everything worse. Janet Flanner noted how the crises affected each other:

even if there were quantities of food in Paris, there would be nearly no fuel with which to cook it. The coal is in the north. There can be no transportation without coal and no coal without transportation. Two months of continuous rain have so swollen the rivers and canals that coal barges are tied up to the banks. Because of the lack of coal, there is no electric power for the city's factories, so they remain closed.... But if they were open, who would fill all the jobs? Eight hundred thousand of the most skilled French factory workers are still labor slaves in Germany.[68]

The acute problems of daily life, while shared by the whole population, were women's problems in that the management of daily life was the responsibility of women. Food was women's business. The daily struggle to feed and clothe children and to keep them warm was the struggle of women, the mainstay of the family. Raymond Ruffin described the daily routine of the housewives:

As early as possible every morning, they have to look in the newspaper to find out which goods are being distributed that day. And so, on the 6th, they learn that 500g of potatoes will be given to anyone with tickets numbered 29 and 30; on the 7th, it will be 50g of butter for GB and GA coupons.[69]

A diary kept by one woman in the Vosges, a Madame Marcel Chabert, was published in *Pour la vie* ('For life') the journal of the Union Nationale des Associations Familiales (UNAF, Union of Family Associations) and tells of how she spent her days in September 1944 during the German retreat:

1 September: You have to get to the bakery very early if you want to find bread. By 10 o'clock it has all gone. People say we are going to run out of flour.
8 September: I'm going to try to find milk and cheese at Bas-Rupts.... We have no bread, no butter. There is no fresh fruit and no fresh vegetables in Gérardmer.
18 September: No electricity.
22 September: I'm going out to try to get butter, milk and plums at Xourupt.
26 September: I went to see Germaine In.... People are talking about bombings and food, nothing else.[70]

Children often helped their mothers. Raymond Ruffin's diary reports his efforts to obtain food, with three hours of queuing resulting one day in buying a pound of lentils. When he proudly took these home, his mother burst into tears as she had no means of cooking them – no gas, no electricity.[71] One and a half hours at midday and an hour in the evening for the preparation of family meals was all that was allowed. A day had to be carefully planned, so that no cooking time was wasted. In one household, the routine was to soak the white beans every morning and cook them quickly in the evening. One day, the mother accidentally upset the pot in which the beans were soaking and so the family had nothing to eat.[72] Any waste or accident was a disaster. The wartime sight of the queue did not disappear and a queue indicated availability of necessary products. Alfred Sauvy tells of the cartoon of a woman looking at a shop with no one outside it, saying, 'I'll come back later when there's a queue.'[73] During the summer of 1944, the school holidays made the situation worse, as children had previously received a midday meal at school. Parents were desperately trying to send their children to holiday camps ('colonies de vacances') so that they would be able to eat. Children aged 6–12 had priority and Raymond Ruffin's mother managed to get two of her children sent off, after waiting for four hours to see those responsible.[74]

Pour la vie worried about the effects of deprivation and anxiety on women's health: 'their mental strength is being tested ... many women are suffering from nervous depression without knowing it.'[75] This article goes on to mention the specific practical difficulties faced by women in rural areas, particularly the difficulties due to lack of transport and to isolation: how could they actually get to register for rations? How could products be delivered to them? Government shortsightedness compounded these problems: in one canton, twenty-three pairs of boots were delivered to be shared out among farmers, but no boots were sent for women agricultural workers – they had to do the milking barefoot.[76]

HOW TO BE A WOMAN

Cheerfulness and coping in adversity was the message of the few women's magazines that appeared at the time. *Marie-France* in 1944, and shortly afterwards *Elle* in 1945, aiming at a general women's market, together with the numerous but mostly shortlived broadsheets and newsletters put out by women's groups of Resistance organisations, tell us about the dominant images of women and femininity, about the role women were being called upon to play in the new France, about the actual help given to women, and about the actions in which they engaged. The home provided the central focus for women's lives, but not exclusively so in 1944–6: the magazines looked outwards as well, to see how women could contribute to the rebuilding of the nation. It was suggested that they volunteer for service in the reception centres for returning prisoners and deportees; that they prepare the food parcels to send to prisoners; that they help each other; that (if they were unmarried or perhaps widowed) they sign up to work as a family help.[77] Some commentators, notably Robert Debré, argued in favour of instituting domestic service for girls, on the same basis as military service for boys, but this never got very far. In a 1947 article published in *Pour la vie*, Debré and Alfred Sauvy pursued this theme, arguing that this kind of service was both fair and necessary, and would make proper use of a young woman's natural talents, preparing her for her future role while she served the interests of the nation.[78]

Women were warned that the years of sacrifice were not yet over:

> We all have to learn how to be happy again. Many people believed, naively, that once the war was over, everything would be easy again. Alas! They must understand that there is too much that has to be repaired in France, to be cured, healed, rebuilt.... We all need lots of courage. And we must find this courage within ourselves.... With all our strength, let us help those who need us. Our existence must consist of unceasing effort.... Let us be optimistic. Let us be loving towards each other. The smiles we exchange will make our lives happier.[79]

In the Liberation years, practical information on home-making in difficult circumstances was as important as morale-building. Magazines included pages of practical hints and useful tips, emphasising the need for ingenuity and organisation in the home. In discussing housework, *Elle* even went as far as to suggest that women should learn how to use both hands, doing several household tasks simultaneously, in order to increase domestic efficiency. Suggestions were, however, generally quite sound and probably most welcome, for instance, how to use a pressure cooker (particularly important with the restrictions imposed on gas and electricity), how to make dishes without key ingredients (sauerkraut with no sausage) or how to liven up a dull root vegetable ('turnips à la provençale'). 'Don't be afraid of powdered eggs', said *Marie-France* which also gave women ideas for recipes using substitutes for butter and milk.

Issues that were generally supposed to preoccupy women – fashion, beauty, make-up – took a back seat, while the wartime 'make do and mend' ethos still dominated. *Elle*, the oracle, gave the seal of approval to these practical priorities. It told women that cleanliness and personality counted more than elegance; that they should wear trousers, because 'day dresses are a hundred times less warm and a thousand times more inconvenient than trousers';[80] *Elle* reassured women that they really could go out in the evening in a day dress (just add a piece of jewellery), and gave useful tips about little adjustments whereby one dress could be worn in seven different ways. During the war, many women had adopted the turban as a way of hiding the lack of a good (or any) haircut or lack of shampoo, and some – most famously Simone de Beauvoir – kept this on as a fashion after the war.[81] Leather shortages meant that women wore shoes with rubber or cork soles. Lack of fuel for heating made keeping warm a priority in the cold winter of 1944–5. *Elle* gave recipes for keeping warm (lentil soup), household hints (make padding for doors to keep out the draught), patterns for making trousers. Necessity was sometimes turned into a game: *Marie-France*, for instance, ran a competition on making warm clothing for small children.[82]

While this kind of information was worthy, necessary and probably gratefully received, the content of the magazines also highlighted the abnormality of the times: women's magazines usually stressed femininity and shared with readers the secrets of how to achieve it. In the Liberation years as in the Occupation, women had permission *not* to worry about their appearance, *not* to spend time and money working to be a 'Real Woman'. Nor were readers assailed by advertisements and incited to buy: at that time, there was not enough paper for adverts, and little enough to buy anyway.

Fashion, as a major preoccupation for women, did not return to centre-stage until Dior's New Look of 1947 caused controversy on the front pages. The image of women promoted by all during the Liberation was that of helper of others, of nurturer, whether in the family or in public service. But the woman's role in the family was the most important.

THE FAMILY

During the Occupation, the family had found itself elevated to the status of national symbol. The Vichy motto had been 'Travail, Famille, Patrie' ('Work, Family, Fatherland'). Legislation had made divorce more difficult, promoted traditional roles for men and women, and attempted, albeit not very successfully, to prevent married women from working in the public sector.[83] The reality of the family was, of course, quite different from the rhetoric of Vichy speeches and from the imaginary family of Vichy legislation. War and Occupation did not mean unity within families but profound disruption: between spouses, between parents and children, between siblings. Choices and survival strategies were made for economic, ideological and pragmatic reasons, and the choices made or positions adopted during the war continued to weigh on individuals and their relationships afterwards.

The personal disruption of war was epitomised by the situation of the families of prisoners of war and deportees. Henri Frenay, Minister of Prisoners of War, Deportees and Refugees at the Liberation, estimated that the relative numbers of those absent from France were as follows: 1.2 million prisoners of war; 150,000 deported for political or racial reasons; 50,000 deported for criminal offences; 700,000 deported to Germany through the STO or working voluntarily in Germany; 200,000 inhabitants of Alsace-Lorraine who had joined the Wehrmacht of the Waffen SS either voluntarily or under duress. On top of this there were thought to be 2.4 million refugees of different kinds (who had lost their homes at the exodus of 1940 or through bombing, or who had been expelled from Alsace-Lorraine when it was incorporated into the German Reich); and 100,000 foreigners of different nationalities in France for a variety of reasons.[84] This vast population somehow had to be given homes and jobs, and had to be reintegrated into French society.

In anticipation of the return, an entire network of organisations was set up under the auspices of the Ministry, the Red Cross and the National Movement of Prisoners of War. Centres were opened at border towns, staffed by up to 1,150 people, including many women volunteers. The centres were supposed to provide medical treatment, financial help and moral support while also fulfilling an administrative function. Up to 50,000 returning prisoners and deportees a day were expected at times, and most of the centres were woefully inadequately prepared, although some – such as the centre at Dieppe – were hardly needed at all. In the discussion on the proposed budget of the Ministry in the Consultative Assembly, many delegates deplored the way in which prisoners and deportees were being received. M. Jean Dechartre told one anecdote from the camp at Nancy:

> Sixty-eight comrades arrived at this repatriation camp. The following dialogue took place:
>   'How many of you are there?'

'Sixty-eight.'

'What are we going to do with you?'

They were settled in on straw mattresses in the corridor and told, 'It's Saturday today, we can't do anything today. Tomorrow we won't be working because it's Sunday. We'll deal with you on Monday and you'll leave on Tuesday.'[85]

Another delegate, M. Pierre-Bloch, also told the Assembly similar anecdotes, singling out the case of North African and Senegalese prisoners who complained of disgraceful treatment and virtual incarceration at the Versailles camp.[86]

Mutual incomprehension and false expectations characterised the return. PoWs had little idea of the state of France (although 500,000 copies of the newsletter *Votre France*, edited by the Ministry, were parachuted into the camps every week, according to Frenay[87]); the deportees had even less idea of what they would find. Nor did those organising the return or the families of the deportees and prisoners have any idea of what to expect when the return began. Vichy propaganda had led PoWs to believe that they were the returning heroes, the 'future saviours of France, purified and strengthened by their suffering, expected to undertake the task of national renewal when they returned'.[88] However, they found that the Resistance had replaced them in public affection and acclaim. On top of this, their suffering was considered insignificant in relation to the experience of deportees returning from concentration camps.[89] PoWs expected a warmer welcome than they actually received. Vichy propaganda had also led them to believe that they would find 'faithful wives, knitting warm socks by the fire, their only concern being to look after their prisoner, raise their children with dignity under the paternal wing of the old Marshall'.[90] When the prisoners returned, reunions were frequently far from joyful. In spite of Vichy legislation which had made adultery with the wife of a PoW punishable by imprisonment and a fine,[91] women had sometimes formed other attachments, as had their partner. The ordeal of captivity had also changed the personality of the PoWs and reintegration into the world of work as well as into personal relationships was by no means simple or straightforward:

When a separation has been long or fraught with extraordinary events and time has passed oh so terribly slowly, the result is sometimes such a clumsy breach that when you try to bring the two halves together again, they don't match; this happens with every war, every revolution: the one who has lived in constant danger, suffering hunger, cold, fatigue, fear and outrage has some difficulties upon rejoining a wife or friends who have been living in safety.[92]

In Paris, prisoners and deportees were received in centres including the Hotel Lutétia, ironic in that it had been the Nazi headquarters in occupied Paris. Olga Wormser-Migot, attached to the Information Service of Frenay's Ministry, wrote: 'Heartbreaking reunions took place every day, and for some there was the certainty that there would be no reunion.'[93]

At the Lutétia, photographs were pinned to walls bearing messages from families or the question 'Does anyone know this person?' Personal histories complicated the business of the return. One young woman tried to find out when a particular man was returning, saying that she would be stopped from seeing him if his wife knew the date first.[94] Other simply refused to believe that their son, husband, sister, mother would not be coming back and camped out in the hotel, waiting.[95]

For the women whose partner did return, things could be just as hard: their husband had become a stranger after sometimes five years of absence. During the Occupation, PoWs' wives found themselves in a paradoxical position. On the one hand, they were forced into independence, running a home, earning a living, making decisions; on the other, this independence was in direct contradiction with the image of the family promoted by Vichy with emphasis placed on the role of the mother in the home.[96] Their whole existence, in the eyes of officials, was one of waiting, focusing on the future when their husband would return, and they were supposed to anticipate this with joy rather than trepidation. Yet the women had often been strengthened by their experiences, while the men returned from captivity diminished in many ways, their physical and emotional health damaged. Records of the Ministry of Health studied by Sarah Fishman showed a range of short-term and long-term health problems including tuberculosis, digestive disorders and dental problems. Returning PoWs had prematurely aged, with their memory, movement and skin affected. They were prone to depression, insomnia, fatigue, anxiety and trembling, among other symptoms.[97]

Of the prisoners of war, roughly 55 per cent were married. Mostly young men between the ages of 20 and 40 when they were taken prisoner (60 per cent were under 30) they had not been married long before the outbreak of war. Those who were fathers left behind children who were very young indeed.[98] For these children, the intrusion of a strange adult man was an unwelcome disruption. The absent men had little idea of what conditions had been like in France and wives did not take kindly to the criticisms levelled at them by the returning husband about how they had run the farm or the family business when they were alone.[99] Women questioned about the return who claimed that their marriage had successfully survived the traumas of war sometimes acknowledged that the price of this 'success' was that they were obliged to bow to the husband's will.[100]

It was not only men who returned. Janet Flanner wrote about the return to Paris of the first contingent of women deportees in April 1945:

> These three hundred women, who came in exchange for German women held in France, were from the prison camp of Ravensbrück.... They arrived at the Gare de Lyon at eleven in the morning and were met by a nearly speechless crowd ready with welcoming bouquets of lilac and other spring flowers and by General de Gaulle, who wept.... There was a general, anguished babble of search, of finding or not finding. There was almost no joy; the emotion penetrated beyond that, to something nearer pain.... In a way, all the women looked alike: their faces were gray-green, with reddish-brown circles around their eyes, which seemed to see but not to take in.... As the lilacs fell from inert hands, the flowers made a purple carpet on the platform and the perfume of the trampled flowers mixed with the stench of illness and dirt.[101]

Les Françaises à Ravensbrück gives moving accounts of the difficulties that these women – the few who returned from this camp – experienced: a sense of the unreality of the world around them; learning of the death of their partner and/or children; or discovering that the gulf that now separated the two partners was too wide to be overcome. One woman told of finding that her family was not pleased to see her as they had divided up an inheritance without her. Women returned and some found that they were rejected by their family, that they were somehow held responsible for their arrest and were treated as though they were unclean; they found a fiancé married to someone else, a husband who had a mistress; they found that even in their former Resistance group, they were not always welcome.[102] Sociologist and social psychologist Marie-Jo Chombart de Lauwe wrote that:

> The return was very hard ... maybe we had dreamed too much about it. The attitude we most frequently encountered was one of scepticism mixed with an unhealthy curiosity. And then people said such banal things: 'My poor girl, you've lost the best years of your life.'[103]

Another deportee, Régine Beer, wrote of her homecoming: 'My mother opened the door, she looked at me without recognising me at first. And when she recognised me, she fainted.'[104]

On a personal level, therefore, the Liberation was often an intensely painful time: 'When I saw Paris again, and I learned that my father died at the camp at Dora, my brother at Buchenwald and my sister had been shot ... no, I didn't celebrate the fact that we were free.'[105] Returning deportees found reintegration into the everyday life of French society extremely difficult: some could not sleep, one was afraid to take a shower, another was convinced that her babies would die; most were severely depressed and there was little in the way of support for this aspect of their return, apart from the groups they formed themselves.

After the war, some prisoners and deportees wanted to put the war behind them and hurried to marry and have children ('les enfants du retour'), but many prewar couples were disrupted. Divorce figures peaked in 1946, many of them sought by returning men.[106] The artificially high postwar rate was partly due to postponed divorce after the lifting of restrictions imposed by the Vichy government, but must also have been due to the separations of the war years. One can guess that an attempt was made for a year or two to pick up the threads but that it had failed. Divorce figures tend to show that more wives than husbands initiate the proceedings and that the husband's adultery is far more common than the wife's: in 1945–7, these patterns were reversed.[107]

MOTHERS

If the present was to be endured, the future had to be created, and new roles carved out for women in the new France. Women were seen in the three roles of mother, worker and citizen, with the first shaping all public discourse on women, whether motherhood, women as workers or women as citizens was being discussed. Woman-as-mother was clearly the image that the new provisional government wanted to promote in the new France. Women's specific contribution to the reconstruction of France was to be reproduction: General de Gaulle, as anxious about falling birth rates as his predecessors had been, called, in a speech made on 5 March 1945, for French women to produce 12 million bouncing babies for France in ten years. Legislation therefore had to be introduced that would facilitate this maternal role and encourage women back to the marital bedroom.

One serious problem was housing. 'A house shared is a home destroyed' wrote *La femme*, and urgent measures had to be taken to give young married couples the privacy they needed.[108] It was estimated that 290,000 'residential buildings' had been destroyed during the war – most particularly as a result of the Allied bombings during the Liberation itself – which meant that between 500–550,000 households were without homes.[109] Furthermore, there were approximately 950,000–1 million partially damaged residential buildings, or 1.7–1.8 million homes lost.

The Ministry of Reconstruction and Town Planning was created in November 1944 with co-ordination of a building and rebuilding programme as one of its most urgent tasks. The programme had to compete for funds with the equally urgent rebuilding of factories and the revitalising of the soil for agriculture; the difficulties of reconstruction were compounded by the lack of raw materials, the destruction of the transport system and lack of skilled workers in the building industry. These difficulties were further compounded by the demographic trends of the French population. Marriage was popular again; the birthrate had been increasing since 1943; the composition of households was changing: more were constituted but the number in each household was dropping.[110]

The government began its housing programme with the Ordinance of 11 October 1945. Laws regulated the demolition of housing and the use of buildings; housing could be requisitioned to be given to those who had priority status:

> civil servants who have been moved around the country as part of their job, those who had volunteered for the Free French at least three years previously, returning prisoners and those returning from deportation if they had lived in that department prior to their deportation, those who had lost their homes, and students.'[111]

A further series of regulations specified different types of families as priority cases for housing:

Families with four children, couples with no children who have been married for less than four years, families with two children if married for less than six years and three children if married for less than eight years, if moving would undermine the stability of the family.

At the beginning of 1947, about 200,000 requisitions had taken place, at least partially solving the housing crisis for about 500,000 people, but requisition was never a popular solution to the problem.[112]

The provision of housing was complemented by new family legislation. The regulations quoted above indicate certain norms of family size to be encouraged and the speed with which these sizes should be attained. Further legislation concerning marriage and the family gave advantages to the large family, or 'famille nombreuse'. All governments in France had been pronatalist since at least the turn of the century and there was remarkable continuity of approach between the prewar 1939 Code de la Famille (Family Code) Vichy legislation (creation of a Family Ministry, various family allowances, repression of abortion) and policies at the Liberation.

Postwar demographic anxiety led to the creation of a Ministry for Public Health and Population, with a Minister specifically responsible for family affairs; the creation of a High Consultative Committee on Population and the Family, attached to the Prime Minister's office; the creation of the Institut National des Etudes Démographiques (INED, National Institute for Demographic Studies) to study demographic trends; the institution of prenatal benefits; a family quotient for tax purposes; and the creation of UNAF in March 1945.[113]

The family was to hold a significant place in postwar French society. Even in the Conseil National de la Résistance (CNR, National Resistance Council), plans were elaborated to support and sustain the family (or, as it was sometimes put, 'the worker and his family'[114]) and the Constitution of the Fourth Republic was to include in its preamble an undertaking that: 'The Nation guarantees to the individual and the family the conditions necessary for their development.' This guarantee took concrete form in legislation promoting the family.

In 1945–6, many proposals for laws designed to encourage and support young couples were discussed in the French National Assembly and some were passed. It was suggested that a loan should be given to a young couple upon marriage. Robert Prigent, Minister of Public Health and Population, opened the debate by evoking the financial difficulties of many young couples following the war: they had no savings, their parents could not help them to set up a home, and the housing shortage affected their plans to start a family. Prigent spelled out the goal of the marriage loan: 'we want to encourage the establishment of young and fertile households'.[115] The conditions under which a couple could apply for a loan indicate the family ideal and the underlying nationalistic concerns of the legislators. Only the French family, with legitimate offspring, was eligible for a loan. The man had to have completed military service; he could be a foreigner if he had at least three years' residence in France or if he married a Frenchwoman who kept her French nationality; he could – after much discussion in the Assembly – be over 30 when he married or marry a woman who was over 30. The loan was allocated by a local committee comprising representatives from trade unions and family associations, and two mothers designated by local women's organisations; the repayment was reduced on the birth of each child.

Further discussion set out the conditions for family allowances, which were to be allocated by an autonomous fund (Caisse d'Allocations Familiales, CAF) separate from the social security funds, and which were only allocated on certain conditions. The CAF also had a social work function, assisting those families who received allowances as and when they needed help. CAF intervention could be concerned with housing, holidays, home helps for mothers, youth work, extra benefit for household goods and other loans.[116] For a mother to receive maternity benefit, her first child had to be born within two years of marriage and further children within three years of the preceding one; to be eligible for benefit, the mother of an illegitimate child had to be under 25. Half the allowance was payable on birth and half six months later if the child was still alive. The right to receive family allowances began with the birth of the second child and continued while the child was of school age. Every type of allowance was subject to these conditions, which concerned the timing and number of children but were not means tested. The most contentious of the allowances was the 'allocation de salaire unique' or single-wage benefit, paid to families which depended on one wage and, later, to families of self-employed workers when the mother was not employed.[117] As Pierre Laroque wrote: 'The state knew the kind of family it wanted and adopted a coherent set of measures which favoured these families and penalised others.'[118]

Between 1944 and 1946, the two years of Liberation, French

women had to contend with continued – or increased – material hardship combined with legislation that placed them firmly in a maternal role. In this, the French state was unambiguous. The ambiguity lay in the repercussions that this view of women's role was to have not only on family policy, but on legislation over working conditions, childcare facilities and education: in other words, it was to have serious implications for the potential for full participation by women in France's political and economic life. Yet the Liberation brought a change in women's political status, and the economic situation of France required their participation in the labour market; their public, if not their private, role had changed.

2 Women in public life: the political arena

At the end of the war, French women were enfranchised. This was the most obvious way in which a revised public presence for women in postwar France was anticipated. Women's suffrage was claimed, mainly by the Left, as a reward for their Resistance activities. This was stated as though it was simply an accepted fact. Former Resister Lucie Aubrac said: 'To sum it [the war] up as far as women were concerned? Much suffering, but not in vain. We won the right to vote and thereby the chance to make other changes.'[1] There was no suggestion that women had the same right to vote as men for the simple reason that women were human beings with 'inalienable rights'; no acknowledgement of the fact that women had been demanding the vote for decades.[2] Aubrac's statement reflected the commonly held view that women had 'proved' that they were worthy of citizenship and that political rights marked the beginning of equality for women. Other changes in women's status, it was thought, would follow on naturally.

THE VOTE

Women were enfranchised not through debate in the National Assembly and a favourable vote but by a decree issued by the provisional government of the French Republic towards the end of the Second World War.[3] The question of women's suffrage ought to have been resolved before the war and the principle had indeed been accepted by the Chamber of Deputies (lower house) after the First World War, but had always been rejected by the more conservative Senate (upper house). Those who theoretically supported women's right to vote (mainly the Left) were nonetheless anxious about its likely electoral effect, as it was believed that women would vote massively for the parties associated with the Church. This was a particular fear of the fiercely anti-clerical Radicals, who therefore voted against granting the vote to women. The more conservative right-wing groups objected to women's suffrage on ideological grounds.[4] By the end of the Second World War, France was lagging behind other western nations in its support for women's suffrage, and granting women the right to vote was probably no more than a measure aiming to correct this anomaly – as well as to provide electoral support for General de Gaulle, in whose gift the vote seemed to be.

Once achieved, however, each political group was keen to claim responsibility. According to the PCF, women had won the vote through the Resistance and the efforts of the party; the Socialists also cited Resistance activity as the primary reason, but reminded women that Socialists had always championed the cause of women's suffrage; the Radical Party, somewhat ill at ease, conveniently forgot that it had opposed women's suffrage, and stressed that, before the war, it had been responsible for much of the social legislation which had been so important to women; the new Christian Democratic party, the Mouvement Républicain Populaire (MRP, Popular Republican Movement), claimed for de Gaulle the status of liberator of France and liberator of women. As the party of de Gaulle and of the Church, the MRP was looking forward to beginning its parliamentary life by attracting a significant women's vote. The role of feminist groups who had campaigned for women's suffrage in the Third Republic was, on the whole, ignored.

The Third Republic in France had been swept away by the 1940 defeat and by the Vichy régime of Marshal Pétain. Once the war was over, a new régime had to be installed, purged of those who had participated in the Vichy system. The shape of postwar France was already being planned by the CNR and then by de Gaulle's provisional government before the end of the war. De Gaulle's Ordinance of 21 April 1944 set out plans for the organisation of power in postwar France. With no elected representatives in place, the provisional government under de Gaulle planned the changeover from war to peace, and appointed delegates (chosen for their role in the Resistance) to a Consultative Assembly whose task would be to oversee the re-establishment of democracy. In the name of democracy, it was decided that the French people would determine the future political system of the nation themselves, making their views known via referenda. They were first asked whether they wanted France to readopt the Constitution of the Third Republic or whether the Assembly they were about to elect should draw up a new Constitution and inaugurate a new Republic. They were then asked to decide whether – assuming that a new Constitution was chosen – the new Constituent Assembly should be given similar powers to those of a National Assembly, or whether its powers should be restricted, and a time limit imposed for the preparation of a new Constitution. After a campaign which had already divided Gaullist from Christian from Communist, the French public voted for a new Republic and for a time limit of seven months to be imposed on the work of the new Assembly.[5]

The Ordinance of 21 April 1944 had stated in its first Article that the Assembly set up to draft a new Constitution for France would be elected by all adult Frenchmen and women. To make this even clearer, the Ordinance stipulated that women would be able to vote and to stand for political office on the same terms as men. Thirteen million women swelled the ranks of the electorate, forming 53 per cent of those entitled to vote. Women were to be as responsible as men for whatever the future of French democracy was to be.

Women voted for the first time on 29 April 1945 in the first elections to be held in France since 1936, electing local and departmental councillors in certain areas. There had been some discussion over the timing of these elections, as the prisoners of war and deportees had not yet returned, and it was felt that the massive influx of women voters meant that the results would be 'biased'. These first elections were swiftly followed by more: local elections (September 1945), elections to the first Constituent Assembly (October 1945), the referenda on the role of the Assembly and then on the proposed Constitution (which was rejected – by more women than men) (October 1945, May 1946), elections to the second Constituent Assembly (June 1946), another Constitutional proposal (this time accepted) (October 1946) and finally elections to the first National Assembly of the Fourth Republic (November 1946). In the re-establishment of democracy at local and national level, women had ample opportunity to exercise their new right.

CITIZENS

It appeared that women needed to be coaxed into citizenship. Public discussion focused on making sure that women would actually register to vote and go to the polling station. The message to women citizens was that voting was a duty, a new responsibility, rather than a right. It was felt that women would respond more positively to the call to vote if it was presented as continuing a feminine tradition of duty and thinking of others: duty towards France, Christian duty, duty towards their 'dear lost ones', towards their men, towards the Resistance. Each political group used this argument in its own way and most used a vocabulary and images that they thought women would understand: 'we must give birth to a more humane and just France'[6] called on the maternal nature of women and also evoked the need to start everything anew; 'we must bring the enlightenment born of our faith to the City'[7] was an unambiguous religious message; 'France needs you, this new France that we want to be noble, great, pure', wrote the Communist-dominated women's organisation the Union des Femmes Françaises (UFF, Union of French Women), referring to the fact that the Communist Party had been the party least contaminated by collaboration, and most visible in the Resistance.[8] Only one voice preferred to use arguments about women's self-esteem to encourage them to vote: journalist Françoise Giroud, writing in *Elle*, emphatically urged women to vote:

> If you believe that your opinion should not count, if you believe that the local tramp or your caretaker's nephew or your boss or the garbage collector is more intelligent, more reasonable, better informed, better qualified than you, then abstain. Otherwise, vote![9]

As new citizens, it was believed that women needed to be educated so that they could play their new role responsibly, and in discussion of women's suffrage in newspapers, women's magazines and political parties, the emphasis was on information. 'What is a Constitution?' or 'Voting: a practical guide for women' were not unusual titles for articles. Underlying all discussion was the assumption that women, novices in the public world, would only be able to understand politics if it was presented to them in terms of home and family. Registering to vote was as important as registering at the dairy for butter rations;[10] the national budget was merely a large-scale version of a household budget, and so on. France was 'une grande Maison' and the housewives of France could now take care of it. The political education of women was therefore a simple affair of showing them that France was no more than a large household, and that those who ran the country shared the concerns of the housewife and mother: looking after the moral and physical welfare of the family.

Hardly any voices of protest were raised against the notion of the political ignorance of women. The Ligue Française pour le Droit des Femmes (League of Women's Rights) had given itself the job of monitoring the misogyny of the political world and quoted the

Socialist newspaper *Le Populaire* which wrote in 1946: 'elections today hardly seem to interest anyone, especially women who, mostly, don't know what it is all about.' The League commented: 'Is *Le Popu* quite sure that men, "mostly", *do* know what it is about?'[11]

Women's abstention rates were in fact slightly higher than men's in the first local elections, and then more noticeably so in the subsequent national elections and the referenda. Three experiments were carried out in the towns of Vienne, Belfort and Grenoble, where men and women placed their ballot papers in separate boxes. Nothing conclusive emerged: political scientists commented that the overall voting trends of each area studied had not changed between 1936, when the electorate was male and 1946, when women voted too. They suggested that apart from two differences – slightly higher abstention rates among women and clear female support for the MRP – women tended to vote like men from the same social class.[12]

However, debate on women's relationship to the political world for at least the first decade after the war stressed women's lack of interest in and ignorance of public affairs: they did not understand politics; they did not understand the electoral system; they failed to grasp the significance of voting; they lacked experience and they lacked confidence. There may be truth in all of these arguments. Yet assumptions made about women's nature and women's vote before they had even voted seemed both to determine discourse about women and politics and to shape the conclusions drawn afterwards. It was never thought that political parties should rethink their programmes or include women at all levels of decision-making in order to attract women's vote: the way women voted was thought to be predetermined by their nature.

HOW DID WOMEN VOTE?

In 1945 the political landscape was unsettled, with many groups and unfamiliar labels appearing on electoral lists. For instance, the results of the April 1945 elections show that the following political parties and groups had put forward candidates: Communists, Socialist-Communists, Section Française de l'Internationale Ouvrière (SFIO, Socialist Party), independent Socialists and Republican Socialists, Radical-Socialists, unspecified Left, MRP, independent Republicans, left-wing Republicans and Democratic Alliance, Republican Federation, unspecified Moderates and Conservatives, Conservatives, unspecified numbers of representatives of Resistance groups.[13] It was not therefore surprising if there was a certain amount of confusion: it was not always possible to distinguish between the groups and to know exactly what you were voting for by choosing one or the other. Furthermore, all the groups claimed to support the demands of the National Resistance Charter. As Pierre Villon (PCF) noted: 'in 1944, it simply was not possible to declare oneself openly hostile to the struggle against the occupier, to the struggle for democracy, freedom and social progress.'[14]

As the system settled down, some parties tried to attract women, each pointing to its past activity to show why it and it alone was worthy of their support. The Communist Party dwelt at length on its wartime Resistance record of heroism. Unwilling to let the public forget that it was (or rather that it claimed to be) the 'party of 75,000 martyrs' and thereby morally unassailable, Communist Party speeches and publications contained constant references to Danielle Casanova, who died of typhus at Auschwitz, and to the courage and sacrifice of Communist women. Women who survived the camps (notably Marie-Claire Vaillant-Couturier who testified at the Nuremburg trials) were honoured, as were the widows of Communist Resistance heroes, such as Mathilde Péri.[15]

The MRP, formed at the end of the war, could not claim Resistance glory as a party, and so celebrated Resistance actions on a more individualistic level: 'we simple women suffered through the Occupation. How many of us hid Jews, welcomed and clothed parachutists, fed the wives of absent Resisters?'[16] Very many women did support the MRP, whose appeal depended, ultimately, on its association with General de Gaulle, its association with the Church and its claim to be the defender of the family. Germaine Poinso-Chapuis, MRP Deputy who was (briefly) Minister of Health, wrote: 'In a nation, women are the element that represents tradition, continuity. If women are drawn to our programme, it is because they have seen that we are guardians of a French, religious, tradition.'[17]

The Communists and Christian Democrats were the only parties which made a concerted effort to reach the female electorate. Women in the Socialist Party tried to indicate that the party should follow this example, but both the SFIO and the Radical Party failed in this respect; and the conservative groups had no effective voice at the Liberation at all, compromised as they had been with the Vichy régime.

The PCF and the MRP were, accordingly, the two parties which attracted the largest number of female voters in the various elections of 1945 and 1946 (see Table 2.1). The MRP in particular won the support of women, and this led to a number of assumptions being

Table 2.1 Women in the electorate

Legislative elections of November 1946

Party	Results %		Men %	Women %
PCF	28.6 ⎫		60	40
SFIO	17.9 ⎬ 58.9%		53	47
RGR	12.4 ⎭		51	49
MRP	26.4 ⎫		42	58
Moderates	12.8 ⎬ 41.1%		46	54
Other	1.9 ⎭		47	53

Legislative elections of June 1951

Party	Results %		Men %	Women %
PCF	26.7 ⎫		60	40
SFIO	14.5 ⎬ 52.3%		53	47
RGR	11.1 ⎭		51	49
MRP	12.5 ⎫		39	61
Moderates	12.8 ⎬ 47.6%		47	53
RPF and	21.8 ⎬		48	52
others	0.5 ⎭		–	–

Source: M. Dogan and J. Narbonne, *Les Françaises face à la politique* (Paris: Armand Colin, 1955)

PCF	(Parti Communiste Français)	Communist Party
SFIO	(Section Française de l'Internationale Ouvrière)	Socialist Party
RGR	(Rassemblement des Gauches Républicaines)	Radicals and Radical Socialists
MRP	(Mouvement Républicain Populaire)	Christian Democrats
RPF	(Rassemblement du Peuple Français)	Gaullist Party

made about the women's vote. Women were said to be innately conservative; because they supported de Gaulle, it was said that they voted for the person and not for the programme; because many abstained, it was said that they were a-political; because of their a-political nature, it was said that they voted like their husbands – without the contradiction appearing to concern the commentators.[18] There was no equivalent explanation of why women voted for the Communist Party.

The political scientists who studied women's voting patterns during the elections of 1946 and 1951 did stress that their conclusions were only provisional. However, their analyses confirmed the influence of assumptions about women and about definitions of political behaviour. For instance, it did not apparently occur to them that women might have voted for de Gaulle after much consideration and thought, for the political ideas he was putting forward rather than for what he symbolised. Nor, in suggesting that women were a-political, did they seem to realise that 'political' could mean anything other than supporting a political party: a distinction was often made between 'political', 'social' and 'technical' activities, and 'political' was always used to mean 'party political'.[19]

Questions could also be asked about the way the gender gap in voting was discussed. A gender gap seemed to be evident since, in the legislative elections of November 1946, it was estimated that women voted 47.3 per cent Right and 52.7 per cent Left, and men 35.2 per cent Right, 64.8 per cent Left. If the MRP and moderates were defined as the Right, and Communists, Socialists and Radicals as the Left, women still voted in greater numbers for the Left than for the Right. However, in those early days, the MRP was not as obviously located on the Right of the political spectrum as it soon became, born as it was of the Resistance, inspired by left-wing Catholicism and associated with de Gaulle who was, after all, perceived more as the 'liberator of France' and the 'First Resister' than as a potential right-wing autocrat. Furthermore, analyses of the election results in terms of gender failed to account for other factors which influence voting behaviour – age, geographical location, education – and failed to note the exceptional circumstances of the 1945 elections which, on the one hand, saw many women not yet registered on the electoral roll, and, on the other, saw a disproportionately high number of elderly women in the voting population – age tending to indicate caution, resistance to change and attachment to the Church. Yet both the press and political parties seized on the traditional notion of women's natural conservatism and women's place within the family as the central focus of their analysis, and this was reflected in the strategy adopted by the parties and in the way the issue of women and politics was dealt with in the press.

'WOMEN'S ISSUES'

The two parties which attracted the largest number of women voters were those which had put together what were called programmes of women's demands. The contents of these programmes were affected by the same ideas about women's nature which underpinned notions about women's priorities and interests. Women were said to have special interests, special needs and a special contribution to make to politics. The MRP saw this in almost biological terms:

Germaine Poinso-Chapuis believed that women's citizenship finally made the body politic whole, and stressed the theme of the complementarity of the sexes, each with its own noble mission, equal but different. In texts across the political spectrum, allusions to one aspect or another of women's nature were frequent: their sense of the concrete made them more realistic and less credulous;[20] their intuitive nature meant that they could see straight to the heart of a problem whereas men took far longer to reach the same conclusions;[21] their sense of morality would filter through to men and would ensure the high moral calibre of candidates.[22] Women's nature would improve the world of politics at every level.

The frequency of elections meant that political parties and their affiliated groups were constantly putting forward programmes for action to be taken on a range of issues, and addressing the interests of specific groups (women, farmers, workers) as well. Women's interests, were, predictably, considered to be anything concerning family, children, school and social welfare. On this, there was cross-party agreement.

In spite of the fact that 'women's issues', as social issues, were subject to widespread consensus and were therefore generally defined as not being truly political, certain differences along the lines of party political divisions were in fact visible from the earliest postwar days. This can be seen most clearly in the programmes of the Catholic MRP, supported by the Union Féminine Civique et Sociale (UFCS, Women's Civic and Social Union), on the one hand, and of the PCF, supported by the UFF on the other. In 1944, for instance, the UFCS in its widely read newsletter *La femme dans la vie sociale* set out women's concerns as: the fight against alcoholism; priority to large families in allocation of housing; respect of family wishes in deciding on the type of school for their children; abolition of prostitution and closure of brothels (which were closed by the so-called Loi Marthe Richard in April 1946); action to support single women.[23] The political and religious perspective is very clear in the emphases on the 'social evils' of alcohol and prostitution, on freedom of education (which, in France, always means support for religious education) and on priority for the family and material help for families. The reference to single women may indicate support for war widows or for those women considered to be 'surplus to requirements' following the death of so many young men – the condition of being a single woman was cause for concern, particularly in Catholic women's publications.

In 1945, the Catholic, conservative UFCS set out its 'general

programme of social and civic action' in which it called for 'legislation and practice that acknowledge both a woman's personal dignity and her specific role in the family and in public life'.[24] When
the programme discussed women's work and women as mothers,
the priority was always on the latter. When discussing the vote, the
UFCS asked for the vote to be made obligatory, for a family vote
(giving greater electoral importance to fathers and mothers of large
families), for the sale of alcohol to be banned on election day and
for owners of brothels to be denied citizenship. Again, the importance given to morality, religion and the family is evident.

The earliest leaflets and statements published by the MRP took
up the theme of the family: 'It is with the French family, it is within
the French family and it is through the French family that we intend
to make our contribution to the reconstruction of our country.'[25] In
1945, MRP women called for a new Declaration of Rights, as the
Declaration of the Rights of Man in 1789 had ignored women. They
wanted to include the following statement in a new Declaration:
'Woman, in the Nation, has equal rights with man, allowing her to
fulfil, in accordance with her nature, her duties in the home, in her
profession and in public life.'

This statement rather confusedly incorporates equality and difference, suggesting that women's nature determines their desires and
their choices, while still claiming for women a public role and professional life. Yet another MRP leaflet published in 1945 stressed
the family in a different way, demanding for:

> the man, in particular the working man, the right and the power
> to fulfil his responsibilities as husband, head of the family and
> educator; for the woman, in particular the working woman, the
> chance to accomplish her civilising mission, her vocation as wife
> and mother.

The reference to the man's ability to fulfil his family responsibilities
is in fact a call for a family wage – a theme dear to the Right –
which would give a man enough money to make it possible for his
wife to stay at home. There is also, implicitly, the notion of a man's
right to paid employment and, explicitly, the acknowledgement of
inequality within the family. The reference to the woman's role
reiterates the common notion of a woman's primary duty, expressed,
however, not as 'responsibility' or 'duty' but as 'mission' and
'vocation', giving it religious overtones and stressing the family as
the natural place for women's fulfilment.

In 1944, the Communist Party wanted to warn the French people that the Resistance Charter was already in danger of being forgotten. The party's ideas mostly reached women via the activities of the UFF, which, at the Liberation, took up this warning and reiterated the themes of the Left: the struggle against inflation, the fight to control the black market and ensure better food supplies and fuel, the theme of the purification of France. The UFF and the UFCS saw this in different terms, with the UFF focusing on the condemnation of collaborators and in particular the execution of Pétain, rather than on prostitution and public morality in a sexual sense.[26]

In December 1944, the UFF set out a National Women's Charter which stressed women's role in the Resistance, the needs of war widows and the defence of the family.[27] The UFF understood 'defence of the family' somewhat differently from the UFCS. On the one hand, the tone was pronatalist, and one of the most powerful slogans of the time was 'to avenge our dead, let us give birth'. On the other hand, there was the demand to make it possible for women to contribute to the renaissance of France as workers as well as in their maternal role:

> Women's working conditions must be improved so that a greater number of women can contribute to the reconstruction of France. They must be provided with crèches, mothers must be allowed to breastfeed their babies during working hours, the 20 per cent wage differential must be abolished.[28]

The UFF also stressed women's rights and wanted a statement specifically concerning women to be included in a new Declaration of Rights to be inserted in a new Constitution, again somewhat different from the UFCS's version:

> The Frenchwoman is a free human being. Mother, worker, citizen, married or unmarried, she has, in every domain, equal rights with men – economic, social, legal, political rights. In particular, she has the right to work, according to the principle of equal pay for equal work.[29]

The UFF and the Communist Party then expressed their commitment to the family in different terms from those of the Catholic groups. The UFF was unclear about the attitude to take towards the housewife: its members, themselves highly active and politicised, wanted support for mothers, and wanted to attract full-time mothers to the PCF and the UFF (and away from the Church) although they believed that the working woman was morally and politically superior to the housewife.[30] The result was 'a contradictory discourse, a curious mixture of political slogans modelled on the PCF and a bland, anodyne language thought not to terrify women'.[31]

The political lines, then, were drawn over the respective roles of Church and state and the intervention of these institutions into the daily lives of French families (for instance, over whether state support should allow married women to keep on working or encourage them to abandon paid employment), and in consequence over the perception of women's 'proper place': at home with her children, subordinate to her husband, or working for France's reconstruction (at a lower rate of pay) as well as caring for husband and children. In other words, women were offered a choice between total dependence and subordination or taking on the double burden of paid employment and domestic responsibility.[32]

Interestingly enough, women's rights (as opposed to women's 'issues') were not on the general political agenda in the early postwar years. Those feminists who, before the war, had fought for women's suffrage, rather naively believed that gaining political rights meant that equality had been won and there was no further need for a feminist lobby. Feminism had been equated with loss of femininity, with adopting the unfeminine posture of making demands, of speaking out, of complaining. This was no longer necessary, they thought: in the words of the admittedly right-wing Gaullist organisation the Rassemblement du Peuple Français (RPF, Rally of the French People): 'Women have won equality. And they have refound their femininity, their taste for soft, silky fabrics, for flowers, for embroidery and for pearls.'[33]

Few of the many women's associations in the 1950s called themselves 'feminist': only the Ligue Française pour le Droit des Femmes was proud to claim this label.[34] Women politicians were eager to prove that they were 'as good as men' and did not take on promotion of women's *rights* as their particular function, but, rather, were perceived as defenders of women's *interests*, which were not thought to be the same thing – and were in fact sometimes seen as being in opposition. The vote and admission of women to the world of politics paradoxically demobilised them rather than offering a new impetus to – and a new forum for – discussion of women's rights.

WOMEN IN LOCAL POLITICS

Organising the transition from Occupation to peace was a complicated political task at local as well as at national level. The plans for the move towards a new democracy had to account for local government as well. This included setting up Comités Départementaux de Libération (CDL, departmental Liberation committees) which would oversee the passage towards elections, run the municipalities in the absence of elected officials and assist the new 'Commissaires de la République' – appointees sent from the provisional government – and which would be composed of Resistance activists representing different Resistance groups and former deportees.[35]

The work of the CDLs was concerned, at local level, with the issues of national importance described in Chapter One: the purge of collaborators, considered particularly by the Communists to be the most urgent task; the organisation and distribution of food and fuel; the elimination of the black market; the problem of housing the homeless. These were defined as 'women's issues' because they were concerned with daily life, family and food. Women were also thought to have a special interest in the more personal issues, such as providing support for the families of the war dead and prisoners and for war orphans.

Women were eligible to participate in these committees and some were chosen as delegates, though not many: in seventy departments, with 1,653 CDL members, only 125 were women (7.5 per cent), and four departments had committees with no women members. Nine departments had over 12.5 per cent women members, but only four included women in their executives, one department (Charente) having a woman leader.[36]

The Resistance was praised as a school for women's responsibility, or as generator of the solidarity that was evident in women's activities at the Liberation.[37] The women delegates in the CDLs represented a number of Resistance groups, from the UFF (52 per cent) the non-Communist Mouvement de Libération Nationale (7.2 per cent), Ceux de la Libération and the Familles de Fusillés et Déportés (2.4 per cent). They represented a variety of professions, with schoolteachers – particularly primary schoolteachers – (30.4 per cent), housewives (30.4 per cent) overrepresented and women in higher levels of management underrepresented (3.2 per cent). There was one agricultural worker and two shopkeepers among the women representatives.[38] In terms of class representation, working-class women were more visible than women of the bourgeoisie who possibly had more to lose, materially, by Resistance activity, and possibly were more likely to have supported Pétain and the world view of the Vichy régime. The provisional government chose twelve Commissaires de la République to be the 'extraordinary representative of the provisional government [in the provinces] who shapes and organises public spirit and maintains order and legality'.[39] No women were among them.

INSIDE THE PARTY

By the time that elections had been restored, and representatives elected by the people rather than designated for Resistance activities, the CDLs no longer had any real function, and massive popular support for de Gaulle effectively ended their existence.[40] Once elections had been restored, numbers of women active in local politics began to drop. Access to office of any kind was once more channelled through recognised political parties which were on the whole unwilling to include more than a token number of women. Once women sought a voice within a political party or indeed sought office, they were treated as competitors by the men who controlled the entry points for political responsibility.

The admittedly unreliable figures for party membership show very small numbers of women; they drop further for women activists, and yet again for women in decision-making roles.[41] Political parties wanted to attract female support but did not want it to be independent or even particularly active. The (unacknowledged) ideal for all parties was to have women as 'visible non-participants':[42] seen to be there, but not rocking the boat in any way. The SFIO unwittingly expressed this ideal by asking women at the 1946 Congress to be the 'solid companion of the socialist activist'. Writing about the Radical Party, one political scientist observed that 'the Radicals have always loved women, which is why they don't really want them to intrude into the life of the party (although they would deny this).'[43]

In order to gain female support, all the political parties set up women's sections, whose purported role was to organise propaganda concerning women. The PCF was the most effective in this, and had both its women's section inside the party, whose purpose was to carry on outreach work (its 'travail parmi les femmes', 'work among women', programme) and the UFF outside. From 1948 onwards, the Confédération Générale du Travail (CGT, General Confederation of Labour – the Communist-dominated trade union confederation) also set up women's sections. In the earliest postwar years, the UFF also attracted non-Communist women, who were placed in prominent positions within the organisation, no doubt to support the claim that it was independent of the party line. Even so, the UFF was obviously controlled by the PCF and was led by the wives and companions of PCF leaders.[44] The UFF claimed to have over half a million members at times and its weekly newspaper, *Femmes françaises*, sometimes sold 140,000 copies. *Femmes françaises* was said to address primarily non-working mothers, as working women could read the newspaper published (from 1952 onwards) by the women's section of the CGT. The glossy monthly magazine *Heures claires* came to complement the weekly magazine and offer some kind of alternative (although hardly competition) to the mainstream glossy women's magazines.

The MRP's work with women was less direct. While the party had a 'women's team' and published a bulletin for its women representatives called *Pour l'information féminine*, the propaganda work on behalf of the MRP was carried out more by religious groups, linked either directly (such as the Ligue Féminine d'Action Catholique (Women's Catholic Action League)) or indirectly (such as the UFCS) to the Catholic Church. The association of the MRP with Catholicism was an effective way of attracting women to the party particularly as voters (rather than activists), calling them to vote against Communism and for Christianity.

The other political parties were less successful in their attempts to reach out to women via women's sections and a militant press. The SFIO had a women's committee, and published a weekly women's magazine, *La vie heureuse*; women of the Centre-Left Rassemblement des Gauches Républicaines (RGR, Rally of the Republican Left) formed the Rassemblement des Femmes Républicaines (Rally of Republican Women), while women in the Radical Party formed the group Femmes Radicales, both with their own newsletters, which mostly appeared irregularly.[45] It is impossible to establish reliable figures for membership of these groups or readership of the newsletters. What can be learned from the publications is the individual party approach to 'women's issues' and the way in which women were addressed.

La vie heureuse, for instance, demonstrated the inability of the SFIO to find an appropriate way of addressing women. Discussion inside the SFIO women's committee indicated that Socialist women assumed that the wider public of women were not interested in politics and would be put off by a too overtly political publication.

They therefore decided to keep the obviously political content of the magazine to a minimum. Written anonymously, the magazine always opened with a political editorial called 'Letter to our readers', addressing a specific problem such as how to vote or the falling birth rate. The only other sign that this was in fact a party political publication was its regular column called 'How they live' which looked at the private lives of Socialist and Communist women representatives; there was no further mention of or comment on anything that could remotely be accused of being 'political'. Even the 'How they live' column pandered to what it was assumed that women wanted to hear about their women politicians and showed the women firmly ensconced in family surroundings, sitting with their children, darning their husband's socks or standing by the stove, stirring something. The MRP was more at ease with its female audience – and its newspaper *Forces nouvelles* had a women's page – as it had a clear view of women's nature and role and was certain that women agreed with its view.

The centrist groups were unable to broaden their appeal to include working-class women as active members of the party. The most obvious examples of this were the women from the Rassemblement des Femmes Républicaines. Middle-class and well-meaning, this group organised classes in oratory style for prospective candidates, held 'feminist teas' during which invited speakers told of their experience in the USA or in which women's rights were discussed, and seemed to accept that its role was a kind of training-ground for women's political education.[46] The way in which these groups operated assumed both the time and the education which made it possible for women to participate: its audience was, not surprisingly, generally limited to middle-class women – and, even more specifically, to women in the professions and to wives of politicians.

The likely function – as opposed to the declared function – of these groups was to keep women in their place: by setting up a women's section, political parties could avoid taking on any far-reaching implications of women's political rights and push women's political activity into a corner labelled 'women's issues'.[47] It was a way of dealing with the party appeal to women voters and of dealing with women inside the party at the same time.

CANDIDATES

The scant attention paid by most political parties to women is obvious in the absence of space given to women and to 'women's issues' in general party publications, in the cavalier way women were treated at party congresses,[48] and in the attitude within different parties towards putting forward women candidates. The PCF was a notable exception, consistently fielding the largest number of women candidates, but even this apparently pro-woman party was not immune: Jeannette Vermeersch, the most prominent woman in the PCF, reported that one Communist candidate refused to have a woman on his electoral list, saying, 'You wouldn't do that to me, would you.'[49] Socialist women complained increasingly, and increasingly desperately, about the lack of support they received from their male colleagues; Radical women were still regretting in 1956 that there were no women Radical Deputies in the National Assembly;[50] the Gaullist Rassemblement du Peuple Français claimed to be setting up a women's committee but there is no evidence that it ever did so. There is no indication at all that the Gaullists wanted women candidates. The Duchesse de la Rochefoucauld wrote in her memoirs of her experience in the political world of the RPF when she was hoping to be a candidate as a seat became vacant in the Marne:

> One day, I received a courtesy visit from Jean Taittinger. 'Is it correct', he asked me, 'that you are standing for election? For if you are not, I will stand myself.' I withdrew. Jean Taittinger went on to have a brilliant political career.[51]

The problem for the MRP was one of doctrinal logic as far as women candidates and representatives were concerned: if the party strongly supported the place of women in the family, what could justify putting women candidates on their electoral list? When questioned, MRP women representatives put forward the argument of fulfilling a maternal mission in a different domain; they were looking after the future of their children on a grander scale.[52]

Dogan and Narbonne claimed that women were excluded from prominent positions within political parties because of their lack of experience and not because they were women – as if these two facts were independent of each other.[53] Women disagreed. Inside all the political parties, women complained that they were not given a fair chance of being elected to the National Assembly. The electoral system in 1945–6 was a form of proportional representation and generally only first place on an electoral list gave the candidate a real chance of success. In the 1946 legislative elections, women constituted only 16 per cent of the candidates in first or second place on party lists and only 7 per cent of those who were finally elected (see Table 2.2).[54] In the preparation of the electoral list,

Table 2.2a Candidates for election in November 1946

		PCF	SFIO	RGR	MRP	Moderates	Others
Total	2801	544	537	554	543	482	141
Men	2419	437	469	487	472	437	117
Women	382	107	68	67	71	45	24
% of women		19.7%	12.7%	12.1%	13.1%	9.3%	24%

Total % of women candidates = 13.6

Table 2.2b Women candidates in November 1946

	PCF	SFIO	RGR	MRP	Moderates	Others
Number of women	107	68	67	71	45	24
Women 1st or 2nd on list	27	10	5	8	2	11
% of women 1st or 2nd on list	25%	15%	7%	11%	4%	46%

Total % of women 1st or 2nd on party lists = 16

Source: M. Dogan and J. Narbonne, *Les Françaises face à la politique* (Paris: Armand Colin, 1955)

women were 'thought useful but rarely placed high';[55] Léon Blum, writing in 1945, seemed unaware of his tokenism when he said that he hoped to see at least one woman candidate (or, as he put it, 'un candidat femme') on every party list, but was not interested in making sure that any of them were in fact elected: 'even if they aren't placed in positions where they will be elected, their very presence will change the electoral campaign.'[56]

What could women do to improve their chances? In direct contradiction with the suggestion that women had a special contribution to make to the world of politics, women were told that to be good candidates, they should emulate men as far as possible. 'It isn't as women that we must act, but as competent individuals. We must demonstrate that we are capable of dealing with issues like men. We must try to show that although we are women, we are competent'.[57] *La vie heureuse* interviewed Andrée Vienot, Deputy and, briefly, Under-Secretary for Youth and Sport, and said: 'after a few minutes conversation, we had completely forgotten that we were talking to a woman.'[58] The Radical-Socialists wrote:

> We want women to become accustomed to opening their intelligence to everything that is noble and good ... not simply to follow others like sheep. We want them to think like men. By this, we mean that they should have free, proud and generous spirits.[59]

Prospective women candidates were taught how to speak in public and how to dress, in order to make themselves appeal to the electorate. Think like a man but look like a woman, seems to have been the message: 'for goodness' sake, let us remain feminine in our appearance, simple and always carefully turned out, with a hint of elegance'.[60] An expert brought in by the SFIO told his female audience to avoid being frivolous but also to avoid being bluestockings. According to him, the way to make an audience forget that 'you are only women' was to display both elegance and common sense.[61]

Another strategy for gaining political office, this time in keeping with the notion of woman's nature, was to limit ambition. Political parties felt that women's place in politics was likely to be at local rather than national level. Local government was in line with women's nature and interest in their immediate environment. Furthermore, women's lack of political experience or supposed competence was less likely to matter at local level: local government was perceived primarily as a question of administration, of supervision of

Table 2.3 Women in local government 1947–65

Year	Women local councillors		Women mayors	
	Number	%	Number	%
1947	14,889	3·1	250	0·7
1953	13,832	2·7	300	0·8
1959	11,246	2·4	381	1·0
1965	11,145	2·3	421	1·1

Source: Mariette Sineau, 'Femmes élues: la percée. Bilan historique', *Citoyennes à part entière*, No. 20, May 1983, p. 9

the concrete aspects of life – schools, hospitals, roads – and not as 'political' at all. One unstated reason for accepting women at local level more easily than at national level was that male candidates felt less threatened, aspiring as they mostly did to national importance: where real power was not at stake, women's participation met with less resistance.

In spite of this, figures do not show that women were elected in large numbers to local office. The Ligue Française pour le Droit des Femmes noted that in the local elections of October 1947 in a commune in the Ardennes (Condé-les-Vouziers: 400 inhabitants) there was one list of candidates who were all wives of the 'gardes-mobiles' and policemen, putting themselves forward to defend the interests of 'their men', who could vote but who could not stand for office. The League also notes that one commune (Echigey in the Côte d'Or) had elected a women-only town council in 1945 and that a fierce wrangle was going on in the 1947 elections because the men wanted to take back their local power.[62] These examples are of course noteworthy because of their novelty and the numbers of women local councillors dropped consistently over the next twenty years (see Table 2.3). This was interpreted as bashfulness on the part of women, who hesitated to put themselves forward. No attempt was made to make it more possible for women to take on a career in politics and reconcile the several roles they were supposed to play; indeed, the mere fact of attending the meetings required of candidates could work against women. One MRP woman wrote, 'I wonder what influence a woman who left her children with anybody in order to run around public meetings would have.'[63] This image conjures up fast and loose women, 'running around' and 'public meetings' hint at prostitution or at least loose morals, and the woman in question does that most terrible thing, leaves her children with 'anyone' (their father?). Hardly subtly, we are told that a woman who so blatantly denies her feminine role could not be worthy of office.

DEPUTIES, SENATORS, MINISTERS

With so many obstacles, visible and invisible, practical and ideological, in their way, who were the women who managed to reach national office and intrude into the misogynistic world of French national politics? What was their experience as the first generation of female elected representatives?

In spite of the obstacles, some women were determined to play a public role in the new France. During the parliamentary debates celebrating the Allied victory in Europe, Mathilde Péri spoke in the name of the women of France, praising their contribution to the Resistance and claiming that 'out of the chaos of war, a new woman has emerged'.[64] While this may have been an overly dramatic formulation of the foreseen changes, women *had* gained new political rights. Female suffrage and eligibility for political office, it was felt, was bound to lead to public discussion on women's 'proper place', and it was widely believed that perceptions about women's role might be susceptible to change. The tension between competing discourses about women's nature and women's role characterised discussion about women and politics not only in the earliest postwar years, but at the very least through the decade of the 1950s. It gave the first generation of women politicians the complicated task of taking on masculine roles in a male-dominated political world without any female models to imitate; and it made them aware that they were carrying the burden of setting the tone for generations to come.

The participation rate of women in politics for the whole of the period up to 1968 was hardly glorious (see Tables 2.4 and 2.5). Indeed, it was better in 1946 than it was in 1968. Women barely figured at all in government. Two women, one Socialist (Andrée Vienot) and one MRP (Germaine Poinso-Chapuis), served briefly in governments in typically 'feminine' posts (Youth, Health), but from 1949 to 1959 no woman was in a French government.[65] General de Gaulle, who according to his supporters was the liberator of women, mocked the idea of a woman in government, laughing it off as absurd: 'What, appoint an under-secretary of knitting?' he reportedly said.[66]

A sociological study of women politicians of the 1944–68 period

Table 2.4 Distribution of seats 1945–68

Senate

Elections	Seats	Men	Women	%
12.1946	314	295	19	6.1
11.1948	320	307	13	4.1
5.1952	319	310	9	2.8
6.1955	319	311	8	2.5
6.1958	314	308	6	1.9
4.1959	307	302	5	1.6
9.1962	274	269	5	1.8
9.1965	274	269	5	1.8
9.1968	283	278	5	1.7

National Assembly

Elections	Seats	Men	Women	%
10.1945	476	443	33	6.9
6.1946	476	446	30	6.3
11.1946	621	579	42	6.7
6.1951	627	605	22	3.5
1.1956	596	577	19	3.2
11.1958	586	578	8	1.3
11.1962	482	474	8	1.6
3.1967	487	477	10	2.0
6.1968	487	479	8	1.6

Source: Distribution des sièges entre hommes et femmes dans les Assemblées nationales (Union Interparlementaire, Geneva, 1987)

Table 2.5 Percentage of women Deputies in each political party

Year	PCF	SFIO and other non-Communist Left parties	MRP	RPF; UDR; UNR (Gaullists)	Centre Right
1946	16.0	3.0	6.0	0.0	0.0
1951	15.0	3.0	3.5	0.8	0.0
1956	12.1	2.2	2.8	0.0	0.0
1958	0.0	5.0	3.8	1.0	0.0
1962	7.3	2.6	3.9	0.9	0.0
1967	5.9	0.8	0.0	2.1	0.0
1968	6.4	1.8	0.0	1.8	0.0

Source: Ministry of the Interior

has yet to be written. Mattei Dogan in his study of the social origins of Deputies elected in 1951 specifically excluded the women, on the grounds that they constituted only 3.5 per cent of the total and that 'many of them were housewives, and were therefore considered as being without a profession'.[67] The pioneering political women of the Fourth Republic were mostly appointed or elected because of their own role in the Resistance or because of the activity of their husband or father. Dogan reports that eight-tenths of the Deputies elected in 1945–6 were former members of the Resistance.[68] The large number of Communist women (twenty-six Deputies in the first legislative election of 1946) reflected the importance of the party at the time and the significance of Communist women in Resistance movements. Yet as the numbers of women representatives declined through the 1950s, it is not clearly indicated that a prior role in the Resistance played a part in determining who stayed and who went. Most former Resisters who stood for re-election in 1951 were successful, but by then the influence of the Resistance in politics was declining. Only three women who had been appointed to the first Consultative Assembly in 1944 remained in the National Assembly or in the Senate (called the Council of the Republic during the Fourth Republic) in 1958.[69] A total of only nine women were elected to both Constituent Assemblies and all three Legislatures of the Fourth Republic.[70] In the Senate (where elections were held in different ways and at different times) this figure drops to seven.[71]

Women politicians at national level, whether they liked it or not, had their role carved out for them in advance: they were there to 'defend women' in whatever way they interpreted this task. Some embraced this role, others contested it, and their response was not dependent on party affiliation. Germaine Degrond, Socialist, said: 'I want to represent women, mothers and housewives: I'm one of them and am proud to know their joys and their fears.'[72] Madame Lefaucheux, a conservative (PRL, Parti Républicain de la Liberté) however, disagreed: 'Not every woman has the vocation to be a social worker... the most brilliant financial analysis I have ever heard was by a Communist local councillor, Madeleine Marzin.'[73] For the MRP, the apparent contradiction of doctrine and behaviour was resolved to their satisfaction by pursuing the notion of the household of France. For instance, MRP Deputy Germaine Peyroles said:

> I don't think that women should be limited to dealing with questions of childhood and hygiene. Women are used to holding the purse-strings, their role is to feed and clothe the family. Do you really believe that economic and social questions are so foreign to them that they can't deal with them on a national level? Do

Table 2.6 Membership of parliamentary committees 1945 and 1946

	Number of women			
	1st Constituent Assembly	2nd Constituent Assembly	1st National Assembly	2nd National Assembly
Family, population, health	8	9	7	5
Education, youth	6	6	8	2
Food supply	5	5	8	–
Employment and social security	6	4	3	1
Justice	3	3	2	1
Economy	1	0	5	2
Foreign affairs	1	1	2	1
Public administration	1	2	1	0
Industry	1	0	1	2
Agriculture	1	0	1	1
Defence	0	1	1	0
Finance	1	1	0	0

Source: Maurice Duverger, *La participation des femmes à la vie politique* (Paris: UNESCO, 1955)

you think women have nothing to say about international events? Believe me, no major problem remains unknown to them.[74]

Yet in reading the parliamentary debates of the Fourth Republic, it is patently clear that women only spoke about issues recognised as 'women's issues': if they were allocated the role of speaking about health or the protection of the child, then that is what they did. They rarely spoke in open debate, but confined their contributions to speaking on behalf of those parliamentary committees in which they were involved – generally concerned with social or cultural affairs. In the first Legislature of the Fourth Republic, there was a significant presence of women in the committees dealing with health, education and the family, but they barely made a dent in the committees concerned with industry and reconstruction (see Table 2.6). The high-prestige committees were finance, foreign affairs, and defence, from which, unsurprisingly, women were almost completely absent.[75] Any woman keen to exercise her expertise in economic theory or agriculture in Parliament would thus be frustrated. The international issues that tore apart the French nation in the 1950s – the wars of decolonisation in Indochina and Algeria, the question of European defence – did not leave women politicians untouched,

Table 2.7 Interventions in the National Assembly on topics of general interest in 1947

	Men	Women
Public health, family, housing, leisure	17	49
Education, youth	7	13
Employment and social security	4	13
Finance, economy	65	10
Public administration	57	6
Foreign affairs	12	1
Agriculture	12	0
Defence	5	0

Source: Maurice Duverger, *La participation des femmes à la vie politique* (Paris: UNESCO, 1955)

but did keep them silent. The 'special contribution' that women would make was kept in its special place (see Table 2.7).

Male politicians apparently resigned themselves to the presence of women in the Assembly, but did so with bad grace. Their misogyny, conscious or unconscious, was revealed by innumerable small signs. A case was reported of a refusal to listen to a proposal brought to the house by two women, who were told to go away and solve it 'entre bonnes femmes' – a particularly derogatory and dismissive way of referring to women.[76] Attention was paid to men – a barber on the premises, tobacco rations – that was not extended to women, who were made to feel like the interlopers many of their male colleagues felt they were.[77]

Women politicians had a difficult task: to negotiate a new public identity for which there was no model; to prove that women were worthy and capable, that they could fit into the political world; to be truly feminine women but behave like competent men; in other words, to fulfil the ideal gendered behaviour of both men and women simultaneously.

DISAPPEARING WOMEN

If, in the early days, women politicians spoke in the name of women, on behalf of women and about women's issues, this apparent women's voice gradually disappeared over the course of the next decade. The consensus issues of the Liberation years moved from centre-stage and the international situation dominated French politics. A study of the themes of the 1956 electoral campaign put 'women' as one of 'various social issues' at the bottom of a long list of electoral priorities.[78]

Women representatives diminished in number as has been observed above from forty-two to eight in the National Assembly and from nineteen to six in the Senate in the 1946–58 period. In percentage terms, the drop was from 6.7 to 1.3 per cent in the National Assembly and from 6.1 to 1.9 per cent in the Senate.

Why did this happen? Explanations must include factors both internal and external to the position of women inside the parties, taking account of both pragmatic and ideological reasons. The general evolution of the French political scene was one of the most powerful factors. In 1945, the PCF was the strongest party in France, and participated in government until May 1947. As the Cold War set in, fear of Communist influence and power led to a change in the electoral system in 1951, which effectively marginalised the PCF's representation if not the percentage of the vote it continued to attract. The PCF lost eleven women Deputies between 1946 and 1951, reducing their number to fifteen, which, however, was still higher than the other parties. Also, in 1945, the MRP had appeared to be a new party, attractive to women, with its roots in social Catholicism and its attachment to the person of General de Gaulle. When de Gaulle founded the Rassemblement du Peuple Français in 1947, he intended it to be a cross-party grouping. In spite of this, the RPF soon functioned as a classic political party, in direct competition with the MRP, which suffered dramatic losses from which it never recovered. The RPF did not put women cadres in place, but rewarded the Gaullist faithful with political responsibility. As the PCF and the MRP had had the most support from women and the majority of women representatives, their electoral fortunes were obviously reflected in the fate of the women candidates. The first elections of the new Fifth Republic in 1958 saw the Communist Party all but eliminated, and the actual elimination of all women Deputies of the Left.

During the life of the Fourth Republic, every government was a coalition and the parties were constantly negotiating for power. Political opportunism was an effective barrier both to women's advancement within the individual parties and to their candidacy.[79] As we have seen, men were less than willing to share power with women and in times of uncertainty, candidates new to politics – as women necessarily were – were replaced by 'experienced activists'. The old arguments (women do not vote for women; women are incompetent; women are conservative) were used to keep women away from potentially powerful positions. All the attitudes described in this chapter concerning women and politics conspired to increase rather than decrease the gulf between the private, domestic world of women and the public, political world of men. Women were locked into perceptions of their role based on motherhood and on their truly feminine nature; deviation meant that they were not 'real' women (and would they therefore be good representatives?), but conformity meant that they accepted women's inferiority and their place in the home – and how could they then put themselves forward?

Political scientist Maurice Duverger noted this powerful blend of practical male opposition to female political competitors and ideological opposition to women politicians as early as 1955. In his article 'Are women anti-feminist?', he wrote that men's resistance to women in power was the first and most significant obstacle to women's effective participation in politics:

> Giving a place to a woman means taking one away from a man: in these conditions, the positions given to women are reduced to the minimum required for propaganda purposes. . . .
>
> The elimination of women for competitive reasons is dissembled behind a very effective justification: showing that politics, by its very nature, is an essentially masculine domain, into which women should be admitted only exceptionally and in strictly limited areas of responsibility.[80]

Duverger argued that this situation was the reflection of dominant perceptions of women's role and nature in France, and that for women's participation in politics to change, meaningful reforms would have to be introduced that would combat the notion of women's 'natural inferiority'.

THE FIFTH REPUBLIC

In 1958, General de Gaulle was brought back to power, when the politicians of the Fourth Republic finally recognised that they were unable to end the crisis in Algeria. It was widely believed that de Gaulle would be able to take France out of the Algerian impasse, and public opinion demanded a solution. He was supported, although sometimes reluctantly, by members of all political parties except for the PCF, but the most enthusiastic were those who wanted to keep Algeria French and who thought that this was de Gaulle's intention.

One of de Gaulle's conditions for accepting to head the French government in 1958 was that a new Constitution should be drawn up which would redistribute power in such a way as to eliminate the confusion, instability and immobilism that characterised the Fourth Republic. This was agreed. In complete contrast to the elaborate and public discussions that surrounded the preparation of the Constitution of the Fourth Republic, the Constitution of the Fifth was prepared quickly by a small committee of Deputies, Senators and experts in constitutional law. It was adopted by the government on 3 September 1958, presented to the population on 4 September and accepted by almost 80 per cent of those who voted in a referendum on 28 September which saw an exceptionally high turnout. The 'yes' vote may have been a personal vote for de Gaulle; a vote against the shambles of the Fourth Republic; a vote for the end of the Algerian war. Whatever people thought they were voting for, the result was perceived as a massive vote of confidence in General de Gaulle.

This confidence was expressed more by women than by men. Polls showed that women voted consistently for de Gaulle, while men preferred the Left. Gisèle Charzat gives the following figures for the first presidential elections to be held in the Fifth Republic (in 1965): 38 per cent of women voted for François Mitterrand and 62 per cent for de Gaulle; 52 per cent of men voted for Mitterrand and 48 per cent for de Gaulle.[81]

In 1958, political victory went not just to General de Gaulle but to the new Gaullist Party, the Union pour la Nouvelle République (UNR, Union for the New Republic), which won over 200 seats in the new National Assembly. Legislative elections showed women voting more for centrist and Gaullist candidates than for the Left, providing 55 per cent of the Gaullist party's electors.[82] The main losers were the Communists. Four years later, the MRP, a party associated with the Fourth Republic, lost votes, while the Gaullist vote increased by over 2 million.[83]

The 1960s witnessed the confirmation of the Gaullist hegemony: in 1962, the people voted to elect the President of the Republic by direct universal suffrage; the Gaullist party, with sympathetic minor parties, held an absolute majority in Parliament. De Gaulle himself seemed immoveable and did not favour women in politics: he may have issued the Ordinance of 21 April 1944 giving women the vote, but he did not do it so that women could participate freely in political life. De Gaulle's views on women in politics did not evolve over the 1960s and he did not hide them. When asked about the possibility of having a woman in the government, he is reported in *L'Express* in 1963 as follows:

He did not hide from his audience that, in his view, it is more appropriate for a woman to keep busy with house and children than to take on ministerial or other political responsibilities. . . . He replied in a rather frivolous way 'a woman in government? . . . her presence, especially if she is young and pretty would potentially disrupt the already hardly laborious Cabinet meetings.'[84]

The first legislative elections of the Fifth Republic in 1958 were disastrous for the representation of women: there were fewer women candidates (2.31 per cent) than before and a low percentage of them were elected (8.8 per cent); the number of women in the National Assembly reached a low point which continued until the early 1970s.[85] There were no Communist or Socialist women Deputies elected in 1958 and although a couple of PCF women were elected in 1962, there were no Socialist women in the National Assembly throughout the decade. In the 1967 legislative elections, Mitterrand's non-Communist left-wing grouping the Fédération de la Gauche Démocrate et Socialiste (FGDS, Federation of the Democratic and Socialist Left) reserved seven constituencies for women candidates, at Mitterrand's insistence. The seats chosen were not those where the women were likely to win and, in the event, they lost.[86] In the Senate, the percentage of women was reduced from a high of 6.1 per cent in 1946 to a low of under 2 per cent, maintained until 1974. Between 1958 and 1968, there were fewer women Deputies and Senators than at any time since 1946. Apart from Nafissa Sid-Cara in a junior ministerial post from 1959 until April 1962, no woman was in government until after the events of May '68.

The first decade of the Fifth Republic, then, was not good for women in politics in France. Party membership figures are not reliable, but nonetheless offer an indication of the low numbers of women involved. Charzat's figures show that in 1968 there was one woman member of the PCF for every twenty women who voted communist; one woman member of the non-Communist Left for every 200 voters; and one woman member of the Gaullist Party for every 500 women voters.[87] Gaullist women seemed to fulfil the ideal of the 'visible non-participant', while, as before, Communist women seem to have been the most committed to party and to politics. Not that the party treated them particularly well: one woman (Vermeersch) out of seventeen in the politburo and only 12 per cent of the central committee in 1966.[88] This was, however, a more favourable level of representation than in the other parties. Women with local political office (particularly mayorships) had begun to increase in number in the 1960s, but the noticeable jump of women local councillors from 2 per cent to 4 per cent did not take place until the beginning of the 1970s.

In the political arena, then, the hopes and expectations of the Liberation years were disappointed. Instead of opening up a new forum for debate, women's rights slid off the political agenda in the 1950s; instead of a progressive integration of women into the political system, they were marginalised; instead of becoming increasingly visible, women disappeared. The revised electoral system of the Fifth Republic, which abandoned proportional representation in favour of the single member constituency vote, may have brought stability to Parliament but made it even harder for women to be elected.

The new Republic also considerably reduced the power of Parliament as political power was concentrated in the hands of the President, his advisers in the presidential office and the higher levels of the civil service. This was not necessarily negative as far as women were concerned, and theoretically meant that they could be appointed to positions of power and influence, bypassing the misogynistic processes of selection and election. However, for this to function in favour of women, the will to appoint them had to be there: and in the 1960s it was not.

While women national representatives disappeared, the question of women's rights reappeared in the mid-1960s, brought to the fore controversially by Mitterrand's endorsement, in 1965, of the campaign to legalise the dissemination of information on birth control and to make contraception available and, less controversially, by the campaign to reform the status of married women.[89] Important women's rights legislation was, perhaps paradoxically, enacted in the 1960s with very few women able (or willing) to speak in favour of it from inside the political arena. The eight women elected to the National Assembly in 1958, standing as members of the Gaullist UNR, the MRP or as independents, were not prepared to speak out for women's rights. Jacqueline Thome-Patenôtre, Radical-Socialist Senator, became a Deputy in 1958 and led the campaign for reform of the marriage laws, but hers was one of the very few female names that recurred as champions of women's rights in the National Assembly in the 1960s.

The stranglehold that Gaullism seemed to have on parliamentary life had a number of consequences for women. As Mariette Sineau has explained, Gaullist confidence in its female electorate meant that there was:

no pressure to introduce to Parliament a policy of reforms affecting women. Nor did it [the Gaullist Party] feel a need to bring women into its organisational structure or parliamentary body. The Gaullists simply catered to the conservatism of a constituency they thought they were certain to maintain under any circumstances.[90]

Furthermore, the left-wing parties which provided the only potentially viable opposition to Gaullism were not yet motivated to consider women and women's rights and concerns as an essential part of their programme and practice. The disappearance of women from the French political scene over the course of the 1945 to 1968 period was by no means confirmation of an a-political feminine nature, as was claimed at the time, but shows how the mechanisms of exclusion successfully kept women out, or strictly in the place that was allowed to them.

However, the consequences of this Gaullist domination of politics and the Left's relative lack of interest were not only negative. As women disappeared from national politics, other avenues of action and debate were sought. Women's political activity, by necessity, took place off-stage, within the parties, in the political clubs associated with them, in the unions and in issue-oriented pressure groups.[91] The many political clubs that operated as fora for ideological debate (now that Parliament did not have this function) included the left-wing Mouvement Démocratique Féminin (MDF, Democratic Women's Movement) and the Socialist Club Louise Michel. Other single-issue pressure groups and informal women's groups were already in existence. The failure of the Republic to include women, and of parties to reassess programmes and, in particular, practices, led to increasing disaffection and disengagement from the formal arena of politics. This was generally used to confirm the belief that women were not political animals. Women, however, realised that the important battles to be fought on behalf of women were going to have to be prepared elsewhere.

3 House and home

> A woman is the soul of the home: she sees to the material needs of its occupants, providing them with food, clothing, a roof over their heads; she creates the moral atmosphere of the family and thereby contributes to a great extent to the health and happiness of everyone.[1]

Women found out in no uncertain terms that, in spite of the vote and the optimistic belief that they were going to play a full and equal part in the new France, the ideology of femininity rooted in the home was still strong. Women's world was still defined as private, as domestic; women's fulfilment was still thought to be wrapped up in house and home; women's biology was still destiny. A good woman was a good mother; a good mother was a wife and a house-wife; and, for at least fifteen years after the war, no vision of fulfilled femininity involving anything other than domesticity and motherhood was readily available to women.

This emphasis on women in the home and in the family was represented as the re-establishment of normality, after the upheaval of war. Yet, as Judy Giles has said when discussing the situation of British women after the First World War, the impact of war could have a range of meanings for women's relation to the home: it 'might mean a rejection of older versions of domesticity, but it could also mean the re-intensification of women's relation to the home and the private sphere.'[2] These two possibilities were not in contradiction. After the Second World War, new versions of perfect domesticity overlapped with the old, with the core components of housewifery and motherhood still in place but updated. Furthermore, notions of home and women's role within the home varied according to social status, geographical location and profession; and the undoubted influence of the vision of women primarily as housewives and mothers on their position and aspirations in the labour market was matched by a reciprocal impact of women's work on the vision of the housewife.

The next two chapters will explore the implications of the 'woman equals housewife and mother' equation as it affected government policy, public discourse on housewifery and the home, matching the discourse to women's experience of the home and of motherhood, while Chapter Five will focus on women's paid employment. All three chapters will examine the way in which the relationship between home and work altered for women during the decades following the war.

THE DOMESTIC IDEAL

In the immediate postwar years, the 'home' was that which had been upset by the war, when both housing and family relations were in crisis. The majority of French families experienced housing difficulties – shared lodgings and inadequate provision of basic facilities such as running water and electricity. The home was at first discussed as 'housing', a political question requiring government action. During the 1950s, the home reappeared as a private a-political space, women's domain. The domestic world was presented not as the location of the daily battle for survival that it had been during the war, but as a haven from that battle, the location of the harmony and stability that had been lacking in the war years. At the heart of the home, providing the stability and the harmony, was the woman. According to Robert Prigent, Minister of Population and Public Health, women's true fulfilment lay in 'accepting their feminine nature', expressed in their life in the home.[3] Being a housewife and mother was a mission, a vocation, they were told by the Church, by teachers, by government ministers, by their parents and later by their husbands.

Being a wife, a housewife and a mother was a full-time occupation. Being a wife was not in itself particularly time-consuming, although middle-class women were expected to participate to a certain extent in their husband's career. Being a housewife, on the other hand, was a job, and a job represented as more noble than others as it was accomplished for love – and because of women's nature – rather than for money:

> it is impossible to quantify the amount of devotion, of love, of giving that a wife and mother does ... this is why there can be

no question of 'payment', but we must try to make her work easier, to respect it, because it is a vocation that finds its reward in the work itself.[4]

Housework itself held few charms and nobody pretended that it was fun. It was boring, repetitive, monotonous and unrewarding; and yet it apparently provided women's fulfilment. On the one hand, as has been noted above, women were told and taught that this was so; on the other, notions of women's innate selflessness complemented the first argument. As sociologists Marie-Jo and Paul-Henri Chombart de Lauwe noted, current opinion accepted that a woman's purpose was 'not to live her own life but her role and "vocation" was to serve and love her family.'[5]

The domestic ideal of the postwar years was that of 'la femme au foyer'. It means more than the word 'housewife' in English, which corresponds to the French *ménagère*, although, according to sociologist Evelyne Sullerot, the word *ménagère* is rather disparaging, and evokes a woman in a housecoat, with 'her shopping bag, her large broom and her huge bosom'.[6] The word popular in the USA, 'homemaker' may be a little closer, but still does not provide an exact equivalent. The *foyer* is the home and the hearth; the woman, 'la femme au foyer', is present in the home, inside. The home is placed in opposition to the world outside. *Foyer* indicates family, which the woman chooses above a life outside. 'La femme au foyer' also has religious overtones and was used by Catholic organisations and right-wing political parties whereas the Left preferred the term *ménagère*. The 'femme au foyer' had no occupation outside the home, the home was the family and the woman was at the service of both. In one much-read book, *La femme au foyer*, the author (a Mme Foulon-Lefranc) spelled out the destiny of young women:

> Whatever her artistic or intellectual gifts, a woman cannot do better than to start a home [*fonder un foyer*]; she would also be wise to remain there unless financial need obliges her to work outside it. Her absence from the home weakens family life, deprives the children of the maternal care so vital to their spirit as well as to their bodies.... Stay at home and you will have made the right choice. Create a united, loving family and it will be the source of the purest and strongest joy in your life.[7]

Mme Foulon-Lefranc, like other authors of books of moral instruction for young people, set out the qualities and virtues that the woman in the home most required, first as a 'maîtresse de maison', the mistress of the house, who must display love of hard work, foresight, order, cleanliness and economy. But the woman was more than mistress of the house, she was called upon to be a wife and mother, for which she needed: devotion, goodness, patience, tact and an even temper.[8] These qualities added together made the perfect woman.

After the war, housewifery was represented first as responding to women's own innate needs, but also as a valuable occupation in its own right. While women's contribution of love and devotion was of primary importance, their financial contribution was also brought into play. Women were told that they were indispensable: they were contributing to the household income by staying at home, saving the cost of services that would have to be paid if someone else did them.[9] Articles such as 'What is a woman worth?' in *L'Express* in 1956 added up the cost of the different tasks a housewife and mother accomplished and acknowledged that nobody could actually afford such a woman's services if they had to be remunerated.

A woman's domestic skills were also said to play a part in the husband's professional life. It was an apparently proven fact that a man whose wife kept a good home was more reliable, a better worker, and never needed an advance on his wages.[10] As well as being the guarantee of the man's stable and successful professional life, a good housewife meant a harmonious household. However, a harmonious home tended to mean that the woman simply went along with her husband's demands or requirements as opposed to decisions taken as a result of discussion and agreement. Women were constantly warned, either subtly or openly, that if they were not competent housewives, if they failed in any aspect of their wifely or housewifely duties, they were likely to drive their husband away and would be fully responsible for their own abandonment.

LEARNING TO BE A HOUSEWIFE

Housewifery, then, the guarantee of future happiness, was to be treated as an occupation, as a science requiring training, preparation and understanding:

> It is her job to create a home, an atmosphere of confidence and mutual understanding ... woman must create happiness. She will do this best in her home. The home and only the home is her true professional milieu, where she is both employer and worker.[11]

Schoolgirls had had compulsory domestic science lessons during the occupation and many continued to do so after the war. Textbooks with words such as 'science' and 'method' in the title proliferated. The various components of domestic science can be learned from the contents of these books and from directives sent to teachers. Girls learned:

> the rational organisation of domestic work, upkeep of the house, making and looking after clothes and linen, laundry and ironing, keeping household accounts, elementary notions of law, theoretical and practical childcare, hygiene, elements of psychology and the ethics of family life.[12]

Teachers of domestic science stated their goals which included showing young women where their fulfilment lay:

> Our goal is not only to teach and help them understand but also to make young women love their work in the home, their role in the family and in society.... If this book helps young women understand that their true happiness lies in the home, if it helps them find it there, it will have reached its goal.[13]

A gendered division of household work was always assumed. Domestic science teachers' manuals described how the subject could be taught to boys: they should learn just enough to allow them to lend a hand when they became fathers. 'Obviously there is no question of asking them to take on the role of a girl', wrote one author, in whose view boys ought to know how to: wash up, make a bed, wax the floor, clean windows, do the washing, sew on buttons, peel vegetables, do some simple and quick cooking. In a mixed group, different tasks would be allocated to boys and girls: while the girls would prepare an entire meal, the boys would work out its unit cost, weigh out the ingredients and so on.[14] Even in the classroom, the more prestigious tasks of direction were allocated to the boys while the girls carried out the less valued work of execution. As Dena Attar has pointed out in her study of domestic science in schools in Great Britain, it is no accident that the target audience of domestic science lessons consisted of the least valued group of pupils: working-class, low-achieving girls.[15]

For young women who had left school, there were centres which offered domestic science courses, either privately run or sponsored by the state under the auspices of the CAFs (Family Allowance Funds) and directed primarily at a working-class female public.[16] In rural areas, domestic science training was proposed for young women when they finished their schooling, in order to give them some qualifications. These rural centres of agricultural domestic science followed a similar curriculum to that of their urban counterparts, but added on areas of specialisation in agriculture. In 1957, a survey by the Jeunesse Agricole Catholique Féminine (JACF, Women's section of the Young Catholic Farmers) in which 114,588 young women participated, showed that 43 per cent of farmers' daughters attended these classes.[17] When questioned, however, it appeared that parents were less interested in giving their daughters a training geared to a life in agriculture than in potentially allowing them to earn their living using non-agricultural domestic science skills, in careers such as social work. Moreover, the dream of women in agricultural families was less of being competent farmers themselves than of being able to stay at home and raise their children – like real housewives.[18]

The need for proper domestic science training for women was emphasised by Mlle Monin, an inspector of domestic science education, in a speech she made at the Salon des Arts Ménagers (the Ideal Home Exhibition) in 1948. She illustrated women's domestic incompetence and need for education with the example of one of her students in a cooking class:

> Without reading the recipe carefully, she crossed the kitchen, went to the cupboard, brought back a bowl, realised that she needed a knife, went back across the kitchen; she began to peel her vegetables, realised suddenly that she should have put some paper down on the table to catch the peelings, went to get some, remembered that she should have put some water on to boil, went back to the cupboard, took out a pot, filled it, stopped for a moment because she didn't know how much water to put in, went back to reread the recipe . . . and accomplished during that evening an extraordinary number of superfluous movements and awkward gestures.[19]

Mlle Monin was convinced that domestic skills had to be learned, and could not be left to chance: 'It is quite probable that all the women, and there are – alas! – many of them, who have turned their home into a hovel, with all that that implies both materially and morally, dreamed of something quite different when they married.'[20]

Among the most popular books on domestic science were those of Paulette Bernège, who, perceiving herself to be the direct heiress of Xenophon, Descartes and Taylor, introduced methods of organisation and rationalisation into the home. Her nod of recognition to Descartes is evident in the title of her bestselling book

De la méthode ménagère, written in 1928, and described as essential reading for the mistress of the house. The book ran into many editions in the postwar period.

Paulette Bernège claimed to provide a theoretical framework for her conceptualisation of the housewife's role. If housewifery was a job, then the home was a place of work and should be treated as such. Taylorian notions provided her guiding thread, and she emphasised the distinction between direction and execution of tasks, and the organisation of both time and space in order to increase productivity and reduce unnecessary effort and movement. For instance, Bernège drew up plans for the ideal utilities room, in which the appliances required for the efficient dispatching of washing-related tasks were placed one next to the other in a room given over solely to washing, so that the housewife never had to retrace her steps. According to Bernège, this should be the guiding principle of all the housewife's tasks. 'Work should move constantly forward, in a straight line, without coming and going or retracing steps. Study the doors, the relationship of one room to another, so that it is possible to accomplish your work in a straight line.'[21]

The extent of Bernège's influence is obvious in the women's magazines of the 1950s which contained useful advice for women on how to organise their time, economise on their effort and use their space efficiently. Her methods dominated domestic science teaching, and the journal *Education ménagère* paid due homage to her in a special issue in 1960: 'What women owe to Paulette Bernège'. The introduction sums up her contribution to women by saying:

> It is owing to her:
> – that society today is beginning to recognise that housework is a profession and, like all professions, deserves the status that it will shortly have;
> – that domestic appliances are no longer considered a luxury but an absolute necessity;
> – that we realise that housework cannot be done in a haphazard way, but must be thought out, prepared, ordered, co-ordinated, so that the woman who is doing it is not a thinking robot, but a fully aware worker who is in control of her work, so that she can free herself from it.
>
> We can therefore conclude by reasserting the fact that Paulette Bernège was a 'pioneer' and women will never be able to thank her enough for what she has done for them.[22]

For Bernège, domestic tasks had to be approached in a scientific, methodical, logical way. Her motto was 'order, care and foresight'; she believed that there was a right way and a wrong way of doing everything; a right place and a wrong place for keeping different utensils; a right kind of pot and a wrong kind of pot.

Housewives were turned into amateurs, no longer able to trust their own way of doing things or follow the advice handed down from grandmother and mother. The expert was brought in to show women what to do appeared in various guises: advising women from the pages of *Marie-Claire* and *Elle* in special regular features on the organisation of the home; or coming into a woman's home to advise her on the type of fitted kitchen to install. An expert spoke to women every morning on the radio in programmes such as 'Woman and home' or 'Good morning, Madame'. From September 1957, the radio station France-Inter broadcast 'Advice to housewives', and the morning news included a few words on shopping tips. TV programmes before the 8 o'clock news were also aimed at the housewife ('Art and magic of the kitchen', 'Women's magazine', 'The woman at home').[23]

The emphasis on science and technical expertise paradoxically both claimed to elevate the occupation of the housewife to that of a worthwhile profession with specific skills, its own vocabulary and job satisfaction, yet also infantilised the housewife by increasing her level of dependence: economic dependence on her husband in that she no longer earned a wage and he had to provide everything including the equipment necessary for her to do her work in the home; and dependence on the expert. To do a job properly – and there were clear ideas about what constituted 'properly' – she had to do it the right way, that is, their way. This was true for arranging clothes in a cupboard, for organising the day, the week, the season, the year.

All domestic science textbooks provided model timetables for the housewife, detailed down to the fifteen minutes in the morning for preparing the *café au lait*. Different timetables were provided for different situations: whether the woman was also in paid employment, whether she had children, and if so how many and how old they were. These timetables were established in accordance with the idea that not only was there a right way of doing something, but there was a right time for doing it and a right amount of time to spend on each task. The fact that these timetables made their appearance in mass circulation magazines such as *Marie-France* shows the enthusiasm for the Taylorisation of the home of the 1950s and maybe represented a response to women's need for advice. The stated aim of domestic science teaching was to save a housewife's most valuable resources: time and energy, and as such, there is no doubt that it was useful. Rigid routines were adhered to:

> On Monday, my mother would disappear into her laundry and from then on the washing-machine would be running all day. On Wednesday, sheets, table-cloths, towels and cleaning rags were put through the mangle, folded and ironed. Thursday was mending day. . . .
>
> In addition, a daily rhythm supplied its own counterpoint: every morning the bedding was aired at the windows, beds were made, dishes washed and the kitchen given a quick mop down.[24]

The weekly and daily routine must have given women a sense of control and achievement. The discourse of domesticity of the 1950s, however, was caught up in a discourse of femininity that prescribed limits for young women, affected their future possibilities and their sense of their own worth, while making them totally responsible for the success or failure of their family life and their marriage.

'MOULINEX LIBÈRE LA FEMME': THE MODERN HOUSEWIFE

The push for improved housing conditions, better household equipment and proper domestic science training for women was intended to make housewifery a more attractive prospect. Liberation from drudgery would make housewifery more fun, give women more time and more control. Organisation was one element of liberation. Most importantly, however, domestic appliances made a dramatic entry into the middle-class home. The refrigerator, the vacuum cleaner and the semi-automatic washing-machine were signs of the modern woman, who was represented as free from household chores. The goal of this freedom was to allow a woman to seek higher things: her own cultural development and increased time with her children in particular. The authors of *Les arts ménagers* (1950) were enthusiastic in their reception of new machines and techniques:

> In control of her mechanised kitchen and of her various machines, in command of her mechanical slaves and raising her children according to the principles of hygiene, the woman of the future will do less physical labour than her peasant ancestors; but she will have to reflect, foresee, measure . . . think . . . it has been decided that women will become intelligent.[25]

Advertisements for appliances always stressed their labour-saving aspects. An advertisement for a Thomson washing-machine shows a couple relaxing together in armchairs, presumably while the machine does the washing;[26] another brand of washing-machine (Flandria) shows a woman sitting doing her embroidery, and all the while her 'weekly wash will be soaking, boiling, washing, whitening, rinsing, drying with the incomparable semi-automatic washer-dryer Flandria'.[27]

Women were hungry for consumer durables, particularly after the war during which they had been deprived of even such basic materials as soap. Everything that distanced them from the war and brought them into the modern era was welcomed. Modernity meant new materials, new appliances, and lots of them. Modern materials which were practical, easy to clean, cheerful and bright, probably disposable, included formica, plastic, nylon, stainless steel; modernity was measured partly by the materials a woman used, but also by the number of appliances she had at her disposal. *Nouveau fémina* showed the woman of 1955, her open arms indicating freedom, with her twenty-five appliances, compared with the woman of 1930, who only had thirteen.[28] *Elle*, in 1956, published a quiz ('Are you a modern woman?') which included some questions on the home: Do you own printed sheets? Do you use disposable napkins? Do you have an electric coffee-grinder, mixer or hairdryer? Have you had lino put down on your kitchen floor? Novelty, disposability, technology: these were the signs and the aids of the modern housewife. The modern era was characterised by *Marie-Claire* in 1954 as the age of 'abundance, emancipation, social progress, airy houses, healthy children, the refrigerator, pasteurised milk, the washing-machine, comfort, quality and accessibility'.[29] Jumbled together in this list are notions of healthy living, women's emancipation through modernity, mechanised help in the home which facilitates the task without sacrificing the quality of the achievement, and all these aspects of modern life theoretically available to all.

WASHING MACHINES AND FRIDGES

Modernity and healthy living clearly required significant expenditure. During the 1950s, there may have been a boom in the buying of domestic appliances, but their distribution in the population was extremely uneven. Paris was generally ahead of the rest of France in ownership of appliances, although an interesting exception was the ownership of washing-machines. Washing seems to have been the most resented and difficult of household tasks, obviously the more so when there was no running water in the home and not enough space to hang the washed clothes up to dry: indeed, one 1956 study of daily life in working-class families reported that washing was the most common cause of complaint by women.[30] Machines were supposed to free women from these chores. According to *La maison française*, the relatively low level of ownership of washing-machines in the Paris area was attributable to the way that washing was done: well-off families either had domestic help in the home who took care of this chore, or sent their heavy laundry out to a laundress.

Some initiatives were taken by working-class family associations to help those who could not afford a washing-machine. In the Lyon area, a washing co-operative was set up, which lasted from 1950 to 1961. In Roubaix, washing-machines were bought by one local family association, either with a loan from the CAF or with money collected from all the potential users. Somebody made a handcart for the machine; a weekly timetable was drawn up, and the washing machine was shared between families who each had it for half a day and then took it on to the next family. In Lille, one neighbourhood had a 'machine committee' composed of one representative from each street participating. Housewives registered for a time to use the machine each week, starting at 6 a.m. on a Monday and continuing all week. Each user put her money in a box attached to the machine; nobody stole or cheated. Most of the machines were second-hand demonstration models, and purchase was made easier because the Hoover representative lived locally. There were ten machines owned by this group, eight in constant use and two in reserve in case of breakdown. This particular initiative continued until 1965.[31]

Laundromats were gaining in popularity in Paris, whereas in other areas, washing was still generally done in the home.[32] The laundromat, or 'Lavaupoids', was not universally liked, however, as women felt that it was not kind to laundry, and sheets wore out more quickly than they did when washed at home. It is also interesting to note that whereas husbands would often 'help out' with shopping and other chores, they would almost never do the washing.[33]

Those least likely to own a washing-machine or any other domestic appliance, were agricultural workers, only 9 per cent of whom had a fridge in 1954, when 34 per cent of households of senior managers owned one.[34] The same disparity was obvious with every type of household convenience, from running water to vacuum cleaners. Labour-saving appliances were simply too expensive for most housewives. A survey in 1956 showed that 60 per cent of housewives wanted to improve their kitchen equipment but could not afford the substantial initial outlay.[35] If a family could afford the initial purchase, with the help of credit or a loan from the CAFs, they still lacked the space for an item as bulky as a washing-machine or fridge, let alone a utilities room.

Attitudes towards the value of a fridge indicated class status, lifestyle and values. *Maison et jardin* in 1951 claimed unequivocally that a fridge had become as indispensable as a cooker, while *Bonnes soirées* noted in 1956 that it was still a luxury item waiting for manufacturers to find a way of reducing the price. Later that same year, *Bonnes soirées* ran one of its popular major surveys on 'the refrigerator: luxury or necessity'. Those in favour of the refrigerator believed that its purpose was misunderstood. It was perceived as a place to keep drinks cold and make ice cubes rather than as a means of economising on time, by shopping less often, and on money, by buying in bulk: gone for ever was the necessity to go to the shops every day or even twice a day, the ads proclaimed.

Women's magazines, where women found out about modernity in the home, knew their markets well and each catered to a specific audience. The home and interior decoration featured differently in different publications: *Maison et jardin*, the most upmarket, took readers into the homes – mansions, châteaux – of the rich and famous, with a heavy presence of Americans, representatives of modernity and progress.[36] *Elle* and *Marie-Claire* both ran regular features on aspects of interior decoration and DIY (mostly aiming at a younger audience), while *Femmes d'aujourd'hui* and *Bonnes soirées* had regular features on practical hints for home improvers. While magazines such as *Maison et jardin*, *La maison française* or *Arts ménagers* addressed women who could afford not only to visit the Salon des Arts Ménagers but to make purchases there, those with a more modest leadership such as *Femmes d'aujourd'hui* or *Bonnes soirées* tended not to advertise expensive appliances but limited themselves to ads for more accessible household aids such as washing powder. These magazines wrote little about interior decoration or how to host a cocktail party, but included advice on how to create the illusion of more space in a small flat and how to cook a nourishing meal quickly. The magazine produced by the CGT for women, *La revue des travailleuses* ('The working women's journal', which changed its name to *Antoinette* in 1955), specifically addressed the problems of working-class women who ran a home and worked outside the home as well. While always looking to the

Soviet Union as a model, and focusing on the situation of women at the workplace, the magazines did include some household hints as well, such as providing a list of essential items for the 'housewife's laboratory'. As a militant rather than a commercial publication, however, it was not dependent on advertising revenue for its existence and was not a major source of information about domestic technology or the art of being a housewife. And as a militant publication, it reflected the views of the CGT which claimed that the housewife was a construct used only when it suited the capitalist bourgeoisie.[37] The CGT could hardly denounce the ideology of the 'femme au foyer' with one breath and provide a positive image of her with the next.

THE REALITY OF HOME

The idealised discourse of the home as haven was belied by the reality; the discourse of domesticity as women's fulfilment was contradicted as soon as anyone asked women what they actually felt and wanted, or as soon as sociological studies were undertaken about living conditions.

The housing crisis, mentioned so often in the National Assembly and elsewhere as being one of the major social evils of the time, was nonetheless not a priority for government investment in the 1940s. Priority, as it appeared in the first plan for modernisation and infrastructure (le Plan Monnet) was given to 'productive investment', the results of which would be visible in terms of industrial and agricultural output. In the 1950s, the military budget was drastically increased because of the wars in Indochina and Algeria, while the housing budget remained insignificant. Shocking stories were told about insanitary conditions, overcrowding, dangerous buildings, illness. A *taudis*, or slum building, was defined as: housing that should be destroyed, that clearly constituted certain danger for the health and safety of its occupants.[38]

It was estimated in 1945 that there were 280,000 urban slum buildings, and 200,000 in rural areas. The 1946 census showed that 20 per cent of buildings in Paris had no running water, 77 per cent had no bathroom and 54 per cent had no inside lavatory.[39] In the 1954 census, 22 per cent of the housing stock was considered to be in a state of 'critical overcrowding', defined as three people living in one room, four in two, six in three or eight in four. In 1957, this was estimated to have dropped to 12 per cent in the Paris area.[40]

The postwar migration away from rural areas had caused a

population increase of 53 per cent in towns of 50–100,000 inhabitants while towns of over 100,000 inhabitants (excluding Paris) had increased by 29 per cent.[41] This migration exacerbated the urban housing crisis.

The state of the housing stock obviously varied from one region to another: rural communes and urban communes both suffered although sometimes in different ways. For instance, the phenomenon of the 'hôtel garni' – hotels providing furnished rooms on a daily or weekly basis – which exploited the occupants shamelessly, was an urban phenomenon, estimated to have concerned about 400,000 people in the Paris area in the early 1950s.[42]

New housing in rural communes tended to give priority to agricultural buildings rather than homes until the end of the 1950s. In the 1960s, the rate of building new homes increased dramatically compared with the earliest postwar years, but in 1968 only 8 per cent of all categories of agricultural workers and farmers lived in a house built after 1945.[43]

To provide the housing needed for the population, 320,000 new homes would have to be built every year, according to INED, but this never happened. Compared with new building in Britain and West Germany, France could be seen to be lagging behind. A half-hearted attempt had been made to redistribute housing through requisitions: rents which had been frozen after the First World War were allowing some – mainly elderly women – to occupy large apartments by themselves, while young families could not find anywhere to live. The extent of the requisitions was never very widespread, however, and failed totally as a solution to the housing crisis.

Some groups and individuals took their own initiatives: the squatter movement, supported by the Mouvement Populaire des Familles (the Popular Family Movement), occupied its first building – a château outside Marseille on 8 October 1948. While the movement acknowledged that the numbers concerned by squatting were insignificant nationally, it nonetheless achieved temporary rehousing for several families and symbolised 'the indignant reaction of workers, aware of being taken for fools'.[44] Women played a particularly important role in this movement:

> sometimes by themselves preventing the police from carrying out expulsions ... sending delegations to the town hall ... going into the police stations to get assurances about housing repair. The occupation of buildings by squatters needed to be followed up

by somebody present all the time and only housewives could do this.[45]

During the 1950s, the building of HLM (*habitations à loyer modéré*, low-rent housing) was underway and by 1960, the development of extensive housing estates, or *grands ensembles*, was considered to be the new, modern way of planning living space, particularly for the less well-off. But housing was never a government priority and there was never enough to provide for the needs of the growing population.

Most of the French dreamed of having their own little house ('un petit pavillon') outside a town but within reach of their place of work. Most ideally wanted a three-bedroomed house for a family of five.[46] Sociologist Paul-Henri Chombart de Lauwe and his team conducted an inquiry into 'The everyday life of working-class families' and attributed the attraction of the little house to the fact that it was the furthest away from the reality of most working-class households, who did not perceive its disadvantages:

> A long journey to work, long distances to nurseries and schools, roads which are hard to maintain and are generally in poor condition . . . difficulties in relationships with the neighbours, lack of leisure facilities for children and young people. . . . These families are often quite isolated, exhausted by the sacrifices they have made in order to build their home, showing hardly any interest in public life, cut off from trade union activity in their place of work.[47]

A little house may have been the dream, but expectations were quite realistic. When asked in 1956, most working-class families wanted and expected to have hot water and a washing-machine within a few years, but wanted and did not expect ever to own a car, a bathroom or their own home.[48]

WOMEN'S TIME IN THE HOME

The home belonged to the woman. The husband held a curious position: he was the centre of the home, the focus of a wife's preoccupations, the absent hero around whom her life and priorities revolved, yet in terms of actual time he was of less significance to her than the house and the children. Indeed, he was peripheral to the wife's concerns as they were represented on the pages of women's magazines. During her day working in the home, he was absent. In spite of being the lord and master of the home and its occupants, the husband was an intruder and a clumsy one at that. But the wife was advised to try not to make him feel like the outsider he probably was:

> We women must make the house pleasant with its colours, its tidiness, the care we take with meals and the prompt serving of meals; we should ask our husband's advice on any changes we want to make to our homes, so that the house feels as if it belongs to him as well as to us.[49]

Women's clear sense that the husband was an intruder in the home is shown in the proliferation of humorous articles about how clumsy and inept men were when let loose in the kitchen or the bathroom: 'Careful, there's a man in the bathroom!' laughed *Elle*, while *Marie-France* wrote out the 'Seven commandments for the model husband' left alone for the summer. Women's domestic superiority was linked with their deviousness and easy ability to manipulate their men when trying to get their own way, illustrated in a regular feature in *Bonnes soirées* called 'His Majesty my husband'. Each week, the husband – who clearly thinks he is intelligent and capable – is shown up as stupid and incompetent, whether at feeding the baby, washing a dish or being taken in by some ruse of his canny wife.

The husband brought the outside world into the home. He was the provider; he appeared in ads for new appliances, pleasing his wife by buying her a new machine. He was the giver of gifts or the technical expert who could fix things around the house. The husband appeared in the home in the evening, after work. For him, home was a place to relax, not to work, and when he was there, he was the focus of his wife's attention. She had to make sure that he was able to get the rest he needed by keeping the children quiet, listening to him but not worrying him with her domestic problems, feeding him: but he still did not belong.

In all discussions about helping the housewife, or liberating the housewife, nobody seemed to think that an equitable distribution of household labour might be an appropriate solution. The husband was sometimes called upon to lend a hand; he was never required to do his share. The primary responsibility of women in the home was never questioned.

INED published studies of the time-budget of married women in 1947 and drew the following conclusions: a woman who worked outside the home as well as running her household spent less time on housework than her full-time housewife counterpart; only one-tenth of working-class households had paid help in the home compared with eight-tenths of households in the liberal professions; the more children a woman had, the less likely she was to be in paid employment as well.[50] More surprising, possibly, is the amount of time per week devoted to housework: 47 hours a week for a woman without children, increasing to 72–76 hours a week for a woman with three children; and yet time and energy devoted to children, considered the most important of a woman's duties, occupied her for far less time than housework, cooking and shopping.[51]

Most working-class women had no paid help in the home although some were lucky enough to have family members, generally a mother or sister, who would help with children, and they depended on these informal childcare arrangements. Many who would have been eligible for a *travailleuse familiale* (TF, home help) did not know either of the existence of this service or how to get hold of one.[52]

By the end of the 1950s, was women's time in the home less preoccupied by housework than before? Did the domestic appliance really 'liberate' women? Did tasks take less time and become less onerous? In 1958, the question of the 'time-budget' of married women was addressed again. The authors found that there was a slight reduction in the amount of time women spent on domestic chores (from approximately 74 hours a week to 70.3) but that for women who both ran the home and held a paid job, the working week took up as many hours as before. Certain household tasks were as time-consuming as they had always been, most notably the washing. The authors concluded that: 'at the end of the war, the number of households with domestic appliances was far from what it is today. In spite of that, the length of the married woman's working day does not now seem to be any shorter'.[53]

Women were, in part, held responsible for this lack of progress. They were said to be resistant to change and to remain attached to their habitual ways of doing things, for instance the shopping. French women were reluctant to give up the daily market. Doing a weekly shop was unthinkable: full-time housewives liked the market which got them out of the house, gave them contact with other people and was an integral part of the structure of daily life.

Furthermore, appliances such as fully automatic washing-machines were not yet available and the machinery that women did use in the home required attention, servicing. The strong notions concerning the 'proper' way of doing something together with the dominant ideas about appropriate ways for women to spend their time and energy combined to inspire guilt in those who took short cuts to ease their routine. Even the busiest working mother was suspicious of time-savers such as tinned or prepared foods. There was also the notion that being a good housewife meant not taking short cuts such as these, but devoting time and energy to looking after the family: the resources that Bernège was hoping to save were in fact being used up quite properly. The relationship between women and domestic appliances was more complex than might at first be imagined.

DOMESTICITY AND CLASS

The discourse of domesticity was presented as gender-based, not class-based. A discourse for and about women, it could appear as a great social leveller and a unifying force, where success as a woman could be evaluated not by money or culture but by the ability to keep house. Indeed, one definition of the 'ordinary housewife' describes her as the 'middle-class wife [who] had finally lost her servants, and the working-class wife [who] had gained or was in the process of gaining a whole house to look after'.[54] This female classlessness was quickly undermined when the question of class and home was specifically addressed.

Judging by all the information on the state of working-class living conditions of the 1950s, the advice of Paulette Bernège was going to be at best hard to follow, and completely irrelevant most of the time. For most working-class women, home represented the double shift rather than a haven from the world of work.[55]

The notion that running a home smoothly was mainly a question of organisation and attitude was insulting to women whose material living conditions made organisation an impossibility. Chombart de Lauwe noted in his study of the everyday life of working-class families that:

> Almost all the women in the study found it difficult to put up with their living conditions ... they had neither the housing, the equipment, the social services nor the local organisations which would allow them to find satisfaction of their most profound aspirations in their lives at home.[56]

Even so, 49 per cent of the women he questioned wanted to stay at home rather than go out to work: women's conditions in the work-place and in the world of work generally was not so enticing as to make them preferable to hearth and home. For many working-class

women, staying at home had both symbolic and practical implications: it meant a significant rise in status, the fulfilling of certain
aspirations and a less exhausting daily routine.

THE RURAL HOME

Women in agricultural families had a quite specific relationship to
the home. The notion of 'being a housewife' did not exist: women in
agricultural families worked all the time. Indeed, being a housewife
represented the dream of a better life. Women could not make the
distinction between what constituted 'real' work and what constituted family work, as both took place in and around the farm and
neither was paid. Domestic labour was particularly onerous in the
farmhouse which was less well-equipped than urban homes. Houses
were old and even in 1962, nearly half of France's rural dwellings
had no running water and 84 per cent had no inside lavatory.[57]

Women were isolated, without the contact provided by the daily
market visits that many urban women could enjoy. The Jeunesse
Agricole Catholique Féminine provided one of the few forms of
social life available for young rural women. The JAC and JACF
educated the next generation of agricultural leaders, preparing
young men and women for adult life and maintaining a clear vision
of male and female roles. Improving and beautifying the home was
a major discussion theme for young women in the JACF. In the
study days organised by the JAC, boys would learn about new
agricultural techniques, girls about the role of the mother, about
hygiene. If they learned anything agricultural, it was about hens and
rabbits.[58]

THE MIDDLE-CLASS HOME

In the postwar period, it was no longer the norm for middle-class
households to have live-in servants. In 1945, there were 36,520
declared servants in Paris and 29,071 housekeepers or cleaning
women.[59] Domestic science lessons – previously (and still pre-
dominantly) for working-class girls – became useful for middle-class
girls as well. The same was true for women once they had taken
on the role of housewife and mother: from being the 'mistress of
the house' who directed and organised others, the woman had to
be involved herself in the daily tasks that composed the running of
the home. This point was stressed by *Maison et jardin*'s early issues,

which showed women of the bourgeoisie accomplishing various tasks ('Mme R. de Crepy effortlessly waxing her floors herself thanks to an electric floor-waxer'[60]) which they would never have done themselves previously. Another lady (Mme Bertrand Larcher) found that 'with Christecla, she only needed to clean her silver once a week'.

Magazines addressing women with disposable income advertised goods beyond the reach of less well-off families, and showed a daily life and material surroundings worlds apart from the working-class home. The first issue of *Maison et jardin* in 1950 contained adverts for silk stockings, washing machines, Lalique glasses, fitted kitchens, Venetian blinds, fridges and perfume, indicating a lifestyle cushioned by leisure and money. *La maison française* published a serious article about the correct wine glasses to use with different wines and another about how cocktail parties had become 'the only way' to entertain in Paris. The women's page in the weekly news magazine *L'Express* contained useful advice on the correct way to wear trousers, on the chores that have to be done at different times of the year (put your fur coat in storage, have the furniture cleaned) and other items of no interest to the majority of Frenchwomen.

Middle-class women were those able to fulfil the domestic ideal as expressed by Paulette Bernège, as far as organisation of space and time was concerned. The readership of *La maison française*, according to its publishers in their campaign to attract advertisers, spent well over the national average on their homes. The readers were 'exceptionally receptive to advertisements because they want to buy and they have the means to buy'.[61] Middle-class women would probably also be able to devote themselves to their children and therefore be 'better' mothers.[62] Most had given up paid employment either upon marriage or on the birth of the first child, and without the economic necessity that permitted (or forced) women to continue working, they had no socially acceptable reason to go on. Most also had some form of paid help in the home although this was rarely a live-in maid. These middle-class women's contribution to the housework was rarely the heavy washing or cleaning, but consisted more of tidying, making the beds, cooking and supervising the activities of the children:[63] the activities defined as the crowning glory of a woman's work.

A caricature of how the wife of a businessman spent her day appeared in an article on leisure in *Marie-France*:

> My dear, I don't have any leisure ... at 8.30 I have breakfast and read the newspapers ... to keep up with everything, I can't just

glance through them, I have to read them properly! Then my mornings are taken up by my two children, because I look after them myself, of course! Then there are keep-fit sessions, the masseuse, the hairdresser... between ourselves, do you know what a woman goes through to keep herself looking good and with what effort she makes and keeps herself beautiful? In the afternoon, there are the children, different charitable activities and the dressmaker, the milliner, exhibitions, openings. When I sometimes have an hour free before dinner, I look at some of the latest books. And I haven't even mentioned my duties as mistress of the house, the way I have to keep an eye on everything... or the receptions, the need to dress, either for dining at home or in town... the galas, first nights... no, really darling, I don't have a minute.[64]

This sounds like a lot more fun than the race against time and the fight against fatigue and inadequate housing that seems to have been the lot of most working-class women. Much of the middle-class and upper middle-class woman's time was spent in maintaining a certain level of appearances, both her own and her family's; her lifestyle was not necessarily free of constraints, and what seems like amusement to others may well have represented obligation and duty for her.

Middle-class women were still tied to being in the home, if not to cleaning it. For instance, in 1954, over 75 per cent of middle managers and senior executives still went home at lunchtime: even if their wives had not cooked the meal themselves, they were required to be there when the husband came home to eat it.[65] The home still provided the core of their emotional and economic lives; 'doing up the home', organising its occupants were as much the focus of the middle-class 'femme au foyer' as of her working-class counterpart, if not more so.

AGAINST HOUSEWORK

Ultimately, housework was the material manifestation of a notion of home, of a nest. For Simone de Beauvoir, a woman's fulfilment was less in the accomplishment of household tasks than in the symbolic function of housework: providing order and ensuring the smooth running of the lives of family members, making their lives possible by sacrificing her own in an endless round of monotonous, never-ending and frustrating activities. The notion of women's innate sense of sacrifice fitted neatly into the scenario of the selfless housewife living through and for those she loved. The home is the woman's universe: by renouncing her life outside, she creates her own universe around her, transforming her prison into her kingdom.[66]

Few women spoke out against the emphasis on women's role in the home. Jeannette Vermeersch, whose views were not necessarily shared by the Communist Party hierarchy, took issue with the Catholic, conservative middle-class ideal of 'la femme au foyer' and was one of the very few to reject it utterly on the grounds of lack of recognition of domestic labour as work:

> it is considered that a woman's role is to make love, to make children, to cook and to clean and wait for her lord and master. Without anyone ever taking account of the exhausting work that she does all day long.[67]

Vermeersch also challenged the notion of women's natural fulfilment in the home:

> People, possibly well-intentioned, claim that woman's place is in the home. Maybe they should ask women about it. Is it such a foregone conclusion that women consider that the role they will always play in life is that of shining the family shoes, doing the washing.... No, women want to be free, conscious beings and don't want to watch life pass by from behind the kitchen curtain.[68]

This impassioned speech, made in 1945, was not repeated in these terms or any remotely like them. The PCF wanted to attract not only women workers but also the stay-at-home wives of male workers, shopkeepers and women from all social classes and did not want to appear hostile to women who stayed in the home.[69] André Barjonet expressed the party's ambiguity during the Week of Marxist Thought in January 1965, saying:

> There is no question of denying the great merit of women who are raising their children or of under-estimating the many services they thereby render the country. But whatever the positive aspects of the housewife's work may be, it is nonetheless true that it is (and is becoming more and more) a-social.[70]

A similar ambiguity was found among women in women's rights groups and professional associations.[71] These women had privileged positions in society; they were not housewives themselves – nor did they want to be. The women involved in groups such as the

Association des Françaises Diplômées des Universités, Les Soropto-
mistes, la Ligue française pour le Droit des Femmes or Femmes,
chefs d'entreprise did not share the experience of the majority of
women. Their experience corresponded far more to that of the
worldly, socially superior 'maîtresse de maison' if they were not
employed. If they were employed, they were preoccupied with other
issues – women's advancement in the professions, education, travel,
women's rights – not with the home. When the home was mentioned,
it was usually with some unease. They did not discuss housework in
their publications; the advertisements were for perfume, typewriters,
fur coats, and not for fridges or washing-machines.

It was rare for women to be asked their opinion of housework.
One survey organised by *Femmes d'aujourd'hui* and published in
Arts ménagers et culinaires in 1956 questioned women on their
attitude towards the out-to-work-or-stay-at-home debate. The opinions given were not flattering to the home. A Mme X wrote: 'I
find housework tedious and demoralising'; Mme G. V. added that
'domestic worries have turned me into an old woman with no joy
in life'; Mme G. said 'My husband demanded that I stay at home
and I felt terribly unhappy about it.' Her advice to young women
was – paradoxically – that 'as soon as you have found a house, stay
at home ... I'm sure it will be hard at first, but you will get used
to it quickly.' The implication is clearly that women should not get a
taste for the outside world, or life in the home would be increasingly
unattractive. Yet housework was acknowledged as an integral part
of married life. The same article quotes a Mlle G. J. who said: 'If a
woman doesn't feel that she has the vocation to be an educator and
a housewife, then she shouldn't marry.'[72]

Simone de Beauvoir was scathing about housework in *Le deuxième sexe*. While the husband has access to the entire universe and
therefore is not really interested in his own home, the home is the
woman's universe and, by controlling her environment, she tries to
find fulfilment. But 'the saddest thing is that this work never creates
anything lasting. The woman is tempted to perceive her work as an
end in itself. Contemplating the cake as it comes out of the oven,
she sighs. What a pity to eat it!'[73]

For Beauvoir, housework could never represent a woman's real
fulfilment: it gives her no autonomy, it is not directly productive or
creative. It perpetuates the notion that women's main function is
the service of others. Other women may not have theorised and
analysed their own dissatisfaction with the life of the home, but
obviously experienced it. This dissatisfaction was not generally

addressed in the 1950s: women had no right not to feel fulfilled by their role as housewife and mother. Many became depressed but did not know why.

A study on overworked mothers prepared by women doctors was published in 1953. The conclusions drawn pointed to housework and not to children as the main explanation for the frequent occurrence of nervous depression among women: 'We have the firm conviction that there is a state of specific, psychosomatic exhaustion due to housework', they wrote.[74] They identified the components of the problem: housework involves at least twenty different tasks; women work in solitude; the tasks are monotonous; there is no legal, economic or social value accorded to this work; there is little in the way of selection or professional training; there is insufficient equipment of the home. But above all there is a basic conflict:

> Women, becoming aware of their personalities, their aptitudes, their possibilities which are as diverse as men's, are disoriented by housework which has retained the dullness that centuries of routine and the indifference of public authorities have given it.[75]

THE NEW HOME OF THE 1960S

Things had improved considerably by the mid-1960s. Households were better equipped than before, domestic appliances having made an impact on all social classes by the mid-1960s, although to a differing degree. The telephone was still considered a privilege in 1967: 80.5 per cent of the homes of senior managers and members of the liberal professions had one by then but only 1.9 per cent of those in the industrial working class.[76] The more privileged social groups were well equipped with fridges, vacuum cleaners, record players and cars, while agricultural workers still generally went without, their ownership of consumer durables well under the national average. The television had made its entry into over half the nation's homes by the late 1960s. That the development of the consumer society was socially selective was a well-documented fact. What statistics failed to indicate, however, was the gender-based implications of consumerism. Who in the family, for instance, benefited from these acquisitions: did women drive and have access to the family car? Who chose the record player, authorised use of the telephone? Who filled the fridge and wielded the vacuum cleaner? Whose life was made more comfortable, easier? Did the acquisition of these goods change the division of household labour? Did it reduce the time spent on household tasks? Did this development of domestic consumerism change the meaning of being a housewife in the 1960s?

THE NEW HOUSEWIFE

If there was a new housewife in the 1960s, it was probably in the new developments, the *grands ensembles*, that she was to be found. The first baby boom had caused a housing crisis, and a new crisis was expected in the mid–1960s as the 'baby boomers' grew up and wanted homes of their own. In 1962 there was also the unforeseen need to house the French who had come back from Algeria after independence. The public-sector HLM office in Paris built 2,500 dwellings a year, but received 14,000 requests for housing in 1962.[77] Housing provision had not kept pace with need in the 1950s and a policy of quantity rather than quality was adopted.

The solution of the 1960s was the *grand ensemble*. The expression covers a range of accommodation, from new towns to housing estates. A certain number of ideas helped to define the *grand ensemble*: it was completely new; a large number of dwellings were involved; use of space was carefully planned, and everyday life was to be transformed.[78] The *grand ensemble* at Sarcelles, north of Paris, was often given as a major example of this new urban planning. Construction on a vast scale was preparing to house 55–60,000 people by 1965:

> Each area has 1,000 to 2,000 dwellings of two to five rooms, either in low buildings of four floors or in tower blocks of ten, twelve or fifteen floors. Each area will eventually be equipped with: schooling facilities (25–30 classes, a nursery school, a canteen, housing for teachers); a small-scale commercial centre ... administrative offices, rooms available for meetings, etc., garages, telephones, public lavatories, a medical centre and a social centre.[79]

The construction company and architects were creating an autonomous area, with its own town centre, shopping and sports centres, industrial zone, hospital and cemetery.[80]

Inhabitants of the *grands ensembles* were mostly young, under 40, with children under the age of 10, and with low to middling professional status. The youth of the inhabitants contributed to the image of the *grands ensembles* as the homes of the future. The birth rate in the *grands ensembles* was higher than the national average.[81]

However, the *grands ensembles* provoked a mixed reaction, as the solution to one set of problems turned out to be a problem itself. On the one hand, they represented modernity, progress, open spaces and fresh air for children, on the other, they represented (for the Left) the alienation of capitalist society or (for the Right) an uprooting from the family past.[82] Criticisms were both practical – isolation, lack of facilities for children, distance from shops – and aesthetic. The most striking feature of the *grands ensembles* was that they looked like little boxes, identical buildings and apartments, on top of each other. 'I live in the 1,002nd window' was the famous title of an article in *Marie-France* in March 1960 about life in Fresnes on the outskirts of Paris, and this 'rabbit-hutch' proximity of dwellings was the primary criticism levelled at the new lifestyle. The housing estates which housed mainly working-class families also suffered from this syndrome. Josyane, in Christiane Rochefort's novel *Les petits enfants du siècle*, describes them:

> There were more and more people in the new blocks. As soon as one went up, plop, in went people. I had seen them being built. Now they were almost full. Long, high, standing there on the plain, they made me think of ships. Wind whistled through, between the buildings. . . . It was big, beautiful, frightening. When I passed close by, I thought they were all going to fall on me. Everyone looked so tiny and the buildings on the estate looked like Lego. They were swarming with people, like insects around lamplights.[83]

On the plus side, hygiene was better, and apartments larger. Josyane says:

> Now we had a decent flat. Before, we lived in the 13th [*arrondissement* in Paris], a dirty place without its own running water. When the area was torn down, they moved us here: we had priority: on this estate, large families had priority. We got the number of rooms we were entitled to according to the number of kids. Mum and dad had one bedroom, the boys another, and I slept in a third with the babies; we had a washroom (the washing-machine arrived when the twins were born), and we had a big kitchen-living room where we ate.[84]

The location of *grands ensembles* outside major towns (and in 1962, 43 per cent of them were on the outskirts of Paris or within commuting distance of the capital[85]) meant that during the day, men were absent and the *ensemble* became a city of women. The isolation of life on the *grand ensemble* threw women back on themselves and their homes. Women who liked this new style of living, according to a 1965 study, were those of middling social status, who continued to work, who liked the collective aspects of life in the *grand ensemble* and were happy to have their children looked after in a crèche. For many of them, the new life represented a serious improvement on what they had had before. Women who did not adjust well to the *grand ensemble* were at the upper and lower ends of the social spectrum. They were the women who did not go out to work and who had over the average number of children. For bourgeois women, the solitude was new and unwelcome, the absence of distractions a problem. For working-class women, the absence of family and the fact of stopping work increased the sense of isolation.[86]

Women seemed to like the green, the space and the ability to create order in daily life; they did not like the boredom, which, for many, 'was the result of leaving Paris and becoming a housewife'.[87] Brigitte Gros, Mayor of Meulan in 1965 (and Senator for les Yvelines), wrote about women's behaviour in the new estate built at Meulan in her book on her experience of local political office. When families moved in, one woman in three was employed; six months later it was one in five. There were no 'jobs for women' nearby; there were 800 women on the estate and thirty-five jobs.[88] She quoted the woman who ran the newsagent's, who noticed that the behaviour of women changed once they moved onto the estate. At first, they ran around getting their homes in order, but later 'they no longer seemed to want to do anything: they stay at home like hens laying eggs. The children do the shopping.'[89] Gros comments that '80 per cent of the 25-year-old women on the estate are prisoners.'

In the planning of new housing, nobody had paid any attention to women's needs as far as the outside world was concerned: larger apartments for growing families, low rent for the low paid, but poor transport, isolation, no jobs nearby (a priority for mothers looking for paid work) and nothing for women to do all day. In some of the new estates, domestic science centres were opened, where women could go to get 'new ideas for making soufflés or rompers',[90] use the sewing and knitting machines that were kept there and meet the other women: 'we feel less lonely when we're together, as the men aren't there during the day.'[91]

The new housing estates mirrored – although in a socially differentiated way – the middle-class suburbs described in Betty Friedan's

The Feminine Mystique, replacing the 1950s image of the happy housewife with the image current in the 1960s of the bored housewife. Life in the *grands ensembles* put the boredom of housewifery into sharp relief. *Le Figaro* wrote on 15 February 1963: 'For the woman who stays at home, every day in a *grand ensemble* is the longest day'; while *Libération* of 26 November 1963 evoked the archetype of the bored housewife, Madame Bovary, in an article called 'Madame Bovary in a housing estate'.

The potential for boredom as a housewife was acknowledged by others. Worry was expressed that when women were not occupied with housework themselves, they would have nothing to do: this could lead to adultery through boredom ('would Madame Bovary have given in if she had had a television?' asked a journalist in *Le Monde*[92]). Paulette Bernège had already thought of this and responded by saying that a woman always had something to do: 'improve her mind, beautify the house, cherish, direct, console, help, love'.[93] However, finding something meaningful to do represented a real problem for some women, for whom the life of the home was clearly not enough.

The extent of middle-class women's discontent was clear by the response to the translation of Betty Friedan's *The Feminine Mystique* in 1964. Yvette Roudy, who translated the book for Colette Audry's collection, wrote later:

> This book was a shock.... These women in their beautiful suburban homes outside New York, who had all been to college but had chosen to devote themselves to their husband's career and to the education of their children and who were suffering from a mysterious illness – I recognised them. I saw them every day. They were my neighbours.
>
> I recognised Mme M who had given up her law studies to raise her daughters.... I recognised Brigitte R and Dominique C. These women had bravely tried to follow the fashion of returning to the home and to cope with the situation they had chosen. But they didn't feel right with it, they also suffered from this indefinable unease that Betty Friedan talked about. This suffering that comes from living below one's full capacity is not the prerogative of American women ... I witnessed serious crises. I saw suicide attempts and suicides.[94]

Simone de Beauvoir, speaking in Japan in September 1966, said that what she was witnessing in France was the depressing sight of women 'understanding' that their vocation was to be wives and mothers shut in their homes, a situation in which, according to Beauvoir, they would never be able to find personal fulfilment.[95] The response in France to *The Feminine Mystique* indicated that many women, whether they could analyse it or not, shared Beauvoir's views.

THE CHANGING FEMININE IDEAL

The fact that married women were increasingly staying in or returning to the labour market in the 1960s held implications for the housewife.[96] Women who did not go out to work began to feel devalued; and the idea that every woman had the 'choice' of going out to work also implied that those women who were still in the home by the late 1960s were there because they chose to be. Of course, for many women, there was no choice: many were obliged to keep on their paid employment. For others, there was equally little choice: they were obliged to give up paid employment upon marriage or motherhood.

Married women's employment did affect public perceptions of the ideal woman. In a radical shift away from the dominant discourses and images of the 1950s, the home was no longer expected to fill women's needs and desires. If the woman in a *grand ensemble* was the new housewife, nobody was singing her praises, envying her her lifestyle, or proposing her as a new ideal. The home was becoming part of a woman's life rather than the whole of it. Journalist Ménie Grégoire found in her survey of women in the early 1960s that the younger women rejected the life of the housewife: 'They don't want that life, restricted to domestic tasks; housework, housekeeping, children and nothing else.'[97] Even the perfect housewife of the late 1960s was no longer what she used to be. The winner of the Angel of the House ('la Fée du logis') competition at the Salon des Arts Ménagers in 1968 was described in *Elle* in slightly different terms from before: yes, she did everything better than any other woman, but Mme Renée Larcher was not completely wrapped up in her home; a non-domestic world was also glimpsed:

> At 19 when she married, she knew nothing about the home ... at school, she loved to draw and if she could have continued her studies, she would have liked to have been an art teacher. ... In a few years time, she would like to find a part-time job, so that she can earn some money and find an interest outside the home.[98]

The perfect home-maker is thus seen to have had other aspirations prior to marriage and she has not permanently lost sight of the outside world. Indeed, the organisers of the competition, UNCAF (the national organisation of the CAF), held discussions in 1968 about whether or not to discontinue it altogether as inappropriate for the new woman of the 1960s.[99]

The interaction between home and work was altering in the 1960s. As women made an increasingly important financial contribution to the family income, it was thought that relations within the family would also be modified. *L'école des parents* ('School for Parents'), in 1966 called on men to help their wives in the home:

> Unless he is shockingly egotistical, the husband home from work cannot leave his young wife to wear herself out in time-consuming but necessary [household] tasks after the day that she, like he, has had in the factory or the office.[100]

Andrée Michel's 1966 study on women's professional status and its impact on the urban couple took as its starting point the hypothesis that women's employment was a key factor in the 'restructuring of the couple towards greater equality in decision-making and in domestic tasks'.[101] Michel found that power within the family was directly linked to the wife's earning: for the wife to gain in authority in the home, she must be earning a salary, not working in a family business. Michel concluded that while there clearly was change, women were not yet satisfied with the degree of change. Michel found that dissatisfaction with the domestic status quo was expressed more openly in households of working women, possibly indicating that when women were not earning money, they thought it was quite fair that they did the household work, but when they were also bringing in money, they felt the unfairness of the distribution of domestic labour.

Other studies examined this anticipated change in the distribution of domestic labour. They found that in spite of their increased participation in the labour market, domestic responsibilities remained stubbornly assigned to women. A time-budget study of couples where both husband and wife were earning, published in 1965, asked: 'How far is a greater equality of status, resulting from the fact that women are working, reflected in a division of daily domestic tasks?'[102] The sample included women industrial workers, office workers and senior managers. The study reached no obvious conclusions based on gender alone, although it was clear that while men spent more time than women on their professional work, the overall time spent on professional plus domestic work was greater for women. Industrial workers, both men and women, had a longer working day and a longer working week than women who were in senior management positions or in the liberal professions; women industrial workers had no paid domestic help, whereas the majority of women in senior management or the liberal professions had full-time domestic help. Women remained responsible for domestic arrangements, either doing household work themselves or paying for it to be done. The anticipated redistribution of household labour was not as much in evidence as might have been expected.

In spite of the enthusiasms of Bernège's disciples, housework did not satisfy and fulfil women, even if they accepted that they were the ones in the household who had to do it. Women felt guilty if they did not accomplish their household tasks properly – and doing it properly took time and effort, which was resented. On the other hand, there was undoubted satisfaction at the proper completion of domestic tasks and pride in the achievement of cleanliness and order in the home. The blend of guilt, envy, resentment and pride characterised the attitudes of women to their home.

By the late 1960s, the disparagement of the role of housewife left those women who were housewives feeling very inferior compared with their superwomen sisters. 'Just a housewife' in English, 'sans profession' in French, commonly expressed self-perceptions, demonstrate quite clearly that women did not believe the rhetoric about housewifery as a profession as worthy as any other. Men did not believe it either. Young socially mobile men, interviewed for an opinion poll on 'young people' (which did not include young women) in 1965, were asked about the qualities of the ideal wife. At the top of the list were intelligence and common sense; at the bottom were domestic skills, which received between 1 per cent and 3 per cent of their votes.[103]

Attempts were made to show women that although housewifery had been made much easier by the introduction of domestic appliances, their own role was as important as before, if not more so: 'women's work in the home may be less exhausting than before, but demands a far greater intellectual effort', wrote the UFCS author of a 1964 article on 'Work and the married woman' in *Pour la vie*, while Evelyne Sullerot suggested that as housework became both less productive and less onerous, a woman's time in the home was given value in other ways ('hence our passion for arranging, decorating').[104] Many commentators suggested that the emphasis on motherhood resulted partly from the devaluing of the housewife's work, for being a mother was a legitimate reason for a woman to stay at home whereas doing the housework had become a debatable way of filling the day.

Nobody contested the fact that the home was women's domain. Men were fighting women's challenge to patriarchy in politics and in paid employment, and the reassertion of the domestic ideal reminded women that, whatever their choices in the world outside the home, they were expected to carry full domestic responsibility as well. The creation of the superwoman model of fulfilled femininity did not carry with it revised male attitudes towards the home.

The distinction between home and work, public (male) versus private (female), was not as transparent for women as it was for men: home *was* work; home was either the primary workplace or the location of the double shift. The 'home' as a place where women were relatively powerful was set in opposition to the 'world' where women were relatively powerless – but the two terms did not have equal value placed on them. It seems clear enough that the acceptance of home as women's domain was predicated on the assumption of the primacy of men in the world outside. The questions that should be asked are why the world outside the home was not welcoming to women; why it was not considered that it belonged as legitimately to women as it did to men; why, in Beauvoir's words, women did not have access to the entire universe.

4 Marriage and motherhood

Motherhood has been a profoundly political question in France in the twentieth century, subject to the scrutiny of demographers and politicians fearful for the demographic future. Measures combating depopulation after the First World War included the 1920 and 1923 laws (outlawing abortion, information about contraception and the distribution of contraceptive materials) which were passed with no opposition in the conservative postwar Parliament. The right-wing discourse in the 1930s on the decadence of France saw both the low birth rate and the question of sexual liberty as fundamental explanations of the decline of the French race.

After the armistice in June 1940, population decline was cited as a major factor contributing to the defeat of France. When Marshal Pétain was invested with the full powers of the French state in 1940, he explained the defeat as the result of 'not enough children, not enough weapons, not enough allies'.[1] The motto of the French Republic – the revolutionary 'Liberté, Egalité, Fraternité' – was replaced by 'Travail, Famille, Patrie' ('Work, Family, Fatherland'), and Vichy pursued clear familialist ideals in its legislation. Pétain's view of the mother's role was spelled out in his addresses to French mothers, praising the part they were playing in the French state during his régime:

> Mothers of France, you have the hardest but the most beautiful task of all. It is you, first of all, who educate. You alone know how to give to all the love of work, the sense of discipline, of modesty, of respect, that makes men healthy and peoples strong. You are the inspiration of our Christian civilisation.[2]

At the Liberation, it was estimated that the French population had dropped to 40.3 million from 41.5 million in 1936. This reflected not only the loss of those killed in combat and through deportation, but also the fact that the generation reaching the age of parenthood in 1940 had already been depleted from losses in the previous world war.

The birth rate, however, had begun to rise before the end of the war, probably due to demobilisation, the return of some prisoners of war, and the incentives offered by the Vichy régime, although this is impossible to prove or to quantify. The birth rate was also measured against the extremely low figures of the 1930s, when deaths outstripped births in at least two years. In 1938, there were 612,000 live births compared with 520,000 in 1941 (the lowest point), rising to 613,000 in 1943 and then to 840,000 in 1946.[3]

The birth rate continued to rise after the war: the reuniting of couples or the constitution of new couples combined with a reaffirmation of life and faith in the future (and, of course, lack of adequate contraception) guaranteed this trend. The high birth rate of the second half of the 1940s became known as the baby boom – and later, as the first baby boom, when it was followed by a second in the early 1960s – but even when the numbers began to drop in 1950, they never fell below 800,000 per year. Each Frenchwoman had, on average, three children, dropping slightly to just under three after 1950. This was a marked contrast to the family size of the interwar period, during which the family with only one child was the reality, if not the norm desired by the state. Most of the postwar boom births were legitimate; always lower than the prewar rate, the number of illegitimate births rose slightly in the 1946–50 period (7.6 per cent) and then stabilised at between 6 and 6.5 per cent for the next twenty years.[4]

WOMAN AS WIFE

Marriage was popular in postwar France, and 1946–50 saw the highest marriage rate ever recorded: 9.7 per 1,000 inhabitants.[5] The British *Daily Mail* noted the marriage boom in Paris and reported that in the town hall of the 18th *arrondissement*, ninety weddings had taken place in one morning.[6] Some of these were marriages delayed because of the war and the marriage rate stabilised at around 7 per 1,000 inhabitants until the mid-1960s. People married at a younger age: from an average age of 27–28 for men in 1946 and 24–25 for women, it fell almost consistently until the 1970s, when demographic trends were reversed.[7]

The French population was generally ignorant about and uninterested in the question of the legal framework of marriage. The vast majority of the French population married without a formal contract. If a couple did choose to marry with a contract, then they chose how to organise their possessions and assets. If a couple did not have a specific contract, then the 'default' law came into operation, and it was this default law, the *régime légal* that concerned the majority.

The basis of the marriage law was in the Napoleonic Civil Code, written in 1804 and modified in various ways over time. Women's rights activists had been pushing for reform of the law since the middle of the nineteenth century, with occasional, piecemeal, successes. For instance, divorce was reintroduced in 1884; a wife could control her own salary from July 1907; married women achieved legal capacity (*capacité civile*) in 1938. After the Second World War, the marriage law still gave the husband rights over his wife's property and other assets, and allowed him to contest her right to take a job if he judged that it was against the 'interests of the family' for her to do so; the children legally 'belonged' to the father; he retained the right to decide on the family domicile. The marriage law still sanctioned the existence of the hierarchical patriarchal family with the husband as head of household.

There was renewed effort in favour of reforming the marriage law in 1945, when a parliamentary committee was set up to look into revision of the Civil Code. This committee never published recommendations, however, and seems to have been quietly abandoned. Women's rights organisations, women politicians and lawyers tried to keep the question of marriage law reform on the political agenda throughout the 1950s, but the first proposal did not reach parliamentary debate until 1959; the law was finally modified only in 1965.[8]

Given the very real material disadvantages that marriage brought to women, it may seem possibly strange that young women still perceived it as their ideal future: 'In spite of the heavy responsibility in store for women's destiny, young women want no more than to become wives and mothers.'[9] Simone de Beauvoir points out in *Le deuxième sexe* that marriage defines women:

> The destiny that society traditionally offers to women is marriage. Most women, even today, are married, have been married, are intending to marry or suffer because they are not married. The unmarried woman is defined in relation to marriage, whether she is frustrated, rebellious, or even indifferent to this institution.[10]

Françoise Giroud wrote a light-hearted article on marriage in *Elle* and received an enormous number of letters in response, to which she in turn responded:

> I may be wrong, but I have great faith in Frenchwomen. I firmly believe that their development will by no means incite them to desert marriage, but will help them consider it not as an indispensable ceremony which allows them to call themselves Madame, wear black and be bad-tempered without fear of being left on the shelf, but as the most propitious atmosphere in which they can exercise their most profound qualities and as the fulfilment of their woman's life. . . . By development, I mean that they will become dynamic and attentive companions for their husband rather than being grumpy servants. But women will always understand that the best future for them is still and will always be in marriage.[11]

There was a clear normative view of the ideal couple, presented by agony aunt Marcelle Auclair in *Marie-Claire* in 1955 as follows: the boy will have finished studying and completed his military service; he will be able to provide for a wife and children, hopefully independently of his parents; the couple will have their own flat; a long engagement will demonstrate strength of character and show proof of seriousness; the young couple must be able to distinguish between friendship and attraction and the real love which alone will guarantee the solidity of the marriage.[12] Marcelle Auclair ends by addressing young men specifically: 'Young men, listen to me: in the unstable situation of an early marriage, the woman, more realistic and more adaptable than the man, will take over as head of the household. This is not normal.'[13]

The only argument put forward in favour of young marriage was that the woman would not yet have her own identity and would therefore be more malleable. This apparently boded well for harmony in the home. The French Institute of Public Opinion (IFOP) published the results of a survey on 'Frenchwomen and love' in 1960, in which one respondent wrote: 'I am very independent; it hasn't made things easy. I should have married when I was younger.'[14]

Once a woman was married, it was expected that she would cease her former life and devote herself to looking after her husband and her home, followed by children and her fulfilment as a woman in motherhood. In women's magazines, where the private, domestic life of women was most visible, the husband seems to take third place in the woman's list of preoccupations after children and home, but the wife nevertheless had certain duties towards him. She must:

guarantee his material and emotional well-being. She must make sure that he lacks for nothing; his clothes must be well cared for and ready when he needs them; meals must be served promptly and prepared in the way he likes them and as his health requires. She must provide him with pleasant home surroundings and must try to please him by her attentions to him and by the care she takes of herself. She will share his troubles and his joys, she will respect his work and try not to trouble the rest he needs with her domestic complaints.[15]

This ideal was fulfilled by Céline, the narrator in Christiane Rochefort's novel *Les stances à Sophie*, whose life as the model middle-class housewife is described as an increasing nightmare. Céline is supposed to fill her days with her home and her duties as wife to an aspiring young executive:

I was as good as gold, I swear. I did everything he wanted. I responded instantly to requests. If, during a period of adaptation, I was sometimes restive, I always gave in in the end. And now I don't try to resist. I just do it. Let women who have never done this throw the first stone. Everything he wants, he gets. Everything he expects from a Real Woman, in the way of Absolute and Total Love, he gets. The socks are washed. The collars are or are not starched, depending. The black socks are black. His suits are impeccable. There is always toilet paper. The table is laid when he gets home. The accounts are kept. I get up when he does and I discuss the day's programme with him. There is a menu planned every day that takes account of his taste and his metabolism.[16]

Mme Foulon-Lefranc would probably have approved; Christiane Rochefort's narrator is horrified. The novel describes the middle-class housewife as fulfilling a certain role and receiving rewards for it, measured in possessions: the mink, the car, the holiday.

Once she had caught her man, a woman had to learn how to keep him. She was told that she must not let herself go. *Marie-Claire* reported one example. When visiting a friend, the reporter was horrified to find her pale, with no make-up and a hairnet on her head: 'Does your husband see you like this?' 'Bah!', she said carelessly, 'I'll be beautiful tonight when he gets home.' The reporter warns: 'When he returns, tired, he needs to find an agreeable companion, pleasant to look at. You are going to spend the evening together and if you are not as attractive as the young girl he married, he may well neglect you.'[17]

A wife had to cater to a husband's needs. If she refused to have sex with him, it was considered that he was quite justified in 'seeking it elsewhere'. And then when he had indeed 'sought it' elsewhere, the wife was advised to forgive. *Marie-France*'s agony aunt, writing in October 1956, advised a disappointed wife, Marie-Odile:

> to be tolerant, to accept her husband as he is, to let things go on without disruption. Let her find areas of agreement with him, let her become involved in everything he loves to do ... without looking as though she is making a special effort.

An unfaithful husband must be forgiven and even a violent one tolerated. Wives were advised to: 'avoid areas of conflict. Don't ever be in the wrong, and this way he will have no reason to get angry ... don't openly contradict him. With calm and kindness, you may be able to regain your peaceful home.'[18] The agony aunt of this women's magazine acknowledged that the woman in question had a marriage which was 'alas, far from the ideal love that you dreamed of', but, she continued, 'is it not preferable to an empty life?'[19]

A husband of any kind was apparently better than none. Single women past a certain age were to be pitied. If they devoted their lives to a career, they were mutilated in their femininity; if they devoted themselves to caring for others, they were to be both pitied and admired. A woman was not a successful woman unless she had a husband: finding a husband was every girl's goal, and her effort went into keeping him. Once she had found him, then she could move to the next stage in her life, which promised fulfilment: making a home and being a mother.

THE IDEAL MOTHER

The ideal mother, in the eyes of the French state, was first and foremost prolific. In 1920, with similar demographic problems in France and similar ideas about overcoming them, the Médaille de la Famille française (Medal of the French Family) had been introduced. It was awarded to women who had:

> made a constant effort, by their enlightened concern, their hard work and their devotion, and in the best possible conditions of physical and moral hygiene, to inspire their children with the love of hard work and seriousness, awareness of their social and patriotic duties.[20]

Bronze medals were awarded to women with five legitimate living children, silver to women with eight, and gold, to women with ten. If a son had been killed in the war, he counted as living, but if a child died in infancy, he or she did not. The medal was still awarded after the war, and the Decree of 14 March 1946 showed that in that particular year 342 gold medals had been awarded, 848 silver and 3,767 bronze.

Mothers' Day ('la Fête des Mères') was celebrated after the war with more fervour than before, and UNAF was responsible for organising the day. It was an occasion that easily lent itself to ideological exploitation of all kinds. Mothers' Day was used by some to press home the ideal of the full-time housewife and mother, the need to raise the birth rate and the importance of family policy, and by others to raise issues concerning women workers and women's civil rights. So while Simone Rollin of the MRP in 1945 called on behalf of mothers for 'the right to remain close to their little ones',[21] the Communist Minister of Labour used Mothers' Day to call for a special diploma to be awarded to mothers who, despite the obstacles, continued to go out to work. A circular from the ministry asked each firm to publish on Mothers' Day an honours list of its women workers who were mothers as well, thereby doing their bit doubly for France.[22]

Marie-France called on politicians in 1945 to give mothers a really happy day by offering women a peaceful future, allowing them to watch their sons grow up. *Marie-France's* sentimental attitude to motherhood was quite representative of this type of discourse:

> Their [mothers'] heroism is made up of humble courage as they face tasks which have to be done over and over again. The job of being a mum [*maman*] is a 24-hour-a-day job, with no Saturdays or Sundays off, with no paid holidays.[23]

Raising children was considered to be the summit of a woman's 'career'. The science of raising children, *puériculture*, had been developing since the mid-nineteenth century. Over the course of the twentieth century, doctors intervened increasingly in the lives of pregnant women and mothers: after the war, if women wanted to receive prenatal and maternity benefits, they had to have three medical examinations during pregnancy. Once the baby was born, there were clear ideas about the respective roles of mothers and fathers in the family. Strict ideas on bottle or breast-feeding, and rules about feeding times, weaning and potty-training had begun to relax, as mothers read the translation of the parenting manuals by Dr Spock and other experts (Spitz, Bowlby) and, later, Laurence

Pernoud's bestselling books on babies and young children, but the division of parental labour and the symbolic function of each parent did not evolve much over the decade of the 1950s. The generally progressive publication *L'école des parents*, which involved doctors, educators and concerned parents, was nonetheless clear about fathers ('he represents strength, knowledge, he puts the money in the family purse'[24]) and mothers. The baby wants the mother's full attention even when breast-feeding ('he likes his *maman* to look at him while he is feeding and not do anything else at the same time, because his joy comes from communication'[25]) and best of all, 'baby needs a united family ... he likes things to be permanent and for his parents to love each other'.

This view was shared by the UFCS, whose middle-class assumptions were only too clear in the way that they extended the conditions necessary for a happy healthy childhood to the surroundings of the family: 'a stable, spacious and comfortable home is indispensable ... for the couple, for the children's mental health and for the mother to be able to carry out her educational tasks'.[26] For supporters of this view, the mother whose employment took her away from her children was quite simply a bad mother.

The ideal mother of the early postwar years and of the 1950s was thus at home with her child, in spite of the new Republic's theoretical commitment to equality and to women's rights as workers. The ideal of the mother at home was never openly contested: it was criticised by the Left as unattainable for many women, never as explicitly undesirable.

MOTHERHOOD AND POLITICS: FAMILY ALLOWANCES

After the Second World War, the French state's family policy and attitude towards motherhood continued the pronatalism of the prewar and war years. In a speech on 5 March 1945, General de Gaulle told the French people that France needed 12 million babies in the next ten years, and, to encourage them, introduced legislation to make life less difficult financially for large families.

There was widespread acceptance that it was part of the state's function to intervene on behalf of families, and numerous government ministries and other agencies were involved in family welfare (Health, Employment, Social Affairs, Education, Finance as well as local government and private organisations), although the prime responsibility for the family lay with the Ministry of Health. The Decree of 24 December 1945 set out the goal of family policy as being to 'co-ordinate principles and implementation of a policy to protect the family, encourage the birth rate and ensure that families are given the necessary means to bring up their children.'[27]

A comprehensive social security system was established at the end of the war, following the example of Britain and other countries, providing protection for working people as far as illness, invalidity and old age were concerned. Families too received a range of allowances aiming to compensate for the extra cost of children. A special system of family allowances was set up by the law of 22 August 1946. Other social security benefits concerned only the employed, whereas family allowances concerned all those with two children or more. The conditions regulating receipt of family allowances, then, had nothing to do with employment or with financial resources, only with the number of children. The family allowance was calculated in 1946 on the basis of 20 per cent of the average departmental salary for the second child and 30 per cent for the third and subsequent children; this was increased in 1953 to 22 per cent and 33 per cent respectively.[28] In the following year, the amount per child over 10 years old was raised. The allowances and the new social security system were constantly amended and extended over the next few years. In 1948, for instance, families were entitled to a means-tested housing allowance on the birth of their second child, whether they were employed, self-employed or receiving the single wage benefit. In 1949, this was extended to include young couples with no children – no doubt on the grounds that if they had enough space, they would start a family. A survey in 1952 disclosed that 83 per cent of those asked believed that couples put off having their first child because of inadequate housing provision.[29] In the mid-1950s, housing benefit became the third most costly and important of all family allowances,[30] followed by financial support to enable families to go on holiday together or to send their children to a holiday camp.

The most controversial benefit was the 'allocation de salaire unique' or single wage benefit, originally intended for families dependent on a single wage, which was complemented by the 'salaire de la mère au foyer' (wage for the mother at home) in 1955 to include families of the self-employed. This was intended to cover agricultural families, in particular those who worked on their own small-holdings, who still constituted a significant percentage of the working population. It also covered the families of small shop-keepers, where the wife frequently worked without salary. This benefit was hated by the Left, who claimed that it actively discouraged women from seeking employment, and penalised those mothers who were employed and shouldered the same domestic responsibilities as mothers who were not. They did not campaign actively against it, however, as they did not want the money to be taken away from mothers who needed it. The single wage benefit was supported by the Right, who believed that it promoted the establishment of the type of family considered to be ideal and by the Confédération Française des Travailleurs Chrétiens (CFTC, French Confederation of Christian Workers) for whom it recognised the 'economic value to the nation of the work done by women who stay at home'.[31] The MRP believed that the single wage benefit gave women the chance to choose freely whether or not to stay at home. But what in their view constituted a free choice in fact implied a financial penalty on women who might choose to continue to work, and the MRP clearly believed that all good mothers would choose to stay at home: 'This allowance makes it possible for children to receive the attention, that essential attention, from their mother, who, because of economic need, can only too often not provide it.'[32]

The constant tinkering with the laws for the first decade after the war was meant to bring improvements to the conditions of family life, and family policy since the 1939 Code de la Famille (Family Code) is thought to have had a definite influence on the birth rate. It was widely held responsible for the baby boom and found approval among the majority of the French, who were apparently quite well-informed about the state of the population and agreed with the government's pronatalism. A survey by INED in 1947 indicated that 73 per cent of those asked thought it was important for the French population to increase.[33] A majority of those asked (63 per cent) approved of family allowances as an incentive and as a means of increasing social justice, by supporting the less well-off. Those who disapproved argued that family allowances did not in fact benefit the children and furthermore were an incitement to laziness, discouraging the efforts of the parents to provide a decent life for their children.

The real impact of family allowances on family size and on the quality of life for large families is almost impossible to assess. Some analysts believe that the allowances improved child welfare but not necessarily the birth rate;[34] Louis Henry, of INED, suggested that the value of family allowances was that they allowed parents the joy of increasing the number of their children without sacrificing material comfort. This argument claimed that family allowances successfully reduced the conflict between family size and standard of living.[35] Others disagreed and pointed to the failure of family allowances as income maintenance, for already by 1956 it had become clear that low-income families were not adequately protected against the rising cost of living.[36]

It was said (although there is no evidence) that families had another child in order to pay for another domestic appliance. Christiane Rochefort's novel *Les petits enfants du siècle* contains scenes of pregnant women discussing what they will buy when their next child is born. One Paulette Mauvin pats her belly saying, 'this is my fridge!' while Josyane, the narrator, lets her imagination run wild:

> She had a boy. She only ever had boys and was very proud of it. They would provide at least one firing squad for the Fatherland. It's true that the Fatherland has paid in advance for them. I hoped that there would be a war in time to use all this fodder, which otherwise wouldn't be much use to anyone as they were all complete idiots. I imagined the day when someone would say to all the Mauvin boys, 'Over the top!' and pow, there they would all be, dead on the battlefield and crosses would be placed on them, saying 'Here fell Telly Mauvin, Car Mauvin, Fridge Mauvin, Mixer Mauvin, Washing-machine Mauvin, Carpet Mauvin, Pressure cooker Mauvin.[37]

THE PROPER PLACE FOR MOTHERS

The potential conflict between the demands of home and work was endlessly discussed, with stereotypes rife in the public perception of women's work. Furious arguments raged about the damage caused (or not) to the woman's health, the child's health, the family's well-being, if the mother had a professional occupation. Sometimes this was overt, as in the family organisation UNAF's magazine *Pour la vie*, in which it was stated that 'a woman is not a complete woman if she is not able to put her job to one side, at least for a while when her home requires it.'[38] *Pour la vie*'s position was unequivocal:

> True feminism is the feminism that knows that a woman's being is fulfilled and enriched more by feeding a baby and wiping its bottom than by completing a philosophy thesis or working in a factory, because there is no personal enrichment without fulfilling one's vocation.[39]

Sometimes assumptions about marriage, motherhood and women's proper place crept through in less obvious ways. *Elle* held one of its popular surveys in 1956 in which 500 women were asked about their personal ways around the conflicts caused by home and work. The underlying assumption that married women ought to be at home was revealed by the questionnaire: 'How much more would your husband have to earn for you to give up your job?'[40] *Bonnes soirées'* 1956 article 'My first day at work' concludes that 'Tomorrow, you will try hard in your job, while you are waiting – and this is what I hope for you – to fulfil the most rewarding job of all: the job of mother!'[41]

For many women, there was no contest: one woman activist in the Mouvement Populaire des Familles (Popular Family Movement) wrote:

> Just after the war, it was men at work, a wage, families with kids, three, four, five; home helps went into families where there were eight to eleven kids.... We women didn't have jobs, on the whole. There was no equivalent between doing any old factory job and raising the kids. Bringing up the kids was the important thing.[42]

Some moral support was given to working mothers, even from the MRP, though couched in terms of benefit to the family, not to the woman. A lengthy article in the MRP women's magazine *Pour l'information féminine* in 1957 ('Women's place in tomorrow's world'), while it stressed that 'all women should be able to stay at home while their children are young', also spoke of the value of work:

> It is normal to find personal fulfilment in work ... [there is a] feeling of pride that comes from work, from active participation in a team, from being useful to others. This achievement, this opening that work gives (or rather ought to give ...) does not only enrich the woman for her own benefit, but also for her family: wanting to confine a woman to the kitchen and her mending closes off an important aspect of her husband's life; if she understands working life from her own experience, she will be better able to prepare her children for their lives as adult, responsible men [*sic*].[43]

Mothers, then, needed a taste of this sense of achievement and pride, for themselves, but, more importantly, to improve their mothering and to make them better, more understanding wives. This argument was widely found in publications supporting women's right to work (and whose audience was composed mostly of working women), but, it seems, unable to come out and say so openly.

Where particular support for mothers was concerned, two contradictory positions expressed competing visions of the nature of state intervention. The MRP and other conservative groups believed firmly in keeping the mother at home, and therefore believed that the state should encourage this particular view of family roles. The MRP pursued the positions of Catholic groups in the interwar period, which had begun to demand the right for mothers to stay at home, and had called for the family vote and for a range of subsidies and benefits to be made available to mothers.[44] Communists and Socialists, on the other hand, believed that while being a mother at home may have been an ideal for many women, it was certainly not their reality, and the state should acknowledge this reality by making it possible to reconcile the dual role of women as workers and as mothers.

In the ideological arguments over the proper place for mothers, those who claimed for themselves the role of champion of motherhood were unequivocal: 'Would a woman not be more free, more independent if she were satisfied simply with being a mother, on condition that the law made it financially possible?' they argued, speaking against the notion that economic independence was liberating for women.[45] MRP Deputy José Dupuis also tried to unite the ideas of women's freedom and the family: 'The MRP is the movement that has liberated women, not to put them in the factory but to give them back to the family.'[46]

Marie-France defined mothers who stayed at home as 'real women', while mothers who went out to work, by implication, were not. The magazine set full-time mothers and working women in opposition to each other, mocking a UFF Congress (at which women demanded rights for working women), saying:

> Should we, we real women, also hold a Congress, a real Congress, in order to demand our rights ... the sacred right for women to be real women, not to be forced to work in an office or in a factory when we want to stay in our place to raise our children with dignity, these wonderful little children that France needs so badly. [47]

The CFTC supported the view that home was the best place for mothers. Jeannette Laot, one of the leading women in this Confederation, wrote that until the mid-1960s, the women's committee shared the view that:

a married woman who went out to work was either a victim obliged to earn her own living and sacrifice herself for her family, or a bad wife and a bad mother who kept her profession for her own personal interests and at the expense of her family.[48]

This censorious attitude was expressed also by the UFCS and by the Mouvement Mondial des Mères (World Movement of Mothers), an organisation founded before the war and reconstituted in June 1947. In 1947, the movement set out its goals in a Mothers' Charter:

> The mothers' charter stresses the primary role of the mother in the well-being of the household, for the normal development of the child in its education.
>
> It emphasises the indispensable influence of mothers in social and civic life.
>
> It calls to our attention the conditions necessary for mothers to be able, in any kind of social organisation, to fulfil their specific maternal mission.
>
> These conditions imply respect for the feminine personality, her preparation for the role of mother, a normal family environment, economic conditions permitting households to flourish.[49]

This clear, if dogmatic, view of the mother's role was promoted by the political conservatives, the CFTC, Catholic women's associations such as the UFCS, and the family associations grouped together in UNAF. They constituted a powerful lobby in the 1950s, represented inside Parliament and government by the MRP in particular, and with delegates on the administration of the social security board, the family allowance board and national consultative bodies.

For the Left, motherhood was one of a woman's three functions: mother, worker and citizen. All three were essential social functions. Although the Right tried to claim motherhood for itself, the Left was not anti-motherhood. The PCF could be perfectly sentimental about motherhood, as in its homage to mothers on Mothers' Day in 1947: 'The whole of France will pay tribute to the mother, whose work is the most beautiful expression of love, of sacrifice, of self-lessness and of courage.'[50] The PCF was also the main proponent of 'accouchement sans douleur' (natural childbirth) in France, first seen in Leningrad and brought to the CGT-run Clinique des Bluets in Paris by Dr Lamaze.[51]

The UFF too addressed women as 'Mother, worker and citizen' in articles in *Femmes françaises*. The UFF National Charter made a number of demands on behalf of mothers and children: children should legally 'belong' to the mother as well as to the father; there should be no discrimination against illegitimate children; pregnant women should have a statutory right to medical care; women should have the right to work as 'the child admires its mother not only for her devotion but also for her personal value' (which, in the UFF's view, was obviously conferred by an activity outside the home); women ought to receive equal pay for equal work; women's working conditions should be improved so that they could fulfil their role as working citizen and their maternal vocation.[52] So while the UFF stressed rights and benefits for mothers at work, the demands were nevertheless couched in terms of work as adjunct to family life: a mother happy in her work would make a better home for her family. The UFF, and by extension the PCF, did not dispute the role of the woman in the family, and still spoke of the 'vocation' of motherhood.

The CGT obviously paid close attention to the needs and demands of working mothers. At each CGT Congress, the women's section put forward demands which included measures designed to make working life more tolerable for mothers. For instance in 1948, they asked for two hours a day with full pay for nursing mothers to feed their babies, and the possibility of a year's unpaid maternity leave with the job kept open and no loss of seniority. Furthermore, the women's section of the CGT asked for more crèches and nurseries both at the workplace and in neighbourhoods, in towns and rural areas (the provision of crèches being very patchy across France); they wanted to see far more in the way of local provision of school canteens, youth centres open during working hours where older children could go until their mothers were available, and other state provisions for the children of working mothers.[53]

By the end of the 1950s, the CGT's programme of demands forcefully 'denounced the reactionary theories of the "femme au foyer", of pin money, as damaging to the interests of the entire working class'.[54] The CGT demanded again that motherhood should be considered as a social function, and completed its demands for mothers by repeating and extending those of previous years.

The Socialist Party too demanded more locally based support networks for working mothers, always in the context of aiming to give women the chance to experience 'this complete happiness, motherhood'[55] without necessarily giving up their paid employment. There was no call for women to return to the home. On several occasions, Socialist publications stated clearly that in their view the issue at hand was about reconciling roles:

Engaging in professional life has not freed us from our natural maternal mission, or from our hereditary role of guardian of the home. We obviously do not intend to desert any of these activities, but we ask to be able to carry on with all of them in conditions that make it possible for us to do so.[56]

Or, again:

for Socialists, the goal is not to bring women back to the home at any cost, in order to be no more than the reproducer so dear to some. The problem is to reconcile the roles of worker and mother.[57]

In between the two positions of the PCF with its associated organisations and the MRP and its supporters, the centrist RGR women's section trod a careful path. In their outline of an ideal family policy in 1951, they included symbolic rewards for mothers of five children or more and increased benefit paid directly to the mother. Suspicious of the collectivist nature of the crèche, they could not allow themselves to be over-enthusiastic, but they did seek the creation and extension of local support networks and rest homes to help tired mothers. Their programmes from the 1950s consisted of a curious mix of traditional and progressive positions on the family, blending the call for part-time work for mothers and a pension for mothers who had raised three or more children, with the call for revising the Civil Code and replacing 'paternal authority' with the shared authority of the parents.[58]

HELPING MOTHER AND CHILD

Legislation specifically targeting mothers approached the question from two angles. First, legislators were concerned to make certain provisions for working mothers; second, they were concerned with the quality of a mother's life inside the home and the type of help the state could or should offer.

The crèche, although it concerned only a tiny minority of children, was the concrete symbol of working motherhood, held in horror by the MRP, encouraged by the Left. In 1959, the issue was still alive. Germaine Touquet, MRP activist, wrote: 'Would it not make more economic sense to open fewer crèches and to increase the single wage benefit?' The UFCS argued that mothers at work represented a danger for children:

When the mother works, the home is empty when the child

returns from school, the mother is unable to supervise the child's schoolwork, make proper contact with the teachers, the child feels isolated, has no intimate contact, is left to his own devices and is vulnerable to numerous dangers.[59]

Jeannette Vermeersch attacked the MRP view in some fierce speeches at Communist Party congresses. She accused MRP women of hypocrisy. Speaking of an MRP woman Senator, mother of six children, Vermeersch said: 'What do these ladies do with their children? Maybe they have maids, but then the maids aren't with their own children.'[60]

By the end of the 1950s, there was still hardly any crèche provision in France: a total of 481 in the entire country, offering 17,476 places for children under the age of 3, plus 173 *pouponnières* (6,316 children) and 786 *garderies* (32,800 children).[61] At that time there were almost 4 million children in France under the age of 4.[62] Furthermore, while the Paris area was quite well provided with crèche facilities, nineteen departments in France still had none at all.[63] Crèches were expensive to run (making companies unwilling to open workplace crèches) and, it was felt, not good for children's health as they were constantly exposed to infection. Nor did crèche opening hours always correspond to the mother's working hours. In spite of these disadvantages, nearly 30 per cent of mothers, questioned as early as 1948, regretted that there was no crèche available to them.[64]

The second approach to the question of helping mothers was that of providing assistance in the home. Women needed more up-to-date facilities: running water, electricity, gas, an inside toilet. By extension, help for mothers could also mean increased availability of domestic appliances, made possible for the less well-off by the introduction of credit facilities.

Financial help was available. Loans for domestic appliances and furniture or for holidays or even for housing or home improvements were available for recipients of family allowances from the CAFs. The CAFs also provided support of other kinds. They ran social centres for young mothers, crèches, children's homes, rest homes, holiday camps and family holiday houses.[65] The CAFs and numerous family associations could be approached by women who needed emergency support in the home. Young women were recruited as *travailleuses familiales* (TF, family workers, or home helps) whose role was to go into the home as temporary relief for a mother who was ill, had just given birth or simply could not cope. Originally set up in 1942 as a voluntary family service which would allow young women to avoid compulsory work service in Germany, the first purpose of TFs was to provide practical and moral support for women who found themselves alone raising children when their husband had been killed, taken prisoner or deported.[66]

TFs' accounts of their job were quite revealing about the conditions with which many working-class mothers had to contend; and, as 'surrogate' mothers, the skills and qualities required of TFs are revealing about the skills and qualities thought to be necessary for mothers. An early appeal in *Marie-France* called on young women to come forward for training. Until 1949, no certificate of any kind was given, but the women received basic domestic training:

> The future mother's help... will attend classes on cooking, cleaning, upkeep of linen, childcare, caring for the sick, household economy, hygiene. She will then be placed in a position in a family for three months, paid 18F an hour and work a forty-hour week.[67]

This article concludes by telling young women that what is being asked of them is, in a sense, to act as an apprentice housewife and mother 'before they are called upon to join their ranks' in their own lives. They would be able to share their new knowledge and skills with mothers before practising them in their own homes.

TFs saw their job as filling three different functions: they had a preventive role, called upon to keep a family going when the mother was under particular stress and things were looking grim; a 'curative' role, helping the family when the mother was ill or absent (for instance, in hospital after giving birth); and an educative role, showing the mother efficient ways of running her home (though taking care not to make her feel incompetent).[68]

In 1947 there were 4,000 TFs, a number considered to be insufficient to the needs of the families. UNAF called for girls to volunteer, and wanted a period spent as a TF to become obligatory for all girls preparing a 'social career', that is, as a social worker or nursery school teacher.[69] Those in favour of this proposal suggested that after their domestic national service, women should remain as reservists, on whom the nation could call when there was a local or national disaster.[70]

Families receiving family allowances could apply for a TF to the CAF or, if there was a health problem, to the social security office. During the 1950s, they could be reached through a number of organisations, both public and private, religious and secular, rural and urban. In particular, TFs were closely associated with working-class family associations which deplored the fact that working-class mothers did not have the same access to help in the home as middle-class mothers. Their work was accomplished in the context of class-conscious family associations which encouraged them to participate in the struggle to improve living conditions and housing of working-class families. Most public figures, however, still spoke of the TF's job in the abstract terms of 'fulfilling a maternal role', bringing sunshine to a family, motivated essentially by a sense of service. This view of the job was sometimes shared by the TF herself:

> Being a TF means that with our hard work, we bring our smile, our good humour, our calmness to the family. We soothe, welcome, encourage, console and love ... our profession allows us to live our lives to the full as women.[71]

More families needed TFs than applied for them. An inquiry into the effectiveness of this aspect of the work of the CAFs in 1958 showed that only 13.8 per cent of their budget was spent on this type of aid to families, while 37 per cent of the budget was spent on housing benefit. Only 7 per cent of families receiving family allowances had had the services of a TF in Paris, which the authors attributed to the fact that most people did not know either of their existence or how to get hold of one. Furthermore, as most working-class families had never had any kind of help in the home, they were not used to the idea of it and did not think to ask.[72] Most mothers struggled on alone.

THE 1960S: THE NEW MOTHER?

The marriage rate, after an average of 397,400 per year between 1946 and 1950, dropped for the next decade to an average of 312,500 per year and then rose to 346,700 in 1964 and 356,600 in 1968, continuing to rise thereafter until the 1980s.[73] The divorce rate, also artificially high after the war, stabilised at between 30,000 and 31,000 per year from 1951 until 1963, when it began to rise.[74] The birth rate remained high during the first half of the 1960s (1964 represented a high point with 874,249 births[75]) in spite of the anxiety of politicians and demographers. It began to drop in 1965, however, and has been dropping ever since.

Women's magazines, as could be expected, kept the sentimental view of motherhood in the foreground: actress and film-star mothers featured heavily on the covers (*Elle*'s cover in January 1960 was

Brigitte Bardot after the birth of her son – 'BB, maternal tenderness'); *Marie-Claire* in June 1960 quoted Grace Kelly on motherhood ('In Hollywood, I thought that my career would be my whole life. Marriage has shown me that I was wrong . . . I do everything I can to spend as much time with my children as possible'); *Bonnes soirées* in 1964 wrote of Grace Kelly and Jackie Kennedy, 'they are still mothers . . . after all, it is their most beautiful role'. In the struggle between career and motherhood, motherhood is always shown to win.

Elsewhere, however, the struggle seems to have been overtaken by reality: mothers *were* working. The emphasis in the mother-versus-career debate changed: the double shift was accepted but not celebrated, and mothers were reminded that they were still responsible for the family.

In the light of these changes, ideas about the ideal mother were bound to change too: the woman who was 100 per cent available to her children was less and less visible and less and less prized. The selflessness of the wife and mother giving up her own life in order to devote herself to the needs of the family was no longer proposed as admirable. By the late 1960s, the dominant view on the mother at home was that she was a luxury that the country could not afford, who was resented by many. Aided by an army of experts – Dr Spock, child psychologists, educationalists – the mother was still encouraged to devote herself to the baby and small child, but once the children had reached school age, she was encouraged to develop other interests or take a job. *L'école des parents* broached the subject of parental roles: 'Mother and father form a new team. . . . It is no longer a question of subordination or hierarchy, but of a real collaboration between the father and mother.'[76] The UFCS did not go this far, but shared a revised view of the mother's role:

> A woman with young children should have the freedom to stay at home. However, increased attention to professional training [before motherhood] and retraining afterwards ought to make it easier for her to return to the work force. . . . Many of the mothers we spoke to in our survey wanted to have three children, but did not want an isolated life in the home. They want time to be 'present' for their family without being the family's prisoner.[77]

Even the most conservative family associations accepted that mothers worked outside the home and that it did not necessarily damage the child. Children too were said to be pleased if their mother had an identity of her own, which, it is assumed, was created by her life outside the home. In 1968, Benoîte Groult wrote that the era of the 'maman poule' (mother hen) was over. For Groult, the equation of motherhood equals sacrifice was finished: 'A happy mother is the best possible example one can set one's children.'[78] *Elle* editorialist Jean Duché proclaimed that 'the quarrel over women staying at home or going out to work is no longer an issue';[79] *Marie-France* was more circumspect: 'the biggest problem for women – to work or not. For the married woman, this can never be resolved without conflict.' The influence of Paulette Bernège lived on, albeit put to different use:

> the woman who allows herself to be completely absorbed in her domestic tasks fails in the essential duty of keeping up her intellect and physique, indispensable for the husband and also for the children... [you must] learn to be more organised, econ-omise time and energy. This might be the way to convince men that professional activity does not destroy femininity... for after all, men don't want to have to eat in restaurants every night once they are married.[80]

Skills of domestic organisation had to be extended to encompass the organisation of the double workday. Time became a most precious resource. The idea of 'quality time', popular in the 1980s, was already in evidence in the late 1960s. A good mother, wrote Yvette Roudy and Lydie Pechadre:

> is not a mother who stifles her child with her constant presence, but a mother who manages to give the child a few hours of complete attention every day.... It is commonly observed that working mothers retain better communication with their adult children. A woman who stays at home, even if she proclaims her full and undivided loyalty to the traditional ideal of the 'femme au foyer', suffers from a deeply felt frustration.[81]

Women were thus told that they were new women, new mothers; but being told that they were new women, new mothers, did not necessarily mean that they were doing anything different from what they had always done: juggling their various activities and responsi-bilities. What, then, was new? Did acceptance of the working mother mean no more than approval of women's right to the double work-day? Did this change of attitude merely recognise that the ideal of the mother at home did not correspond to women's needs and aspirations and that women were taking no notice of it? Was the notion of successful femininity simply being revised in order to accommodate what women were actually doing with their lives?

By the mid-1960s, everyone was talking about women and their changing role in French society: Betty Friedan's book *The Feminine Mystique* had been translated into French in 1964; Michel and Texier's book was published in that same year; journalists such as Ménie Grégoire and Pierrette Sartin, sociologists such as Evelyne Sullerot were all writing books about women. By 1965, a TV series targeting women (*Les femmes aussi*) had begun. In 1967, Ménie Grégoire began hosting a daily radio programme, in which she answered listeners' problems. Everyone agreed that the image of the ideal woman was in flux. All these commentators spoke of uncertainty and the unknown where women's roles were concerned:

> the 'métier de femme' has undergone a profound revolution . . . a woman today has to invent her own models, upset the models she knows . . . we don't know exactly what is expected of us, or what we expect of ourselves, or what to tell our daughters . . . but we can no longer ignore the fact that we are undergoing a transformation: the old image is fading, a new one is forming.[82]

The new image apparent by the late 1960s was as artificial as the old one: replacing the mother at home was the new woman, superwoman. The new woman message was applied selectively: particularly to the young, increasingly independent women who read *Elle* and *Marie-Claire*, for whom the 'femme au foyer' was not an ideal and never would be. The image of women promoted by *Elle*, aiming at a young, upwardly mobile audience, attempted to combine both traditional virtues – the feminine woman, and the woman at home (rather than the full-time housewife) – and a moderate feminism – the educated working mother, the so-called liberated woman. *Elle* valued women's employment, was in favour of collective childcare, spoke about women's sexuality while at the same time evoking 'eternal feminine' qualities. This winning combination was exploited by advertisers, who could say, for instance, that 'Moulinex liberates women' encapsulating the notion of freedom in the context of the home. Ménie Grégoire reflected this attempt to reconcile traditional and progressive attitudes in her suggestion that the model for young women was now: 'the woman who is fulfilled, who has her own career and her own autonomy. But careful! Only on condition that all this is done in a feminine way . . . with discretion, tact, grace.'[83] The new ideal woman was competent, yet non-threatening; able to cope in a masculine world, yet remain 'feminine'. What the 1960s

seemed to witness was the 'attempt to construct a coherent femininity which will continue to represent woman in her traditional role
at the same time as recognising the liberalisation of attitudes conse-
quent upon changing social and economic circumstances'.[84]

In line with the altered political configuration of the Fifth Republic, and in line with the altered image of the proper place for
mothers, the family lobby declined quite significantly over the course
of the 1960s. In the face of the baby boom, it was hard to argue for
increased pronatalist policies; with the decline of the MRP and the
dispersal of former MRP supporters and representatives into other
political groupings, the familialist lobby in Parliament all but disappeared. The importance of family associations had been eroded by
the Fifth Republic. Antoine Prost describes them as being 'on the
defensive', with no new ideas or new programmes.[85] The public was
not much interested in matters of family policy, and government
committees themselves were questioning the value of certain benefits which no longer seemed appropriate. Some members of the
committees set up to study the problems of the family in 1960, 1964
and 1965 were keen to abolish the single wage benefit and, although
their recommendations were ignored by the government, the changing climate of opinion about the role of mothers was clearly reflected
in discussions at the highest level. The single wage benefit was
criticised as unfair (a company director's wife was entitled to it
whereas a wife earning a modest amount in order to contribute to
the family income was not); it was thought to be no longer economically viable to give state support to a mother at home.[86] The system
of allowances was reformed in 1967, including reform of the single
wage benefit which had not been raised for eight years, and was
kept at 'ridiculously low levels'.[87] The 1967 Ordinances stopped the
benefit for young couples without children, and made conditions for
receiving the wage for the mother at home more stringent. It was
eventually reformed (means-tested and raised for those fewer
women receiving it) in 1972. Pierre Laroque notes that family allowances in general were allowed to decline in importance, in comparison with the costs of sickness benefit and old age pensions. In 1946,
family allowances had accounted for 40 per cent of social security
expenses, but this dropped to 17.9 per cent by the end of the 1960s.[88]
Furthermore, family allowances were revised in 1967 in line with
the trend of limiting state support to those whose need was proven,
on the principle of redistributing the nation's resources and with
the object of reducing inequality. This marked a considerable depar-

ture from the original desire to promote a particular vision of family and the notion of supporting all families, whatever their means.[89]

These changes in the law, then, sanctioned an altered view of the family, and in particular of the mother's role within it. The ideal number of children per family hovered between two and three throughout the 1950s and 1960s (younger women tending to opt for two rather than three) but the percentage of those who felt that four was the ideal halved between 1947 and 1967.[90] By 1967, an overwhelming majority approved of planned families, family planning centres, sex education in schools and modern contraception, in spite of believing that the birth rate would decline as a result.[91] When asked in a 1965 survey whether they would use modern contraceptive techniques should they be made legal and available, 80 per cent of women of childbearing age said that they would, although they too believed that this would accelerate the drop in the birth rate.[92] Many of the babies born during the baby boom, it can therefore be assumed, were babies of reluctant mothers.

MOTHERHOOD VERSUS MARRIAGE: 'WITH MY FOURTEEN CHILDREN, I WAS VERY, VERY TIRED'[93]

The changes of the 1960s did not drop out of the sky with no warning; this chapter and the previous one have demonstrated how the ideal of the full-time housewife and mother was challenged as inappropriate, unattainable or (more rarely and often indirectly) as undesirable. The political parties of the Left and the CGT kept up pressure for acknowledgement to be made of the reality of women's lives and for improvements to be introduced to help them. As well as this political lobbying, the vision of motherhood as women's fulfilment was questioned by others: by the early family planning movement in particular, and by many women themselves.

What did women feel about their role as mother? Did women want to have as many children as the French state wanted them to have? Women's attitudes towards motherhood can be learned from the few studies that did focus on mothers, asking about their needs and desires, and allowing their voices to come through. More often, however, they can be learned incidentally, gleaned from publications whose main focus was not specifically on motherhood. For instance, the IFOP study on 'Frenchwomen and love' included a chapter on marriage which, in turn, included a section on motherhood. In sorrow rather than in anger, women contested the vision of happily married motherhood. In fact, motherhood was described by many women as frankly spoiling their marriage. Children take attention away from the husband, as many women reported: 'With my one-year-old daughter, I am very preoccupied and less free to maintain the atmosphere that we had in the beginning', said one, while another said, 'The first one represented the fulfilment of our love, the other three, well they have just been a burden.'

Women did not seem keen, to say the least, to compete for the Médaille de la Famille française. 'The first three I welcomed as a gift from God. . . . For those that followed, well I thought that the Lord was being a bit heavy-handed and could have distributed his gifts a bit better.'[94]

The Church seemed to have had some responsibility for women's misery. As late as 1966, the journal with a Catholic rural audience, *Clair foyer*, published a survey on birth control (*3,000 foyers parlent*, '3,000 households speak out') and told of the consequences of the lack of contraception on marriage, health, self-esteem and family life. The 3,000 households which responded to this survey came from all parts of France. 'I feel that I'm no more than a baby-making machine', said one woman, while another added, 'I want to be respected as a woman and not treated like an animal'. Many women spoke of the way that fear of a new pregnancy made them fear sex with their husband:

> Love is a thing of the past. I hate my husband because he is responsible for all my pregnancies. Don't talk to me about conjugal relations, it's a trial for me; when I have to sleep with my husband, the idea of having another child is enough to drive away any thought of pleasure. I avoid sex as much as possible, but try telling a man that he has to go without for any length of time, no, it's not possible, not mine anyway.

Women were not used to the idea of having any right to their own sexual pleasure but were well used to the idea of the husband's conjugal rights and the unstoppable sexuality of men. They seemed to accept the idea that if men didn't 'get it' at home, they were quite justified in getting it somewhere else: 'nine years of marriage, nine pregnancies . . . you can't enjoy sex after that, it becomes an ordeal . . . and so the door opens for the husband, who will go and seek somewhere else the tenderness that his wife won't give him.' Fear of pregnancy frequently meant that the husband and wife did not sleep together at all and the author of the report summed up the dilemma that many women faced: 'have children one after the other . . . or go through the painful experience of seeing the husband seek elsewhere what he doesn't have enough of at home.'[95] Women concluded their responses to the survey by stating categorically that they did not want their daughters to have the same lives that they themselves were leading. In the survey, there is nobody who speaks positively about large families, from any point of view at all; there is nobody who even mentions family allowances; nobody mentions motherhood as a patriotic duty.

The anguish expressed in *3,000 foyers parlent* was also present in Marie-Andrée Lagroua Weill-Hallé's book *La grand'peur d'aimer* ('The great fear of loving'). Weill-Hallé practised (and still practises) as a doctor in the 16th *arrondissement* in Paris and was known for her outspoken support for birth control. Her book, published in 1961, contained case histories from her practice and showed that women from all social conditions and personal situations sought to limit the number of their children. Not all of them were young, single and flighty – in fact, most of them were not:

Mme R. is a doctor's wife. Good mother and good wife. She is alarmingly fertile: four children in eight years and four abortions. Her nerves in shreds. Thirty-three years old, but looks 40. Going grey. Her husband is also 33 but looks like a schoolboy. 'I must do something soon, it's become an obsession with me. P. is fed up with me refusing his advances or finding me asleep when he comes to bed. Our lives have been stolen from us, but soon I'm going to find myself alone and P. will find another woman.'

Mme C. has eight children from 12 years old to one month old. M. C. is a plasterer. Good husband and good father. He is not worried by his wife's repeated pregnancies. 'After the third one, my husband did try withdrawal, but it doesn't suit everyone. And anyway, I was caught five times like that.'

'What does your husband think?'

'Oh, my husband, Doctor, he is used to seeing me pregnant and even ill. I've had two operations . . . when I was pregnant the last time, at three months, they had to remove an ovarian cyst. . . . And of course, Doctor, I do everything in the house. . . . It is hard always being pregnant in those conditions. Never a moment's rest. . . . And as soon as I've had a baby, I'm afraid of having another and it's always the same. . . . My husband isn't a bad man. He's a good man. He brings home his pay packet. He doesn't drink. But he doesn't have anything to do with the children, or with the housework, all that's for me. As long as he finds his food on the table when he gets home, thats all he wants.

I live like an animal and a woman is not supposed to live like this.[96]

These personal tragedies fill the pages, mostly concerning poor health, poor living conditions and husbands who, if they are not always cruel and violent, show very little in the way of understanding, or interest in the children, and give little or no support.

The book is unusual in that it includes, as cases worthy of attention, women who either don't like children or who prefer to organise their lives around a profession – that is, women who received maximum disapproval from society at large:

Mme J., pretty elegant brunette, very much in love with her husband who loves her just as much. Their love is enough for them. No room for a baby.... 'We don't like them, that's all. So when we have an accident and I get pregnant, I make myself abort. I've done it three times.'

Mlle G. loves the career she has chosen and in which she has the chance to help and guide a large number of women in a number of ways. She would like to be able to have a lover without risking pregnancy. [Asked if she would like to have a child] 'Yes, of course, but when the conditions are right. At the moment, I can't get married, but when I can, I would like to have children. I've seen the difficulties that single women have with a child too often to put myself in the same position: it isn't good for the child.'

Mlle G. wants to control her own life as far as she can. Why should she not be able to do so?[97]

Women, obviously, found ways not to have children, in spite of the 1920 and 1923 laws. Recourse to illegal abortion was more frequent than regular use of effective contraception and, because of its illegality, any figures indicating numbers of abortions carried out in France before 1974 are totally unreliable. Some authors claimed that there were as many abortions in France as there were live births; figures given vary from 150,000 to a million per year.

PREVENTING MOTHERHOOD: THE DEBATE ON BIRTH CONTROL

In the overwhelmingly pronatalist climate of the postwar years, it is not surprising that the first attempts to argue in favour of birth control and bring the issue into the open failed. In 1946, a Catholic doctor Jenny Leclercq published a book called *Le contrôle des naissances et le malaise conjugal* ('Birth control and marital discord')[98] in which she discussed the issues from the point of view of a liberal Catholicism. The Pope's intransigence and the Church's insistence that only 'natural' methods of birth control were acceptable had several consequences, according to Leclercq. First, it meant that Catholics were turning away from the Church; those who remained were perpetually at war with their consciences, believing that they were sinning whereas in every other way they were leading irreproachable Catholic lives; young women would marry a non-believer rather than a man who would expose them to the risk of constant pregnancy. Leclercq then became quite controversial, suggesting that male individualism, or egoism, has meant that men have never paid any attention to the difficulties and responsibilities that weighed women down. She also brought other arguments into play: submitting to nature goes against progress and human intelligence; justification for birth control could be found in the Bible; couples needed to express their love sexually, and even if women did not need sexual pleasure in the same way as men, their sexual glands needed 'moderate use' in order to stay healthy; and finally, she pointed out the contradiction by which the Church accepted coitus interruptus but not condoms. The principle of avoiding conception was accepted and decisions about natural or unnatural methods seemed specious to Leclercq.

Leclercq's book was met with silence and was only 'rediscovered' later in the 1950s. In 1949, Beauvoir's *Le deuxième sexe* rather shockingly opened the chapter entitled 'La mère' with a long discussion about abortion. Simone de Beauvoir, alone of any writers on motherhood, declared it to be a trap for women. 'They [women] are not allowed to live; and so, in compensation, they are allowed to play with real live dolls.'[99] Beauvoir's very obvious distaste for the whole business of motherhood is frequently commented on. It has been used to analyse the author more than the subject, leading to claims that she was not a 'real woman' and therefore could not understand women's needs and desires for a child, and making it easy for commentators to dismiss her views. In *Le deuxième sexe*, the joys of motherhood are absent, whether the discussion is of motherhood in theory or of motherhood in capitalist society.

From an existentialist perspective, Beauvoir claims that women cannot escape their immanence through motherhood: 'just as in marriage or in love, [in motherhood] she confers on someone else the problem of justifying her life.'[100] From a materialist perspective, she claims that until society agrees to care for children and to help mothers, motherhood and employment will be in absolute conflict; and until this conflict is resolved, and women participate fully in the economic, political and social life of the nation, there can be no such thing as meaningful motherhood. From a feminist perspective, she points out that 'it was not as mothers that women won the right to vote';[101] she points out too that motherhood is only glorified when it is within marriage, that is when the woman is kept subordinate to the man.

A second attempt to raise the issue in medical circles was made by Marie-Andrée Lagroua Weill-Hallé in 1953, publishing an article in the journal *La semaine des hôpitaux* ('Hospital Weekly') which was widely read by doctors. After publication of the article, she was contacted by some Dutch doctors and by American birth control pioneer Margaret Sanger, but in the two years between this article and the next time she raised the issue in public, not one French doctor spoke or wrote to her about it.[102]

It took the scandal of a trial for infanticide to launch the public debate on birth control. In March 1955, Weill-Hallé, who had been concerned for some time about contraception and had visited clinics in the USA, addressed a meeting of the Académie des Sciences Morales on the subject of voluntary motherhood ('la maternité volontaire'). In this speech, she raised the case of a couple, living in poverty in the Paris suburb of St-Ouen, who were sentenced to seven years' imprisonment for 'causing the death through lack of care of one of their five children'. Weill-Hallé used the case to illustrate the drama of unwanted pregnancy, when the parents, in particular the mother, could not care for the children, when housing and income levels did not permit an adequate standard of living. Would it not be better, she argued, for couples to have only those children they wanted and could cope with, given their material living conditions? Only when women could choose their children would motherhood truly be the joy and fulfilment that it was meant to be.

After this speech, which was received with hostility by the medical establishment but with interest by the press, the editor of *Libération*, Emmanuel d'Astier de la Vigerie, decided to run a series of articles on abortion, and asked the Communist journalist Jacques Derogy to take on the subject. In October 1955, Derogy published his series, called 'Des femmes sont-elles coupables?' ('Are women guilty?') and the following year he published an influential book with the Editions de Minuit called *Des enfants malgré nous* ('Unwanted children'). Full of personal horror stories, the book made a dramatic case for legalising birth control, taking issue with opponents, shooting down medical, demographic and ethical arguments and denouncing press silence on the issue:

> In France, the question of 'birth control', speaking of 'voluntary procreation', 'controlled motherhood', 'conscious parenthood' or 'family planning', sees doors and mouths close, sees you up against a hostile wall of silence, addresses a sort of taboo.[103]

Derogy began his book by discussing illegal abortions, known as 'miscarriages'. It was not unusual to hear a woman say 'I'm going to help my sister-in-law have her miscarriage.'[104] The women would use whatever method came to hand; Saturday nights were the busiest for doctors called out to visit women who were haemorrhaging; Easter and Whitsun saw epidemics as women would not need to miss a day's work, if everything went well. Unfortunately things often did not go well.

Derogy condemned the public attitude and the law which preferred to punish women rather than help them, and which only too clearly punished working-class women rather than the financially secure:

> The situation of women is not equal as far as motherhood is concerned, any more than it is as far as anything else is concerned. For rich, idle women, either married in the bourgeois way or comfortably kept, abortion is merely another possible option. It is not women like these who fill the casualty wards in the hospitals.[105]

He then went on to discuss the effects of lack of contraception on married life, as Weill-Hallé did five years later in her book *La grand'peur d'aimer*. Arguments ranged from the sensible to the dubious: a strained marital relationship made family life hell; a woman who had an illegitimate child might turn to prostitution, probably in order to feed her child; fear of pregnancy was said to be a major cause of women's frigidity; a husband asked to 'be careful' would seek his pleasure elsewhere and so on.

Arguments against birth control were put forward by Catholic doctors at their 1954 congress in Dublin: some methods might cause infection or inflammation of the female sex organs; non-absorption of semen would have a negative effect on the female endocrinal glands; the use of contraceptives would disturb sexual drive and cause frigidity. Only Catholic doctors seemed concerned by these problems.[106]

Derogy ended his book by condemning the official morality proposed by the French state which made motherhood a kind of animal slavery rather than a source of human joy. After the publication of Derogy's book, at least 200 articles were written in the press about abortion and birth control.[107] For the next twelve years, arguments for and against were to be rehearsed endlessly, turned round, examined from all sides, until information on birth control and the provision of contraception were made legal under the Loi Neuwirth in 1967.

In the 1950s, discussions on motherhood focused primarily on the tension between motherhood and employment outside the home. Little was done to reduce that tension in the lives of women who, increasingly, combined motherhood and paid employment. In spite of government incentives, in spite of obstacles placed in the way of a successful professional life, in spite of instruction received at school and in Church, women were deciding to have fewer children and envisaging a future that was not solely defined by family. They were not noticeably responding to the government's financial incentives and keeping out of the labour market; nor were they given sufficient support in the form of childcare facilities to encourage them to keep on producing children while they worked.

At the Liberation, motherhood as a political question was placed in the context of a particular rhetoric of family, and the real support afforded by the postwar state to mothers was worked out within a normative framework. In its postwar legislation concerning the family, the government had a particular ideal in mind: the family with at least three children and a mother at home looking after them.

The direction taken by family policy between 1945 and 1968 reflected increasing government ambivalence towards the role of the mother in a changing society where the desired norms of 1945 were not being met – and were not necessarily the desired norms any more anyway. Postwar family policy had been created in a particular climate, when concerns over demography were paramount; by the late 1960s, this climate no longer prevailed. The government had to respond both to the new notions of social justice and to the unforeseen developments in women's lives, and give legal sanction to the transformations already under way. By permitting family allowances and family policy in general to decline in importance without actually revising the system, the governments and political parties of the Fifth Republic displayed their ambivalence: the 'mère au foyer' was quite out of step with the progressive young educated and employed mother of the late 1960s, but there were still about 8 million of them who could go to vote. Parties could champion neither the mother at home nor the mother at work in safety, and so they tried to do both, making 'work versus home' a matter for a woman's own choice. By 1965, the political debate on motherhood therefore shifted away from 'home versus work'. It was replaced (albeit tentatively at first) with the key question of giving women the right to control their own fertility, to plan their pregnancies or avoid motherhood altogether.

5 Persistent inequalities: women and employment

The postwar period from 1946 to 1975 has been given the name 'les trente glorieuses' (the thirty glorious years), owing to the rapid transformation of the French economy and social structures in a time of economic expansion and modernisation.[1] The reconstruction of the French economy was underpinned by national economic planning and heavy investment in infrastructure. Agriculture struggled to revitalise farming methods and adapt to new conditions as it lost its dominance in the economy and its labour force; the service sector expanded massively. Within the industrial sector, traditional industries such as textiles declined while the newer industries (electrical, chemical, mechanical engineering) thrived. The labour force by 1968 was composed of more salaried than self-employed workers, demonstrating a clear shift away from small independent family businesses, workshops and farms. The labour force was also more urban, better educated, more geographically and socially mobile and healthier than it had been at the end of the war.

This chapter will describe and analyse the pattern of women's employment in France between 1946 and 1968. Some basic questions will be addressed: what were the structures of women's employment during this period? Were they the same as or different from men's? How were women prepared for the labour market? What was done to encourage women into the labour market? How was the view of woman as housewife and mother reconciled with the fact of women's work? How did women experience the world of work? Who fought for women's rights in the workplace?

Studying women's employment is frustrating on a number of levels: building a picture of what women were doing, whether progress was being achieved (that is, whether or not real choices were becoming available to women), involves layers of questions and interpretations. A flat reading of official statistics can mislead: it is possible to assume that 'more' equals 'better'; it is possible to assume that comparing figures for men and women within the same profession is comparing like with like.

The statistics themselves must be treated with caution. An apparently simple question such as 'How many women were economically active in France?' at a given date, will not find a simple answer. Sources which all claim to take their figures from the official statistics office (Institut National de la Statistique et des Etudes Economiques, INSEE) give contradictory information concerning the number of women in the labour market, the percentage of women who were in paid employment and the percentage of the labour force that was female. Information that is crucial for understanding women's position in the labour market is not always considered. For instance, the fact that women worked informally in the family business, shop or farm, as pieceworkers at home, or part-time, or seasonally, is not taken into account in the figures given.

Attention to definitions and categories of occupation is required. For instance, the definition of *population active* (working population) itself changed between 1946 and 1954, when categories were reassessed. A direct comparison between these two dates is therefore impossible. Furthermore, information on employment was derived from census returns and obviously depended on the perception of the person providing the return. In filling in a census form, women might not perceive their activity as 'work' but more as 'helping out' either husband or parents, as was often the case for women in agriculture, or working in a small family business such as a shop, and not receiving their own salary for their labour. After the single wage benefit and the wage for the mother at home were introduced, women might not declare their activity as 'work' for fear of losing the benefit, but not in fact cease their activity. Or, as was more than likely, a married woman's husband would fill in the census form for the family and might not wish to include his wife's activity as work.

Research is still required to explore women's employment both during the war and in the immediate postwar years. In her research on Toulouse, Hanna Diamond notes the impossibility of establishing a clear picture of women's employment in 1946. In many industries and areas, women were laid off (as priority was given to men, and to returning prisoners of war) unless they were the sole family breadwinner, but in others, the demand for labour was high enough to keep everyone employed. However, women did not feature significantly in unemployment figures: Diamond suggests that this could be either because they were happy to stop work or because they found employment elsewhere. For instance, as the textile industry, traditionally a major employer of women, was hard hit by shortages after the war and therefore employed fewer workers, there is evidence that women moved to other industries: food production, chemical production, metal work, banking and commerce.[2]

The qualitative work on women from the 1950s and 1960s is as problematic as the quantitative. As sociologists began to be interested in women as objects of empirical study, the assumptions behind their studies and the framing of questions in their questionnaires often predetermined the results. Time-budget studies did not account for difficulties in establishing what was work and what was leisure for women; or wonder about how to assess the fact that women do several things at once, such as the shopping while on the way home from work (is this transport time or household work time?); or ask whether knitting a child's sweater while listening to the child's homework problems or waiting for potatoes to cook was work, childcare or leisure. Questionnaires used to gauge attitudes towards women's work were of a very limited value, in the view of sociologist Geneviève Texier. Writing in *Les temps modernes* in 1965, she took issue with the presuppositions inherent in these apparently neutral operations. At the outset, questionnaires and surveys tended to pose women's employment as a problem, rather than as a right. Texier argued that negative reasons for women's employment were assumed and positive reasons were omitted. She also disputed the common notion that women should have the so-called 'free choice' between home and work and the assumption that, in the event of a free choice, women would opt for the home. In learning about social attitudes, it is not useful, she concluded, to put forward loaded or insufficient evidence as if it were neutral and she called on sociologists at least to be aware of their own assumptions.[3] Added to Texier's concerns was the influence on the answers of dominant attitudes towards women's employment. If women felt guilty about wanting to work or saying that they enjoyed their work for personal reasons, they might exclude these from their answers. Not wishing to appear selfish, or bad mothers, they might emphasise the negative and omit the positive.

Finally, although it quickly becomes clear that the female labour force displayed quite different characteristics from the male labour force, analysis of women's employment has always used the same criteria, the same terms, the same norms as analysis of men's employment, usually considering employment in terms of 'socio-professional category', and considering women's employment as deviant in relation to men's.

Given these difficulties, the statistics used in this chapter should be considered as indications of trends which can *can* be identified in spite of difficulties in establishing accuracy. With the reservations expressed above in mind, this chapter will build on official statistics in order to assess the employment experience of women, set in the light of the emphasis on women's role as mother, discussed in the last chapter, but also treated in its own right.

First, the figures: the population of France was 40.3 million in 1946, 43.1 million in 1954, 47 million in 1962 and 49.9 million in 1968. Women constituted 53 per cent of the population in 1946, 51.5 per cent in 1962 and 51 per cent in 1968 according to the census.[4] The percentage of the population that was economically active dropped from 48.5 per cent in 1946 to 42.5 per cent in 1962 and 41 per cent in 1968, although, in actual figures, the working population increased slightly, from 19.4 million to 20.6 million between those dates. The census figures show 7,880,000 economically active women in 1946, 7,596,000 in 1954, 6,585,000 in 1962 and 7,123,520 in 1968. At first glance, the drop in numbers between 1954 and 1962 might lead us to assume that there was a massive acceptance of the role of women in the home, particularly in the light of the increased birth rate of those years: indeed it was commonly cited that fewer women worked in France in the 1950s than at the beginning of the century. Before making correlations that are not necessarily accurate, however, it is worth looking in some detail at women's employment structures.

'SOCIO-PROFESSIONAL CATEGORIES'

In 1954, new categories for defining participation in the labour market were devised and used by sociologists, economists and demographers, the *catégorie socio-professionnelle* (CSP, socio-professional category), which allows for a nuanced appreciation of the labour force as a whole (see Tables 5.1 and 5.2). These new divisions and subdivisions are pertinent for understanding the distribution and the evolution of women's labour (see Tables 5.3 and 5.4).

For instance in agriculture, from 1954 onwards the labour force was divided into two: those who worked their own land (whether several thousand acres or merely a small-holding) and those who worked on someone else's and received a salary. This division does not reveal women's place in agriculture, in fact it hides it: the

Table 5.1 Evolution of socio-professional categories in France 1954–68

Category (CSP)	1954	1962	1968	Change 1954/62 %	Change 1962/8 %
Farmer	3,966,015	3,044,670	2,464,156	−3.3	−3.5
Agricultural worker	1,161,356	826,090	584,212	−4.2	−5.6
Employer in industry and commerce	2,301,416	2,044,667	1,955,468	−1.5	−0.7
Liberal professions and senior manager	553,719	765,938	994,716	+4.1	+5.6
Middle manager	1,112,543	1,501,287	2,005,732	+3.8	+4.9
Employee	2,068,118	2,396,418	2,995,828	+1.9	+3.8
Industrial worker	6,489,871	7,060,790	7,705,752	+1.1	+1.5
Service personnel	1,017,798	1,047,312	1,166,252	+0.4	+1.8
Other	513,937	564,023	525,860	+1.2	+1.2

Source: Maurice Parodi, *L'économie et la société française depuis 1945* (Paris: Armand Colin, 1981), p. 248

category of *aide familiale*, or family worker, must be added to make women visible in the figures, as within agriculture men and women held very different positions (see Table 5.2).

The next group, 'employer in industry and commerce', was a large category subdivided into five types: those with more than five employees, those of a more artisanal nature with fewer than five employees, fishermen (*sic*), shopkeepers who employed more than three people and those who employed fewer than three. The same problem recurs in this category, as women frequently worked in the family business without either owning it or receiving a salary for their labour.

The category of liberal professions and senior manager was also subdivided: liberal professions, that is doctors, lawyers, notaries and other independent professions;[5] literary and scientific careers and teachers (but not all teachers); engineers and senior administrators in, for instance, the civil service. There was a lower percentage of women than men in this small category (1.2 per cent of the female labour force compared with 2.9 per cent of the male labour force in 1954);[6] viewed in another way, women constituted 13.8 per cent of this category in 1954, rising to 16.6 per cent in 1962 and 18.8 per cent in 1968. It must be remembered that men and women were included in this category for different reasons, working in different

Table 5.2 Evolution of the labour force in France by socio-professional category and by status 1954–68

		Men				Women			
		Total	Self-employed and employer	Family worker	Salaried worker	Total	Self-employed and employer	Family worker	Salaried worker
Farmer	1954	2,320,211	1,636,045	684,166		1,645,804	279,519	1,366,285	
	1968	1,527,780	1,229,700	298,080		932,060	169,140	762,920	
Agricultural worker	1954	987,422			987,422	173,934			173,934
	1968	527,200			527,200	61,000			61,000
Employer in industry and commerce	1954	1,445,298	1,346,688	98,610		856,118	504,255	351,863	
	1968	1,276,940	1,220,360	56,580		685,040	381,360	303,680	
Liberal professions and senior manager	1954	477,467	102,167	1,056	374,244	76,252	13,149	7,263	55,840
	1968	806,600	116,700	1,040	688,860	186,200	20,800	8,540	156,860
Middle manager	1954	704,196	9,602	174	694,420	408,347	16,290	760	391,297
	1968	1,197,360	17,680	840	1,178,840	816,740	16,900	1,780	798,060
Employee	1954	975,894			975,894	1,092,224			1,092,224
	1968	1,188,300			1,188,300	1,841,600			1,841,600
Industrial worker	1954	5,015,010			5,015,010	1,474,861			1,474,861
	1968	6,128,840			6,128,840	1,569,760			1,569,760
Service personnel	1954	196,841	15,924	146	180,771	820,948	9,478	397	811,073
	1968	245,200	27,600	1,060	216,540	925,860	2,500	2,480	920,880
Other	1954	379,396	68,396	161	311,130	134,250	115,898	436	17,916
	1968	417,420	61,380	260	355,780	105,260	85,040	600	19,620
Total	1954	12,502,026	3,178,822	784,313	8,538,891	6,682,738	938,589	1,727,004	4,017,145
	1968	13,315,640	2,673,420	357,860	10,284,360	7,123,520	675,740	1,080,000	5,367,780

Source: *Bulletin hebdomadaire de statistique*. Cited in Georges Dupeux, *La société française 1789–1970* (Paris: Armand Colin, 1972), p. 242

Table 5.3 Women in the labour market (% of women in each CSP)

CSP	1954	1962	1968
Farmer	41.5	38.7	37.9
Agricultural worker	15.0	11.7	10.7
Employer in industry and commerce	37.2	36.3	34.9
Liberal professions and senior manager	13.8	16.6	18.8
Middle manager	36.7	39.3	40.6
Employee	52.8	58.1	60.8
Industrial worker	22.7	21.6	20.4
Service personnel	80.7	80.0	79.1
Other	26.1	21.8	20.1
Total	34.8	34.4	34.9

Source: *Données statistiques sur les familles* (INSEE, 1975), p. 52

Table 5.4 Occupational distribution of women (% of female workforce in each CSP)

CSP	1954	1962	1968
Farmer	24.6	17.7	13.1
Agricultural worker	2.6	1.5	0.9
Employer in industry and commerce	12.8	11.0	9.6
Liberal professions and senior manager	1.2	1.9	2.6
Middle manager	6.1	8.9	11.5
Employee	16.3	21.3	25.8
Industrial worker	22.1	23.1	22.0
Service personnel	12.3	12.6	13.0
Other	2.0	2.0	1.5
Total	100.0	100.0	100.0

Source: *Données statistiques sur les familles*, (INSEE, 1975), p. 53

professions and earning different salaries. Most of the women in it were teachers, not engineers.

Middle manager as a category included primary schoolteachers, social workers and other health professionals, technicians and middle-level administrators. The number of women involved in these professions rose considerably during the twenty years after the war, to almost 40 per cent of the category in 1962 and 40.6 per cent in 1968.

'Employee' refers to white-collar workers (but not to managerial staff), and to shopworkers. Women formed over 50 per cent of this category, rising most dramatically in the 1950s and continuing this trend throughout the 1960s. It should be noted, however, that while inclusion in the category 'employee' is generally considered as upward mobility from factory work, women frequently occupied positions which were the office or shop equivalent of the unskilled labourer and earned sometimes less than their factory counterparts.

The category of 'industrial worker' was subdivided according to the factory hierarchy and the skills required of each job: supervisors, qualified workers, skilled workers, unskilled workers, miners, sailors, apprentices and labourers. Women were overrepresented at the bottom, as unskilled workers, and a comparison with later dates reveals a deskilling of women workers rather than a move towards more effective training and better prospects for women in industry.

The CSP called *personnel de service* or service personnel, was a mixed bag of occupations. It generally implied domestic servants, housekeepers and maids, but also included waiters, chauffeurs and taxi drivers, usherettes, manicurists and air hostesses. It changed composition between 1946 and 1968, with greatly reduced numbers of servants, but increased numbers of the other occupations which fit rather uneasily together.

When looking at the labour market in terms of CSP, we see an underrepresentation of women at the top (liberal professions and senior manager, employer in industry and commerce) and at the bottom (agricultural worker and industrial worker) and overrepresentation of women among employees and service personnel, constituting 40 per cent of middle managers and close to 60 per cent of employees. Within each CSP, within each industry or profession or firm, the same hierarchical pattern is repeated at micro-level. The tables also reveal clearly that between 1954 and 1968 women were moving at a faster rate than men towards salaried employment in non-agricultural occupations, and were therefore responsible for the major shifts in employment structure, largely determining the overall evolution of the distribution of the labour force.

The CSP must be complemented by other information if we are to gain a rounded picture of women's employment patterns. The CSP does not tell us about civil status; the impact of parenthood on employment; the difference between the public and private sector; the formal and informal obstacles preventing full participation in the labour market; or the different experience of men and women within one CSP.

WOMEN IN AGRICULTURE

When the labour market is perceived in terms of the three economic sectors (agriculture, industry and the tertiary sector), it becomes clear that the loss of women from the labour market in the 1950s overwhelmingly concerned agriculture (from 3,263,000 in 1946 to 2,775,000 in 1954 and 1,272,000 in 1962 according to the INSEE study).[7] The decline affected every age group, and can partly be explained by reasons relevant to the overall loss of women in the labour market: younger women staying on at school, older women able to retire and mothers deciding to call themselves housewives so that they could receive extra benefit. Even so, women were leaving the land. It has been estimated that the number of women with their own farms dropped by 20 per cent between 1954 and 1962, compared with a 12 per cent drop for men, and that the number of paid female agricultural workers dropped by 43 per cent.[8] For women who did remain, the distribution of the female agricultural labour force remained fairly constant, with the overwhelming majority (approximately 75 per cent) occupying the usually unpaid position of 'family worker'. The distribution of male and female agricultural labour was markedly different, as Table 5.2 demonstrates, and women's obviously unfavourable status in agriculture was a powerful motivating factor in encouraging them to leave the land.

Men also left agriculture, mostly to work in factories, but women left the land in greater numbers than men, continuing a trend begun in the late nineteenth century. A daughter rarely inherited the paternal farm, but was expected to work for the family until she married a farmer, worked on his farm, and produced her own children. If she failed to marry, her place on the farm, inherited by the brother, was not a comfortable one, with his wife running the home. Mechanisation also meant that less labour was required and many agricultural families included at least one member who had a non-agricultural occupation.

Agricultural training was not taken up by girls. Boys might be sent to agricultural college or to evening classes, but the most girls could hope for was to be sent to agricultural domestic science classes, in which farming techniques took a secondary place and housekeeping skills were emphasised. One JACF study of girls who attended these classes in 1954 showed that they had limited expectations of their professional futures. Asked what they would like to do as a career, only 5.5 per cent declared that they wanted to be farmers (50 per cent wanted to work in commerce, childcare, nursing or domestic science), while 11.8 per cent expected to work on the family farm as *aide familiale* when they had finished their classes.[9] There was little in the way of leisure time, and not much to look forward to. Leaving the land represented the only way a young woman could better herself, gain some skills and seek a different life. In prewar decades, young single women would move to towns as domestic servants, shop assistants or factory workers, or the more educated among them could find employment as primary school-teachers, or working for the state in the Post Office or in other fairly low-level office jobs. After the war, farmers' daughters continued this trend, with two becoming factory workers for every one who became an office worker and one young woman in every hundred becoming a teacher or manager.[10] Daughters of agricultural workers tended to take jobs in factories or as service personnel.

For young women who wanted to remain in agriculture, the professional organisations provided no incentive: women were excluded from voting in the Fédération Nationale des Syndicats d'Exploitants Agricoles (FNSEA, the farmers' union) if their father or husband was there, and were not welcome to participate in discussions of practice, politics and strategy, even in farming co-operatives. The women's section of the FNSEA, set up at the request of women in 1957, did not seem to play any significant role either in agricultural politics or in furthering the status of women in the profession. The union for the under-35s (CNJA, Conseil National des Jeunes Agriculteurs) was more egalitarian in its practices (for instance, as membership was based on individuals rather than on farms, women who did not run their own farm could still join and vote). The major agent of change in rural France in the postwar decades was the Catholic youth movement, the Jeunesse Agricole Catholique (JAC) and its female group, the Jeunesse Agricole Catholique Féminine (JACF). Like its industrial counterpart (JOC) and the student-based JEC, the JAC was a curious mix of progressive and religious thinking, which on the one hand sought to involve women in the running of the family farms, but on the other maintained a traditional gender-based division of labour. JACF publications encouraged young women to attend agricultural domestic science classes, not so that they could become more effective farmers themselves, but so that they could learn how to beautify the home and support their husband in his labour. Most CNJA (male) leaders had been involved in the JAC and were married to women who had been active in the JACF.

The female rural exodus continued in the 1960s and, if anything, was even more rapid than before. Girls who could not or would not stay on the family farm but wanted a rural career were advised to seek employment as agricultural secretaries and teachers, in social work or tourism, in an agricultural laboratory as a technician, or as a rural home help (*aide familiale rurale*). A career guidance book for girls, *Tous les métiers féminins*, describes this job as being for girls who cannot have their own farm but who love country life. There is, indeed, hope for this kind of girl: 'in the country, the rural home help often acquires the reputation of being a perfect home-maker, which brings her many suitors. Whatever the case, she of course abandons her job when she marries.'[11] In career guidance books, remaining on the family farm or marriage to a farmer are generally presented as the best options and no one presumes to suggest to young women that they might want to run their own farm, or aspire to a career other than those defined as appropriate for women.

It was a struggle for women from agricultural families to gain any qualifications. If a woman wanted to gain a higher diploma in agronomy, she could attend the Institut National d'Agronomie, but very few did: a total of eighty in the thirty-year period up to 1968.[12] Even when women did manage to obtain high-level qualifications, they frequently did not manage to sustain a career in agriculture. For instance, a 1966 survey followed the career paths of fifty-seven (of a total of sixty-one) women agricultural 'cadres' from graduation: four were never subsequently employed; thirteen worked for up to ten years but stopped either on the birth of a child or to follow their husband when his job changed. Forty – of whom twenty-six were married and fourteen were not – did have agricultural careers; of the twenty-six married women, only five actually worked as far-mers; of these two were full-time and three later changed career, becoming teachers or consultants; seven were teachers in agricul-tural colleges (although we are not told if they taught agricultural engineering or domestic science); one was a consultant, twenty-four worked in laboratories, three in professional associations and one in the Ministry of Agriculture. Family obligations and in particular the professional obligations of the husband provided major con-straints on the professional aspirations of women in agriculture.[13]

WOMEN IN INDUSTRY

The industrial sector looks remarkably stable in terms of the numbers of women employed between 1954 and 1968. However, within this overall stability, there were profound changes: the textile and clothing industry, long the major industrial employer of women, continued to employ the greatest numbers but was experiencing a steady decline, whereas other industries were expanding (see Table 5.5).

Table 5.5 Women in the industrial sector

	Number of women employed		% of women employed in each industry	
	1954	*1962*	*1954*	*1962*
Clothing	300,494	259,000	84.0	83.5
Other textiles industries	349,779	282,880	56.5	55.0
Leather, furs	81,792	81,000	47.8	52.8
Paper goods	39,867	44,680	38.8	37.7
Electrical industries	65,508	114,000	32.1	37.1
Chemical industries	92,196	104,000	30.8	30.1
Food production	115,866	126,100	28.8	29.4
Mechanical engineering industries	136,646	194,220	13.6	15.8

Source: Etudes et conjonctures, No. 12, INSEE, 1964

Women's participation in the industrial sector followed both traditional patterns of female employment and the overall trends for each particular industry. So while women remained the overwhelming majority of textile workers, the actual numbers involved were in decline as the industry itself was in decline. Industries making electrical goods experienced an enormous increase in importance and the number of employees rose, particularly female employees.

Women continued to constitute a lower percentage of industrial workers than men. The census figures show that while actual numbers of women working in the industrial sector increased between 1946 and 1962, the percentage of women in the industrial labour market decreased over the same period (to increase again after 1962 and particularly after 1975). One survey carried out by the JOCF in 1956 made the following observations about young (under-25) women workers. Five professions occupied 75 per cent of them: the clothing industry, office work, domestic service, sales, and unskilled factory work.[14] Of female unskilled factory workers, 84 per cent

Table 5.6 Percentage of women in industry according to category

	1962		1968	
Supervisor	5.9	(4.7)	7.2	(5.0)
Skilled worker	17.3	(34.8)	16.3	(36.1)
Semi-skilled worker	26.3	(36.4)	23.0	(36.8)
Unskilled worker	27.9	(24.1)	30.1	(22.0)
Total percentage of women in industrial labour force	22.6	(100)	21.3	(100)

NB: Percentage in parentheses represents the total of male and female workers in each category.

Source: Madeleine Guilbert and Madeleine Colin, 'Les femmes actives en France. Bilan 1978', in *La condition féminine*. Ouvrage collectif sous la direction du CERM (Paris: Editions Sociales, 1978), p. 92

would have preferred to do something else, but could not because they lacked qualifications. A later study showed that in 1961, 75 per cent of women factory workers had no qualification.[15]

Throughout the 1946–68 period, the position women occupied in the industrial sector showed that little was done to improve their chances of reaching supervisory-level employment in the factory. A detailed breakdown reveals that in the hierarchy of the workplace, women tended to cluster near the bottom, as semi-skilled or unskilled workers. Their chances of rising in the factory hierarchy did not improve in the 1960s; in fact, the percentage of women without any skills at all rose disproportionately (see Table 5.6). This was due to a number of factors. Training was offered to boys for industries with expanding needs whereas it was often not available for girls. Women's preference for non-industrial jobs, plus completely inadequate training for women in industry, meant that the women who remained in industry were, if anything, deskilled. Other factors affecting women's employment possibilities continued to be pertinent in the later 1960s: young women were not given to thinking seriously about future careers but were encouraged to place home and family as first priority. Taking the short-term view, they often left school without qualifications. Twenty per cent of the female labour force in the textile industry, for instance, was under the age of 20, the majority engaged in manual labour on the factory floor which required no prior training.

Women who worked in industry, then, tended to be young and unskilled, and did not perceive their job as a permanent feature of their lives: work was a necessary evil, to be endured until marriage might allow them to abandon it. Half of the working-class women questioned by Paul-Henri Chombart de Lauwe's team had no trouble in choosing between factory and home, if such a choice were offered.[16]

There was little to attract them to the factory. Descriptions of conditions found in novels such as *Elise ou la vraie vie* or in autobiographical texts such as the very moving *Une société anonyme* reveal demands for levels of output barely possible to achieve, combined with low pay, long hours, noise and stress.[17] Graphic accounts of working conditions in the metal-working industry tell of impossible demands and physical and psychological strains:

> We have to work fast and it's hard. We work sitting down, but we have to produce 800 to 1,000 items an hour, sometimes 1,500. Our legs hurt, our backs hurt: in the evening we are exhausted and the last two hours are really hard, hard to get through.[18]

> Factory life ends up as a constant struggle: struggle against the heat or the cold, against the rhythms of the machine, against depression, difficulties and obstacles whether they are technical or human... women often struggle alone against themselves, against fatigue, against the clock.[19]

Conditions for women in industry did not seem to improve. The hardships described by women in *Antoinette* or in the articles written for a special issue of *Esprit* on women's work in 1961 were confirmed by a Dr F. Goulène, who reported to the CGT's conference on the reduction of the working week for women in 1965. This doctor practising in Argenteuil, just outside Paris, reported that the most frequently observed problems for factory women were varicose veins, nervous anxiety, irritability, backache and arthritis, fatigue and psychosomatic symptoms aggravated by fatigue.[20] Specific industries brought specific problems: deafness due to noise, skin and breathing problems in the chemical industry, and a high level of work-related accidents in the metal-working industry.

A study of women metal-workers in the early 1960s by sociologist Madeleine Guilbert found that women occupied positions with no responsibility and no prospect of promotion and tended to be paid by output rather than working for a fixed wage. Women's salaries tended to be at least 10 per cent lower than men's, and women were last to be hired and first to be fired.[21] There were clear divisions between men's work and women's work. The work accomplished by women was characterised as work which required less physical effort, was less complex, needed no prior knowledge or training, used simple machines and involved simple manual operations, was more sedentary than men's and more repetitive. Guilbert suggests that there is a remarkable similarity between the tasks accomplished in the workplace and those accomplished during housework:

> The movements involved in a woman worker's tasks reminded the observers of those involved in domestic tasks in many ways. . . . Housework, cooking, ironing, sewing all involve the same type of movement and gesture as in much of the factory work. Furthermore, domestic tasks and those considered to be female tasks in the factory frequently share the fact of being simple and endlessly repetitive. The fact that women workers don't mind doing these jobs is partly due to the fact. . . . that they are used to the monotony of domestic labour.[22]

Madeleine Guilbert's conclusions on the situation of women in the metal-working company she studied were damning. She believed that the placing of women in these lowly and tedious positions was based partly on the profitability of this division of labour, partly on the influence of traditional gendered images, in particular the stereotype of the woman worker in the minds of family, male workers and employers. 'When employers speak of women workers, the stereotypical notions they use are revealing. The image of the woman worker busy with clearly defined simple tasks which suit her and with which she is successful is dominant; other images are absent.'[23] This image of the woman worker persisted in spite of the developments in industry and indeed was not limited to the industrial sector.

The majority of women industrial workers left the factory upon marriage, returning to work once their children were grown up. *Tous les métiers féminins* comments:

> As in all factories, mixed sex working makes marriage between workers likely. It can also lead to emotional complications for married people. Furthermore, factory work is tiring and all-absorbing, which makes it incompatible with the tasks of a young mother . . . [24]

Women who were able to find employment in offices were well-advised to do so and it appears that women made the transition from both agriculture and the factory floor to the tertiary sector. By the end of the 1960s, 40 per cent of women 'employees' were daughters of factory workers.[25]

PROFESSIONAL WOMEN

In the liberal professions, women faced obstacles of various kinds. Women doctors, lawyers, professors fought to overturn barriers against women but it was in the fields of medicine and law, in the universities and in politics that the prejudices against them were the strongest. The first woman doctor qualified in 1875, the first woman lawyer in 1890;[26] educational opportunities were denied until pressure for equality of curriculum and Baccalauréat for boys and girls succeeded in 1924; universities were slow to welcome women, with the Sorbonne open to women only after 1880. Exceptional women could break through (for instance Marie Curie was appointed the first woman Professor of Physics at the Sorbonne in 1906) but the majority of women, even well-placed, well-heeled middle-class women, could not.

The liberal professions were not in any sense liberal: the medical, legal and banking hierarchies were bastions of reaction, hostile to women's participation. *Le Monde* reported in 1957 that in January 1955 there were only 3,000 women doctors and 1,102 women lawyers registered to practise in France. The obstacles to women's full participation in these professions were never-ending. Once a woman had actually completed her medical training, she then had to find the money to open a practice. The difficulty that many of them had is evident in the fact that while women formed 17 per cent of graduating medical students in 1955, they constituted only 7 per cent of practising doctors.[27]

Few women attended the prestigious and professionally oriented *Grandes Ecoles*. These élite training schools were accessible through open competition after a period of intensive preparation of up to two years. Most of the *Grandes Ecoles* have a scientific or engineering focus. In 1964, two of them were still closed to women (the Ecole Polytechnique and the Ecole des Mines); only handfuls of women had entered the others by the early 1960s. An article in the publication of the Association des Françaises Diplômées des Universités *Femmes diplômées* in 1964 tried to explain the absence of women. The author, herself a graduate of and a lecturer in a *Grande Ecole*, suggested several contributory factors: the preparatory classes were not at that time as available to girls as they were to boys; some of the schools – unofficially – imposed a quota on the numbers of girls they were prepared to accept; schoolteachers did not think of directing their best female pupils towards the *Grandes Ecoles*, but rather towards teaching.[28] The overwhelming absence of women in engineering professions is still a fact of French professional life.

The presence of women in professional élites was grudgingly accepted after the Second World War, but in 1957 there was still only one woman in the élite body recognising achievement, the Institut de France (in the Academy of Medicine) and none in any of the other Academies.[29] We have seen the low level of female representation in political assemblies; the magistrature was only opened to women in 1946; the high-level posts in the civil service were all male and the élite administrative training school, the Ecole Nationale d'Administration (ENA), though open to women, received very few applications from female candidates. In the ten years between the founding of ENA in 1946 and 1956, 708 men and only 18 women had passed through the school on their way to brilliant careers.[30] When questioned about this, the Director at the time, M. Bourdeau, suggested that one explanation was the fact that by 21, the age at which candidates could attempt the entry examination, the life decisions of many young women had already been taken. Not so for young men.

Once the young women had completed their studies at ENA and were ready to choose their profession within the state administration, they met with more resistance. Guy Thuillier tells of the two women who in 1952 wanted to work for the Foreign Office, with a view to the diplomatic service. They were told, 'You can come to us if you like but you will never be posted abroad.' Both decided to work within the Conseil d'Etat (Council of State) instead.[31] (Paradoxically, this first entrance by women into the Conseil d'Etat was considered a victory.) The women pioneers at the top of the state did not make it to the Préfecture, the Inspectorate of Finance, ambassadorships or ministerial cabinets until after 1968.

Women's increased participation in the professions must be viewed with caution. Being part of the CSP 'liberal professions and senior manager' did not mean the same thing for men and women: the 1968 census revealed differentiated professional profiles of men and women in this classification. Only 50 per cent of women with degree-level education were in positions classified within this CSP as opposed to almost 70 per cent of male graduates. While the *Grandes Ecoles* were open to both sexes, men held nine-tenths of the diplomas awarded by these institutions. Sociologist Michel Cézard noted that men and women in this CSP had different careers: women with degrees were far more likely to be in teaching than men, whose qualification opened doors for them in the civil service and in engineering. More men than women in this CSP lacked formal qualification: there were many more self-made men than self-made women. Cézard explained women's high level of qualification as linked to their later careers in teaching, which required formal qualification, rather than in other (more prestigious, better paid but less 'diplômé') professions.[32] Even within a given profession, men and women's career profiles and prospects were not the same: men doctors were more likely to open their own practice while women doctors would work for someone else's; women's salaries continued to be lower than men's.

Tous les métiers féminins set out the different careers and jobs available for young women, including the qualifications needed, the number of women employed in each industry or profession and a section on how far each particular type of employment could be in harmony with a woman's role as wife and mother. The book made it clear that the woman was supposed to choose her profession in line with its compatibility with domesticity. For instance, the profession of lawyer was evaluated in the following, unusual way:

> A woman lawyer stays at home in the morning to receive her clients or prepare her cases. She can therefore supervise the running of the house. Returning from court at about five o'clock she can also organise herself to look after her children when they get home from school. Finally, her holidays are almost exactly the same as school holidays, which simplifies things tremendously as any working mother knows.[33]

The journal *Avenirs* published a special issue on 'métiers féminins' in April–May 1965. In this issue, rather than encouraging women to train in medicine, the article is discouraging:

> the training is tough, both physically and mentally. Compulsory daily attendance in the hospital every morning, and the practical work every afternoon, the constant contact with sick people, the frequently painful atmosphere of hospitals, dissection rooms, etc. is often hard for young women to bear, seeing as they are less robust and less emotionally balanced than men. . . . Is it not more agreeable . . . to imagine the satisfactions of a doctor's home, where his wife helps him out?[34]

Colette Audry, commenting on this, remarked drily that for some reason, none of these apparent problems for young women were raised at all in the section on nursing as a career.

CIVIL STATUS AND EMPLOYMENT

Viewing the female labour force in terms of CSPs, important changes in its composition are indicated, but others are partially obscured. For instance, one of the most significant changes in women's employment profile concerned marital status and the number of children of women in the labour market (see Tables 5.7, 5.8 and 5.9). A study based solely on women's presence in the different CSPs does not bring out this fact. What is revealed by an analysis of women's labour market position according to marital and family status is that the percentage of married women in the labour market rose considerably during the 1950s and 1960s, in particular the number of married women with children. The proportion of unmarried women in the labour market is consistently higher than the proportion of unmarried women in the female population (age also plays a part in this); the proportion of married women is lower, but rising, and rising particularly fast where salaried employment is concerned. Women who remained unmarried had a career profile that most resembled a man's, with about 75 per cent of them in employment in 1954;[35] married women's profile showed a significant age fluctuation, with participation rates dropping between the ages of 25 and 34, but rising after 35 and remaining at 39 per cent between the ages of 45 and 54.[36] The increased number of married women engaged in non-agricultural occupations between 1954 and 1962 is quite striking, present in every age group between 17 and 64 and up by over 10 per cent in every group except 35–44.[37] Actual numbers of women with three children or more who also worked outside the home were still low, but even so the figures almost doubled in the eight years between 1954 and 1962. The statement made in 1947 that 95 per cent of women with nine children or more stayed at home to look after them[38] remained true (if ridiculous), but those with three were starting to go out to earn money.

Whether a woman was able to do so and whether she wanted to do so depended at least in part on her occupation. The 1962 census showed that women with two or three children were likely to remain in employment if they were employers, in the liberal professions, or in senior and middle management; if they were factory workers, they were far more likely to abandon their job.[39] Education played a significant role in women's professional ambitions and potential (see Table 5.10). The higher the qualification, the more likely it was that a woman would have a profession and the less likely that she would abandon it. The same is true for women's apparently

Table 5.7 Total female population (by civil status)

Status	1954 %	1962 %	1968 %
Unmarried	23.3	22.4	23.8
Married	57.7	59.3	58.4
Widowed	17.1	16.3	15.7
Divorced	1.9	2.0	2.1

Source: *Données statistiques sur les familles* (Paris: Documentation Française, 1975), p. 37

Table 5.8 Women in the labour market (by civil status)

Status	1954 %	1962 %	1968 %
Unmarried	35.7	33.2	32.9
Married	48.9	53.2	55.3
Widowed	12.2	10.1	8.2
Divorced	3.2	3.5	3.6

Source: *Données statistiques sur les familles* (Paris: Documentation Française, 1975), p. 39

Table 5.9 Activity of married women in non-agricultural occupations according to the number of children

Number of children	Total married women		Active married women		Salaried married women	
1954						
None	3,564,600		1,123,400		815,000	
One	1,668,900		514,000		365,400	
Two	1,127,100		196,900		118,700	
Three +	974,200		95,100		48,700	
Total	7,334,800		1,930,100		1,347,900	
1962						
None	4,068,000	(+14%)	1,310,320	(+17%)	1,024,000	(+26%)
One	1,844,740	(+11%)	681,360	(+32%)	550,820	(+51%)
Two	1,373,040	(+18%)	291,940	(+48%)	217,140	(+83%)
Three +	1,326,900	(+36%)	134,760	(+42%)	89,320	(+83%)
Total	8,612,680	(+17%)	2,418,380	(+28%)	1,881,280	(+40%)

Source: 'L'emploi féminin en 1962 et son évolution depuis 1954', *Etudes et conjunctures*, No. 12, 1964, p. 44

notorious absenteeism. It was commonly believed that mothers were the worst offenders in this respect, taking time off from work to look after a sick child. However, one 1960 study showed that women's absenteeism was more likely to occur if they were in unskilled,

Table 5.10 Women in the labour market by age in 1962 according to educational qualification

Age	No qualification	School certificate	Technical diploma	Baccalauréat	Degree
15–19	66.6	76.9	78.0	–	–
20–24	57.3	69.4	81.1	88.4	85.7
25–29	37.0	47.1	64.9	74.9	80.1
30–34	32.3	41.0	54.9	61.4	69.1
35–39	33.8	41.0	55.0	60.0	65.8
40–44	36.4	42.9	52.2	64.9	67.1
45–49	41.6	46.5	55.2	69.4	69.8
50–54	42.8	46.8	56.2	66.7	69.2
55–64	36.9	40.6	43.2	37.0	59.9
65–74	14.7	16.7	18.0	12.3	20.3
75 and over	4.3	5.0	7.7	6.1	14.2
Total	32.0	43.8	53.0	60.5	68.3

Source: 1962 census. Cited in Françoise Guelaud-Leridon, *Recherches sur la condition féminine*, INED (Paris: PUF, 1967), p. 75

monotonous and tiring jobs, but was highly uncommon if they occupied positions of interest and responsibility.[40]

A comparison between women's employment and men's clearly shows that they followed quite different patterns. Women's employment was discontinuous, interrupted for marriage and motherhood, although this became less and less the case. Men's civil status was never raised as an issue or a problem. Women formed a smaller part of the industrial and agricultural labour force and participated in greater numbers in service industries. A very obvious trend noticeable in women's schooling and employment patterns was the increasing (though still small) number of women who obtained the Baccalauréat or a university degree and who continued their professional activity after motherhood.

The substantial increase in the number of married women in the labour market was the most striking trend in women's employment throughout the 1960s. Charts of women's employment by age and marital status show an increase in the number of employed 25–35-year-old women, confirming the increase in the number of married women and mothers remaining in paid work or returning to it.[41] While mothers with three children of whom the youngest was under 2 participated far less than others in the labour market, the trend for mothers to go out to work was clear and irreversible, and indeed fewer women were choosing to have a third child.

The return of mothers to paid employment was increasingly a fact of professional life, but it was noted that they did not always return to the same jobs as before, or to jobs that were at the same level as before. A significant difference was noted in the experience of women who had 'average' qualifications and who seemed to be increasingly moving towards careers in teaching, social work and health care. Women with higher qualifications were less affected by career breaks; women with no qualifications had 'less to lose' by an employment break. Those who lost out were precisely the most professionally and socially mobile group of women.[42]

A 1966 survey questioned married women about their professional needs and how they envisaged their future. The answers given indicate the diversity of attitudes towards married women's employment, the changing experience of different generations of women, and perceptions of women's immediate employment needs. The sample was limited to women under the age of 50, receiving family allowances, whose husbands worked in the private sector and who had a child aged between 3 and 6. Of these women 61.3 per cent wanted to work again; 70 per cent favoured part-time work; almost all of them wanted their daughters to work. However, they were divided about the ideal length of their daughters' professional life. One-third thought that the daughter should work until she reached retirement age; one third until she had her first or second child; and one third until she married.[43]

PREPARATION FOR WORK

The structure of women's employment revealed deeply held attitudes towards women, shaping their prospects and aspirations from the earliest socialisation in schools and the family. Parents, when questioned, tended to have clear ideas about the future of a son, but not of a daughter: the shape her life would take depended on her marriage.[44] The study of the village of glassworkers, Nouville, carried out in 1953, suggested that parents wanted jobs for their sons that were better paid and had better conditions than their own, but were generally unclear about their daughters' professional future. The children themselves saw their future in limited terms, with the girls mostly indicating that for them work would represent the phase of their lives that preceded marriage, nothing more.[45] Christiane Rochefort's heroine Josyane shows how little thought was given to a young woman's professional future:

> At Careers Guidance, they asked me what I wanted to do. . . .
> 'Well?' said the woman.
>   'I don't know.'
>   'Let's see now: if you could choose anything, let's imagine. . . .'
> She was nice, she asked questions kindly, not like a teacher. If I could do anything. I shrugged my shoulders.
>   'I don't know.'
>   'Haven't you ever thought about it?'
>   'No. I've never really thought about it. Not with a reply in mind; anyway, it wasn't worth the bother. . . . '
> The woman began to get annoyed. She suggested a whole load of jobs, each one more deadly than the next. I couldn't choose. I didn't see the point of busting a gut to choose in advance the job that was going to make you sweat later. People did the job they managed to get and anyway a job was a place you went in the morning and stayed in till night. . . .
>   'So, nothing really tempts you?'
> I thought hard. Nothing really tempted me.

'Your test results are good. Don't you feel drawn to anything, no vocation?'

Vocation. I opened my eyes wide. I had read a story about a girl who had a vocation to go and tend lepers. I didn't want to tend lepers any more than I wanted to work in a textile factory.

'Anyway,' said mother, 'it doesn't matter that she doesn't want to do anything, I need her more at home than at work, especially if there's going to be two of them. . . .'

It was going to be twins this time, they thought.[46]

A 1969 study showed that parents had different aspirations for sons and daughters: of those asked, significantly more envisaged higher education for their sons than for their daughters, with a heavy emphasis on technical training for boys. If they wanted their children to continue studying, they imagined that their daughters would pursue a literary course (32 per cent) and their sons a technical course (46 per cent). Parents hoped that their sons would work in industry and their daughters in education. Parents were more ambitious for their sons than for their daughters: they imagined that their sons would earn a higher salary and hoped that they would be counted as members of the CSP 'liberal professions and senior manager' (46 per cent for boys, 31 per cent for girls); they did, however, have realistic expectations and thought that their daughters were more likely to be employees (27 per cent) than in the liberal professions (10 per cent).[47]

Notions about appropriate male and female socialisation were current in schools: Linda Clark cites the director general of primary education in 1952 who stated that the duty of the male teacher was to form 'the man and the citizen' while the woman teacher's duty was to form 'the housewife and mother'.[48] Lessons in civic and moral education frequently contained clear instructions on male and female roles within the family. One such textbook intended for the final class in primary school, fairly representative of its type, set things out unambiguously in the chapter 'When we have our own home': 'The father's role is to provide for the family. If possible, he should allow the mother to stay at home. The mother's mission is above all the education of children and the adorning of the family nest.'[49]

A young woman's educational and professional prospects were also shaped by class. Viviane Isambert-Jamati found the following in 1954: of 100 daughters of agricultural families, seventy-four received no training unless they attended agricultural domestic science lessons; of 100 working-class girls, thirty-three went out to work at 11 or 12, twenty went on with some kind of education, twelve went to a form of commercial or industrial training, eighteen became apprentices and the remaining seventeen either went to domestic science classes or stayed at home to help their mother; of 100 daughters of the higher level managers or members of the liberal professions, ninety-two were in full-time secondary education at the age of 14. Eight either stayed at home or attended domestic science classes. None of them went out to work at 14.[50]

Levels of schooling and professional training were low for both sexes. Michel and Texier cite one survey of 1,266,300 girls between the ages of 14 and 17 in 1961 which found that almost 47 per cent 'began their lives without either good general knowledge [*culture*] or a trade.'[51] More girls than boys stayed in school until they were 16 (43.1 per cent of boys and 48.6 per cent of girls in 1960),[52] but on leaving school their participation in further training for work suffered.

On leaving school, more apprenticeships were available for boys than for girls (116 possible trades for girls, 248 for boys in training schools in 1959–60).[53] Boys were directed towards those industries with expanding needs, while girls were not. Michel and Texier give the figures for apprenticeships in electrical industries for 1959–60 as 341 girls and 10,040 boys, with 93 girls and 3,353 boys in technical colleges.[54]

Michel and Texier's findings were confirmed by Françoise Guelaud-Leridon. She compared the numbers of young women in a variety of industrial training programmes and apprenticeships with the relative numbers of women engaged in the jobs that logically followed. She found in 1962–3 that the figures showed 86 per cent of the young women in industrial training being prepared for the textile industry which occupied only 37 per cent of women industrial workers.[55] Guelaud-Leridon comments on this disparity and points out that young women were not being trained for work in those industries which were expanding: the needs of the economy were not being met – nor were the needs of young women about to enter the labour market. One of the consequences of this disparity was that women entering the labour market at a young age would end up taking a job for which they had no special training; they would be considered unqualified, with predictable effects on salary, the nature of the job and the possibility of promotion.

Young women were more likely to be trained for office work or other employment in the tertiary sector. Young women predominated in training for tertiary-sector jobs in general and for clerical and secretarial work in particular.[56] Those who gained typing or book-keeping qualifications were very likely to find employment using these skills. Given the number of women involved in clerical and secretarial work, and the trend indicating that this was the major area of expansion in women's employment, surprisingly little attention has been paid to them, their conditions, their prospects, their training. No study has been carried out, to my knowledge, about women's experience of the office that compares with Guilbert's or Michel's on industry; personal tales such as those by Aumont or Peyre, or representation in novels such as those by Rochefort or Etcherelli are not told about office life. Magazines such as *Antoinette* did not specify that their model reader was a factory worker but this becomes obvious in the reading. Why this lack of interest in the office employee? It might partially be explained by the relative novelty of the situation, and by the fact that for many young women office work represented success and satisfaction compared with the factory or the farm. Office workers did not unionise in large numbers and there was no central body to represent them or to speak in their name. The job was neither glamorous nor full of the physical hardships associated with factory work; it was considered to be neither pioneering, and thus worthy of attention, nor a problem, and thus worth a sociological study.[57]

A young woman's chance to participate in the so-called liberal professions depended on her level of qualification. In the general female population in 1962, almost 60 per cent remained totally without qualification.[58] It was clear, however, that the trend was towards a higher level of schooling, and when considered in terms of age and qualification, younger women were making significant strides towards improving their professional potential. Far behind boys in reaching the Baccalauréat before the war, girls caught up quickly afterwards, receiving almost 50 per cent of new diplomas awarded in 1962 and overtaking boys consistently thereafter.[59] More girls than boys were in full-time education at the age of 19, but this trend was reversed thereafter, as boys were more likely to be in training programmes and higher education than girls. An educational orientation by gender was obvious: girls took the Baccalauréat in arts subjects, the humanities and philosophy, while boys opted for maths and sciences in far greater numbers. In 1967, only 1.6 per cent of the young women candidates chose maths and the technical syllabus as opposed to 10.2 per cent of boys.[60] This sexual segregation was repeated in higher education: the overall number of students tripled between 1945 and 1967, and women's share rose to almost half (44 per cent). Women were in the majority in arts subjects and in pharmacy, but still in a minority – although a larger minority – in law, medicine and science.[61]

Training for women had been identified as a priority, but provision fell far short of the ideal. The same laments can be heard at the end of the decade as at the beginning: not enough places in the crèche, not enough part-time jobs, not enough places on training schemes. In spite of this, and in spite of any other discouragements, women with children took a giant leap into the world of paid work during the 1960s and in particular into worlds which required further study, offering careers which they would want to follow through and not simply representing a stopgap job.

THE POLITICS OF WOMEN'S EMPLOYMENT

At the Liberation, several directives came from the government concerning women's employment: in September 1944, the fixing of women's wages at 20 per cent less than men's was abolished; this was confirmed in July 1946 by the Décret Ambroise Croizat which called for equal pay for equal work; the 1946 Statute for Civil Servants gave women access to all jobs within the civil service (although this was later amended to include a clause which suggested that discrimination *could* exist in cases where physical or other aptitudes that women would not possess were 'important');[62] finally, the Constitution of the Fourth Republic stipulated that 'everyone has the right to work'. This had originally been incorporated in the draft Constitution as 'all men have the right to work'. The linguistic ambivalence was removed from the draft, but a real ambivalence remained. There was no directive emanating from high places about the need to encourage women to enter the labour market; family policy and employment policy did not pull in opposite directions because, while there was a high-profile and much-vaunted family policy, there was no policy on women's employment other than these laudable but purely rhetorical statements.

The economic Plans which set out economic goals and priorities for investment did not consider women's employment as a priority until the Third Plan (1956–61). The First Plan (1946–51) stressed pronatalism, while the Second emphasised professional training for adults. The Third Plan's consultative committee on women's employment stated clearly that it would be impossible to attain the economic targets of 1961 without increasing the female and immigrant labour force.[63] The same committee also stressed the need to encourage women to become better qualified and for their training to be adapted to the changing working environment. The committee suggested that 'families should be invited to give the same attention to the professional future of their daughters as to that of their sons'.[64]

UNESCO called for similar changes:

> In view of the fact that the evolution of society demands that women participate more in every activity, the openings for women in technical and professional training should be the same in number and in scope as those for men. Women and men should have equal access to all types and all levels of technical and professional training.[65]

By the end of the 1960s the question of women's work in general was under discussion at government level. The Ministry of Labour set up a committee to study women's work, with the specific goal of 'studying the measures likely to facilitate women's professional activity and the advancement of women in general'.[66] The two main problems raised were still equal pay and access to training. Taking account of all the possible contributory factors, it was calculated that the disparity between men's and women's salaries for doing work defined as being of equal value varied between 7 per cent and 10.1 per cent in the 1960s, and was at 7.3 per cent in 1968.[67] This seems to be quite an optimistic figure, compared with others which suggest a much greater disparity and which also suggest that things did not change much between 1954 and 1972.[68]

Professional training for adults was shown to favour men. In 1967, almost 50,000 men were registered in centres for professional training for adults, and only 2,090 women, of whom 1,810 received training specifically for women, and 280 were in mixed groups. Of the 1,810, almost 1,400 were being trained for office work, the others for work in the textile and clothing industries. Of the 280 in mixed groups, the majority were being prepared for work in the electronics industry.[69] The bias against women was repeated in the centres which retrained the unemployed. The focus in these centres was on building trades and the metal-working industry, male-dominated sectors; and where the centres offered full-time live-in training programmes, women were excluded because the centres had been designed with men in mind and were not equipped to receive women.[70]

The committee on women's employment, headed by Marcelle

Devaud, tried to help alter attitudes towards women's work, and revealed the extent to which complaints against women workers (absenteeism, frequent job changes, inability to take on certain kinds of work) were without real foundation and yet were believed by employers and used both to keep wages down and to keep women out of certain jobs. The committee listed sectors which still had quotas or in which jobs were closed to women in 1966, including positions in the customs inspectorate and other parts of the civil service.[71] The committee, as requested, closed its first report by making suggestions for facilitating women's inclusion in the labour market and professional advancement. There is no evidence of any further action being taken by the Ministry of Labour on behalf of women in the labour market.

SHOULD WOMEN WORK?

Behind public discussion on women's work, there lurked, on all sides, the underlying sense that work had a different meaning for men and for women, was more important for men than for women. Newspapers, magazines, political parties all asked questions about women that were not asked about men: should women work? If they do, what are their reasons? Are there men's jobs and women's jobs? These questions did not really address single women. Single women who went out to earn money were not the object of concern from the state, the Church, the trade unions or anyone else. Single women were not only allowed to work without social reprobation, they were supposed to work, especially at a time when unemployment was not a serious threat and the state specifically needed more workers. But single women were also supposed to give up their job without a struggle, having been encouraged to view it as a stopgap prior to marriage and family.

The prime importance given to motherhood compared to employment was an attitude that persisted throughout the 1950s, held, most particularly, by non-mothers. Françoise Giroud's book *La nouvelle vague: portraits de la jeunesse* ('The new wave: portraits of youth') published in 1958 asked the sample of 18–30-year-olds who participated in the survey (originally carried out by *L'Express*) about how they perceived their future. Giroud concludes the section on unmarried women of under 25 by suggesting that 'most young women rarely think of their future in terms of a profession, even when they have a satisfying job ... they think of work as a period of transition before a better future where husband and children await them.'[72] The older married women in the sample expressed anxiety and frustration: 'my education did not prepare me for the life of a mistress of the house', said one, while another noted that 'it's hard to give up all outside activities and feel tied to the house by domestic chores'. A third said: 'what I miss most ... is being able to do something other than housework and looking after the baby ... the one has already destroyed my mental faculties and I'm afraid that the other will reduce me to nothing.'[73]

Whatever the pressures and arguments which militated against mothers who worked, significant numbers of them continued to do so. For every survey proving that it was harmful for mothers to work, there was another which proved the contrary. The UFF's monthly magazine for women *Heures claires* reported in 1956 on the findings of a Dr Rousseau, who told the PCF's committee on mental hygiene that a mother's employment was beneficial for her children: it helped to place greater value on women; it helped to reduce their tension levels; the children of working mothers were more successful at school; and, in some cases, the mother's employment meant that they all lived longer.[74]

Linked to the question of 'Should women work' came the next most-discussed question, 'Why do women work?' The answers to this question in the various surveys carried out either by women's magazines, newspapers, sociologists, politicians and economists listed economic necessity as the major reason for working, but also mentioned personal fulfilment and the enjoyment of friendship with colleagues. Another popular question in these frequent surveys was about appropriate occupations for young men and women. In Giroud's survey, views of occupations that best suited women included all those that helped to develop their 'feminine' qualities, while the surprisingly conservative *New Wave* expressed worry that women would become more masculine if they worked in men's jobs, and would no longer be 'real women.'[75]

The journal *Esprit* devoted a special issue to 'La femme au travail' ('Women at work') in May 1961. In it representatives of women's organisations were questioned about issues such as a woman's right to work and appropriate jobs for men and women. There was a clear split between those for whom a profession was a question of individual women's choices and ability, and those for whom an appropriate profession for a woman depended on the age of her children and their needs. There was also a clear divide between urban and rural women. To the question 'Should a woman work?', the JACF replied simply that the question was not appropriate for rural women, for whom the idea of the housewife with no professional concerns was anathema.[76]

As well as discussions criticising, or defending, mothers for working, there was also a more positive search for 'solutions' to the problem of reconciling the double function of mother and worker. Legislation, fought for by trade unions, political parties of the Left and women's organisations, improved conditions for working mothers, but not enough. Women on maternity leave (six weeks prior to giving birth, eight afterwards) received half their salary – in one year women worked 3.75 million days which they were entitled to take off, as they could not afford to live on half pay for fourteen weeks.[77] Contracts were negotiated in the civil service to give full pay for maternity leave and to hold open a woman's job during this period. Several other companies and industries followed suit, but this contract was not made the national minimum until 1966.[78] As discussed in Chapter Four, the CGT sought to obtain recognition that motherhood was a social and not merely an individual concern, and that the mother should therefore not have to carry the financial burden herself.

The single wage benefit, designed to keep mothers at home, was in fact considered by some to be the 'solution' to mothers' problems; for others, the solution lay in the development of state childcare facilities such as crèches; and for some women, the solution lay in part-time work. Responses to all these three options were highly ambivalent and all three were discussed at length. The discussions over these three possible solutions remained mostly theoretical: as has been previously noted, the value of the single wage benefit declined over the 1960s; there were never enough crèche places to meet demand;[79] and part-time work did not concern many women.

Part-time work was popular with women, but not with employers or trade unions. Trade unions did not support part-time work for women for the following reasons: if women were to be encouraged to work part-time only, then their professional training would be neglected and they would only have access to low-interest low-paid positions – women's part-time labour would accentuate their lack of qualifications; if part-time work was envisaged as a 'solution' for mothers, then the whole question of the state's provision of childcare could be avoided; the reality of unemployment would be hidden behind figures treating part-time workers as full-time workers; the question of an overall reduction in the working week would also be avoided; the disparity between male and female salaries would increase.[80] Employers were reluctant to introduce it as the cost for them was high; the public sector did not permit part-time work until 1970, and then only with limited conditions of access. So even when women expressed the desire and need for part-time work, it was often simply unavailable – just like a place at the crèche.

EQUAL RIGHTS AT WORK

Any struggle for equal rights for women at the workplace therefore took place in a climate that, if not hostile, was at best ambivalent about what women were doing there anyway. At the top of the equal rights agenda was the question of equal pay. After this one burning issue came equality of access and treatment, and the question of protective legislation for mothers.

Following the directives of 1946, women and men in France were legally supposed to receive equal pay for equal work. This was an improvement on legislation that had previously fixed women's wages at 20 per cent less than men's. In fact, however, women's salary was generally considered to be a *salaire d'appoint*, or pin money, and the efforts of those who saw the home as the ideal place for married women complicated – or indeed undermined – any fight undertaken for equal pay. As is well known, the definition of 'equal work' is problematic. It is also well known that throughout the labour market, women and men rarely occupy the same posts. In 1962, the average female salary was 64 per cent of the male average.[81] Equality was a fiction even – or especially – in the more prestigious professions: if women earned 69 per cent of a man's salary in the factory, a woman senior manager received 63 per cent of the salary of her male colleague.[82] This was not so much because women earned a lower rate than men for the same work, but because women occupied positions lower down the salary scale than men and did not have the same career structure. The reasons for this continued professional sex segregation were above all women's lack of qualification, the interruption of employment for motherhood, and protective legislation (stopping women from benefiting from lucrative overtime or night shifts); plus, of course, the ambivalence that was felt about women being there at all. In other words, women earned less than men because of the very characteristics of women's employment at the time which nobody in power was trying to remedy; and so the arguments fed into each other.

This sex segregation was equally visible in the civil service, in spite of its claims to be an equal opportunities employer. The competitive entry examination kept posts reserved for men, a fact revealed by the SFIO representative Rachel Lempereur in 1957.[83] This injustice still existed in 1968 in a range of positions from the Post Office to Customs and Excise to physical education teachers.[84] Where women could compete for access, they were seen to fail twice as often as men in the oral entrance examination (for internal candidates) whereas they were equally successful in the written entrance examination. As an employer, the civil service did not necessarily respect the law any more than the private sector. Odile Dhavernas cites several court cases in which the Conseil d'Etat was called upon to arbitrate. In Strasbourg, for instance, the statutes regulating employment of municipal workers actually stated that 'Women lose their position upon their marriage or remarriage'; another case was brought in which a man was promoted to the rank of inspector in the Post Office instead of the woman who ought to have been promoted, because the Minister responsible wanted to avoid a situation where a higher number of women than men held superior positions.[85]

TRADE UNIONS

There has been little research carried out specifically on women and trade unions in France after the Liberation and in the 1950s. It is known that women did not join trade unions in large numbers but actual figures and percentages are hard to establish: each of the three major groupings (the Confédération Générale du Travail, CGT; the Confédération Générale du Travail-Force Ouvrière, CGT-FO, after 1948; and the Confédération Française des Travailleurs Chrétiens, CFTC) claimed that approximately 25–30 per cent of its members were women but none has ever provided actual figures. Women were as absent from leadership positions within the trade unions as they were from political parties and from management, even in those unions dominant in professions such as teaching where they formed the majority of members.[86] Women's issues were not at the top of the agenda. The immediate postwar years saw many strikes (in which women participated massively) and the split within the CGT leading to the formation of Force Ouvrière in 1948. Each confederation was closely linked to the ideological perspective of a political party, although this link was generally denied: the CGT was a PCF-dominated organisation; the CFTC was associated with the MRP; and the CGT-FO, on an unofficial and individual basis, was associated with the non-Communist Left.

The CGT was more active than the others: women's sections were

set up (although at national congresses, the *rapporteur* indicated
that this was a slow business and had met with little enthusiasm);
in 1948, a national women's council was organised to look after
women's issues, and a programme of objectives concerning women
at work was prepared. Summing up the CGT positions on women's
work apart from those on motherhood which have already been
discussed, the priorities between 1948 and 1959 were: support for
equal pay and equal access to all jobs and to training; opposition to
part-time work, the ideal of the 'femme au foyer', and the notion
of pin money and the single wage benefit, support for women's
retirement at 55 and (in the 1950s) opposition to the work of the
family planning movement.[87] Madeleine Colin, responsible for
women's issues in the CGT, defined the CGT women's council's
work as being focused on the production of the magazine *La revue
des travailleuses*, later *Antoinette*,[88] which sold up to 35,000 copies a
week. Increased attention paid to *Antoinette* reflected acknowledgement that more and more women could be reached this way, as
more and more joined the labour force of salaried workers. Throughout the 1960s, the CGT's preoccupations can be read through
Antoinette: the magazine's serious articles looked at women's rights
at work (maternity leave and other benefits), conditions at work
(health hazards and beauty tips for tired eyes or rough skin), issues
for working mothers (crèches, social security and the single mother)
or CGT themes such as the reduction of the working day for women
(1965), women's unemployment (1968), reports on conferences.

The CGT attracted the majority of unionised women workers
with high visibility in specific sectors (the Post Office, textiles); Force
Ouvrière seemed to share the CGT demands as far as women were
concerned, while the CFTC, in line with the MRP, made the goal
of returning mothers to the home its priority. The trade union
movement was as divided ideologically over 'women's place' as
political parties, which may help to explain its lack of apparent
success in mobilising women and in fighting any concerted campaigns on behalf of women workers.

Trade unions evolved slowly in their positions and in the early
1960s seemed to make little progress in the struggles over women's
rights at the workplace. The same debates were aired: for and
against the single wage benefit, for and against part-time work, the
length of the working week for women, equal pay, access to training.
At each CGT congress, the spokeswoman for the women's section
set out the same demands, with the focus changing only slightly
here and there.

In 1964, the CFTC voted to end its Christian identification and changed its name to the Confédération Française Démocratique du Travail (CFDT, Democratic French Confederation of Labour.[89] With 'deconfessionalisation', this non-Communist trade union began to develop positions resembling those of the CGT and CGT-FO. The founding document of the transformed CFDT noted the continued existence of prejudice against and exploitation of women in the workplace and sought to involve greater numbers of women in trade union activity.[90] It has been claimed that in spite of the higher visibility of the CGT, the CFDT had a more global appreciation of women's oppression:

> We found in the CGT's feminism a sort of Society for the Protection of Animals and we rejected demands made specifically on behalf of women, such as earlier retirement for women or a reduced working week for women ... I perceived the CFDT as much more open and lively. The CFDT, even before May '68, took on the problem of women in general. The CGT only took on the question of work.[91]

Between 1964 and 1968, the confederations were broadly in accord (and signed an agreement for common action in January 1966), and although different responses to the events of May '68 brought this abruptly to an end as far as more general demands were concerned, their programmes of demands for the rights of women workers did not significantly differ.

Women in the professions were represented by their professional associations and by women's rights organisations.[92] They may have deplored the small number of women in each profession (law, medicine, women company directors) and the poor state of training, but they did very little to change the situation. Concerned to fit in, conscious of their own pioneering status, they chose to fight in ways that did not directly criticise their own profession. They called for more broadly based social reforms: better educational opportunities for girls, and reform of the Civil Code (the inheritance and property laws affecting them, as economically independent women). While they constituted an important pressure group for reforming women's civil status, they were largely ineffective as a pressure group for women's rights at the workplace. Their conclusion to the problem of home versus work was that women simply had to choose between the two or juggle their responsibilities as best they could. They did not analyse the problems that prevented most women from enjoying the same status and privileges as they did. One woman said that, in order to succeed, all you need is to have a good housekeeper and to get up early in the morning.[93]

Nothing as far as women's employment was concerned, not even the most basic principles governing equality of access to education, training, employment, professional promotion, equal pay and conditions, had found even theoretical consensus by the early 1960s. The demands put forward in the early 1960s about pay and conditions were the same as those put forward in the late 1940s. Women found their own individual solutions to their employment needs and problems; some joined trade unions and professional associations; most simply put up with the unfairness of it all.

Education and training were at the top of long-term needs. Women pioneers in the professions had fought and broken through some legal barriers and open hostility, but still faced the *de facto* resistance of men to the inclusion of women in the professions. Women responded to immediate, short-term needs rather than envisaging their professional life as a long-term investment. Women defined their immediate employment needs as: hours that permitted them to run a home at the same time; part-time work; better childcare facilities; a job near home.[94] These needs were not met. Nothing was done to facilitate the reconciliation of family and professional obligations: crèche and other childcare provisions remained at derisory levels in most of the country; and disputes over the desirability or otherwise of crèches or of the single wage benefit blocked any concerted action.

Attitudes towards working women were changing but not quickly enough and not in all circles. It was a sobering reminder to hear Jacques Chirac, then Minister of Labour, saying in February 1968, when asked about the 450,000 unemployed: 'the current economic and political situation being what it is ... there is not enough room for everyone ... a working woman costs the state more than a man, so it is preferable to do without.'[95]

It was clearly not considered that women had the same right to work or found the same personal fulfilment in a career as men. In spite of the acknowledgement that women's labour power was needed for France's reconstruction and growth, it was nonetheless as mothers that women's services were thought to be most useful.

Women went out into a world of work which was essentially defined without them; employment structures and practices of the postwar years contributed to women's exclusion from, or marginalisation at, the workplace; a specific view of an appropriate gendered division of labour at home and at the workplace perpetuated a view of women as the second sex. By the end of the 1960s, the world outside was, for most women, as unwelcoming as before. Women were working, but did not belong to the outside world of paid employment to the same extent or in the same way as men. This is obvious in the lack of incentives offered by government and employers – lack of proper training and inadequate childcare facilities – and in the (frequently unacknowledged) sexism that operated in hiring, promotion, firing.

It is impossible not to agree with Rose-Marie Lagrave, when she says that 'every time women make progress, numerically, in education and in the labour market, there is a new invention which maintains difference between the sexes.'[96] Men were threatened by women's invasion of public space, in politics and in the labour market, and did their best to resist. As women increasingly entered the non-agricultural labour market, the sexual segregation of employment in both occupational and hierarchical terms kept them in typically 'feminine' subordinate positions, as secretaries, as carers, at the bottom of the wage hierarchy. Occupations which became more 'feminised' were devalued; as women gained more and higher qualifications, so too the value of qualifications was shifted from literature and philosophy to the more male-dominated streams of science and mathematics. Women were kept out of economic and political élites. Equality legislation was not respected by employers.

Most importantly, as women played an increasingly significant part in public life, men did not reciprocate in the home. Evelyne Sullerot wrote:

> It is quite striking that women's voices, everywhere, are being raised to demand not protective legislation, not flattery and praise, but education, jobs, responsibility. I can't say that an equivalent male chorus is responding, demanding the right to stay at home to do the hoovering and the washing, look after the children, do the dishes and start all over again once it's done.[97]

Combining family and paid work became a fact of life for Frenchwomen in the 1960s, but this does not mean that anyone made it easy for them.

6 Women's rights

By the end of the 1960s, women's position within the family and in the labour market, their control over their own bodies, and the way in which they could perceive their future were significantly different from what they had been in 1945. While the changing socio-economic and political context was clearly the prime factor affecting women's lives, it also took the determined actions of determined individuals to bring about change: the pioneering work and lobbying activities of women were crucial, and yet are often ignored in accounts of how France became a 'modern' society. Legislation improving women's status does not happen by itself or through the good nature of lawmakers: women have had to fight for change every inch of the way. Yet the achievements of the 1960s (when they are mentioned) are usually attributed to government efforts to make the law match practice, or as a kind of inevitable progress, for which women are given no credit.

WOMEN'S RIGHTS GROUPS

This chapter will investigate the contribution of women's rights groups and feminists of the time to changing women's lives in France. Some of the groups active in the 1950s and 1960s will be outlined, either as examples of women's rights activism at that time, or as being unusual or ahead of their time. The second part of the chapter will describe the two major women's rights campaigns of the 1960s (the reform of the marriage laws and the reform of the law on contraception). There may have been no legislation passed between 1945 and 1965 that specifically focused on changing women's legal position, but there was plenty of discussion over women's 'issues' and women's rights. The discussion – in Parliament, in the press – reveals the generally hostile context in which women's rights campaigners had to operate and it is this discussion that reflects most accurately the dominant atmosphere regarding 'women's place' and 'women's role' in the immediate postwar decades.

Women's groups have been mentioned throughout this book: the women's sections in political parties and in the trade union movement, the groups with specific religious affiliation and women's professional associations. Those with the greatest audience were the UFCS and the UFF, each of which had supporters inside Parliament, but the various groups which defended, promoted and fought for women's rights reflected the full ideological spectrum. The politics of some of the women's groups tended towards social conservatism, while others were more inclined towards social democracy or socialism. Apart, obviously, from the UFF and the women's section of the CGT, they were mostly anti-communist. Some claimed to be a-political. There were single-issue interest groups and groups of women in different professions, usually limited to women already in a political and/or professional élite, who did not seek to analyse anything beyond the situation of women in their own profession. Many of them continued the nineteenth-century feminist tradition of concern with charity and helping those less fortunate than themselves. Apart from the UFF and the UFCS, the audience of each group was very limited, and they did not want to become mass movements.

The groups can be considered in different ways, classified in terms of being on the Left or the Right, women-only or mixed, with political affiliations or not, single-issue or generally concerned with women's rights, religious or secular. Some of them had existed before the war, some of them were newly founded afterwards. There were groups whose focus was on women and those which included women almost incidentally, as an integral part of a different agenda (health, education, employment). The groups intersected in a variety of not particularly coherent ways, agreeing on certain issues, diverging on others, sometimes separated by ideology, sometimes united in spite of it.[1]

Two umbrella groups of women's organisations founded before the war can give an idea of the activities of the more conservative women who were nonetheless promoters of women's rights. The Conseil National des Femmes (National Women's Council) was a long-standing federation (founded in 1901) with generally progressive but moderate views (in favour of an egalitarian marriage law and in favour of birth control, against the single wage benefit) blended with themes of the Catholic parties and women's groups (the fight against alcoholism and prostitution). Its prime mover, Mme Lefaucheux had been an MRP Deputy and Senator, was part of the French delegation to the United Nations between 1946 and 1959 and presided over the UN's Committee on the Condition of Women.

The Comité de Liaison des Associations Féminines (CLAF, Liaison Committee of Women's Associations) united about sixty women's organisations. The spokeswomen for the CLAF were conservative (Mme Devaud in the Senate was first on the Parti Républicain de la Liberté's (PRL) conservative list and later on the Gaullist list; Madame de Lipkowski was a Gaullist). The CLAF's tactics were defined by Michel and Texier as being to keep their demands to the minimum so as to gain something, however little;[2] furthermore, the diversity of opinion among the sixty organisations represented in the CLAF meant that no firm position was possible on any controversial question at all. Mme Devaud was also an active member of the UFCS.

As well as these umbrella organisations, there were the groups with specific audiences: the Association des Françaises Diplômées des Universités (the Association of French Women University Graduates) concerned itself particularly with questions such as education and women's representation in the professions, as did a further organisation representing women in the liberal and commercial professions, the Union Professionnelle Féminine (Union of Professional Women). The activities and positions of these organisations can be traced in their publications *Femmes diplômées* and *Union professionnelle féminine*. The main function of the groups was apparently to provide mutual support for women in privileged minority positions, a sort of 'old girls' network'. Local groups were completely free to operate in whatever manner they chose, but the lecture seems to have been the preferred style. At meetings, members would describe their visits to Poland or Africa; an invited speaker would talk about a new exhibition or a new book. The publications bemoan the small number of professional women but the associations do not appear to have fought actively for increased opportunities for young women and girls in the professions. There was apparently no desire for equality of opportunity for all. *Femmes diplômées* contains a number of articles on education for girls, and on women in the professions, but nothing at all on how to change the status quo. This sense of gentility is even more acute in the publications of women's associations involving only one profession: women lawyers, women doctors, women company directors all produced, for a while anyway, their own newsletters or magazines. They were interested in the aspects of inequality in women's lives that concerned them directly: inheritance, ownership of property, equal pay, quotas limiting the number of women in the professions. They did discuss birth control (some were in favour, others not) and part-time work for women (most were against). However, they mostly did not perceive their – privileged – situation as part of a common female destiny or seek to analyse their own particular experience in terms of a shared discrimination based on sex.

The Ligue Française pour le Droit des Femmes (League of Women's Rights) was yet another of these groups, rightly thought of as bourgeois and dismissed rather hastily as such by later feminists. The League kept a watching brief on the position of women and attitudes towards women in the postwar years. The League was the only one of these groups to embrace the label 'feminist', which it had had since it was founded in 1869. The main figure associated with this group in the 1950s and 1960s was the lawyer Andrée Lehmann; the newsletter it published was called *Le droit des femmes* ('Women's Rights'). Published on a bi-monthly and later on a quarterly basis, *Le droit des femmes* contained several regular features: 'for the working woman', 'jurisprudence', 'women in Parliament'. Most space in the newsletter was taken up with reports of the interventions made in Parliament by women politicians; the League applauded every pioneering act, every time a woman achieved something for the first time – the first magistrate, the first bailiff, the first women in the Conseil d'Etat. In the 1950s, the League tended to remain out of controversial areas, but in the 1960s, there were articles in *Le droit des femmes* on birth control, on professional training for girls, on part-time work, on sex education. The publications were quite insular: there is no mention in either *Le droit des femmes* or in *Femmes diplômées* of Simone de Beauvoir, of the women's groups in political parties, of trade-union activity.

These groups are offered here as examples of the many groups which existed in those years. Others, such as the Fédération Nationale des Femmes (National Federation of Women), or Les Soroptimistes, presented similar profiles. Without suffrage as an issue, some of them took up the question of the political education of women, others mostly sought new causes. The fact that there was no one obvious and unifying cause for them to fight led to a clear malaise:

being a feminist shifted ground and evolved in sometimes barely perceptible ways, so that it has been easy to think that between 1944 ... and 1970 ... the feminist movement was either silent or had regressed. ... It seems, rather, that the feminist movement was seeking a new identity.[3]

Defence of women's rights, as it appeared within these groups, did not seem to occupy progressive ground, but remained the privilege of small groups of middle-aged, middle-class women. Being a feminist, or a promoter of women's rights, was not appealing to a more general audience of women.

The UFCS and the UFF, who placed their activism in the broader context of political or religious ideas, reached far greater numbers of women. The UFCS, founded in 1925, occupied the awkward space of wanting to promote women's rights (such as the vote) within the context of the traditional family. As such, it appealed to thousands of Catholic women, and its journal *La femme dans la vie sociale* sold between 20,000 and 30,000 copies a week.[4] The UFF, founded in late 1944, published a weekly magazine *Femmes françaises* and a monthly, *Heures claires* (which joined together in 1957). Officially at any rate, the UFF did not deviate from Communist Party positions on key issues and fought for better conditions at work and at home, for women's civil and political rights. In spite of agreement with other women's associations over these issues, there was no joint action, no common programme of demands.

FEMINISTS?

What can we make of this range of groups? Were they effective in their campaigning? Were they feminist? In spite of the existence of these groups, the period between the vote of 1944 and the events of May '68 is often represented as a kind of Bermuda Triangle of feminism. The problem is at least partly one of terminology and of how meaning is constructed in a particular socio-historical context. The term 'feminist' did not seem appropriate to many of the women who continued to fight for women's rights after 1945; the word clearly evoked the prewar movement. 'Feminist' was considered to be the opposite of 'feminine', implying aggression, women trying to be like men; the term was not much liked even by those women who would today be described as feminist.

Most women's organisations simply called themselves *féminin* (women's). Some, while not using the label 'feminist', accepted that fighting for women's rights was part of their identity. The expression 'women's rights' was more acceptable than 'feminism' to most of these women, echoing the notion of human rights and the rights of man (*sic*) dear to the Republican tradition, to which they were mostly attached. Women who would not use the term 'feminist' would often be quite happy to describe themselves as being in favour of women's rights.

Neither the UFCS nor the UFF fits easily with the label 'feminist' and both would have rejected it out of hand. The other groups described above hardly made 'feminism' an appetising prospect for other women, although this should not mask their contribution to women's rights reforms and to awareness of women's discrimination in France. The well-known names attached to the groups and the fact that some of the leading women were in Parliament and others in international organisations meant that they had a good chance of influencing policy and achieving some degree of change. The pressure kept up by women in these groups throughout the 1950s in favour of the reform of the marriage laws, for instance, was undoubtedly the motor for the eventual reform of 1965. However, the image of these groups was rather old-fashioned, the participants were not young, and their insistence on the value of law reform (plus their exclusion of men) meant that by the end of the 1960s they were somewhat out of step with progressive thinking on women's issues and progressive politics.[5]

Feminists today seeking to locate feminism in France in the 1950s and 1960s would recognise contemporary understandings of the word in the work of a number of groups and the thinking of a few individual women – either slightly ahead or frankly at odds with the time – which served as precursors for a later more radical brand of feminism: Jeunes Femmes; the Mouvement Français pour le Planning Familial; the Mouvement Démocratique Féminin. The women whose work was pioneering included Simone de Beauvoir, Andrée Michel, Evelyne Sullerot, Françoise Giroud, Colette Audry.[6] None of these women would have defined themselves as feminists, in the sense that feminism was understood at the time (that is, trying to achieve rights that were still denied); but in a variety of ways, they fit a more recent understanding of feminism: that is, they put women at the centre of their analysis; they sought to increase women's autonomy; they challenged the view that being a wife, housewife and mother was a woman's destiny.

JEUNES FEMMES

Jeunes Femmes was a Protestant young women's group, like a consciousness-raising group before the term had become current. Founded in Paris in 1946 as a group in which a specifically 'women's' perspective could be brought to questions concerning members' own lives, small groups mushroomed throughout France. The remarkably open-minded groups sought to become 'a place where every woman can express herself, even aggressively and particularly so when we examine difficult questions'.[7] From the early 1950s, the movement, which was small (500 subscriptions to the journal) but influential, discussed issues that specifically concerned women but which were still more or less taboo in France at the time: male–female relations, psychoanalysis, and birth control. They read and discussed *Le deuxième sexe* and other controversial publications. They looked at these issues from the perspective of the Bible and the Protestant Church. They analysed and compared their own positions with those of the Catholic Church. They sought to question rather than to find answers; there was no particular 'line' dictated by a central authority. By 1967, there were 6,000 members of Jeunes Femmes in 270 groups throughout France, and Protestant women, frequently members of Jeunes Femmes, were found in leading roles in many groups that supported women's rights, most notably in the family planning movement. Being Protestant seemed to make a difference to women's attitudes towards women's rights for a number of reasons: Protestantism emphasized the individual rather than the family; individual responsibility rather than acceptance of doctrine; reading the Bible rather than accepting the priest's word.[8] Protestant women were not weighed down by the powerful moral and religious taboos of the Catholic Church. It might then not be surprising to find them in large numbers at the forefront of feminist activity.

THE MOUVEMENT DEMOCRATIQUE FEMININ

A key group of women's rights activists in the 1960s was the Mouvement Démocratique Féminin (MDF, Democratic Women's Movement). Given the apparent ideological stagnation of French political life in the early 1960s, many intellectuals participated in a number of political clubs, independent from political parties but in sympathy with one or another of them. In 1961, the MDF, a women's political club associated with the non-Communist Left, was founded and was to play a pivotal role in the development of feminism in France in the 1960s and 1970s, with individuals in the group active in both pre-'68 women's rights campaigns and the post-'68 women's liberation movement.

This club saw its goals initially as to: 'help women achieve their liberation and their advancement and give them the means to make a choice and achieve fulfilment according to their individual qualities, in the family, in their profession, in society, in the country.'[9] Several personalities dominated the MDF: Yvette Roudy (who later used ideas from the MDF for her programme as Minister for Women's Rights after 1981); Marie-Thérèse Eyquem, who was appointed the first Minister for Women in Mitterrand's 1965 shadow cabinet but died before she had the chance to take up the post; and Colette Audry, teacher, writer, trade unionist and intellectual. According to Audry, the MDF prepared the ground for the post-'68 women's liberation movement in spite of the fact that the two brands of feminism never got along.[10] The MDF's strategy was to make concrete demands, to try to use political parties and those in power on behalf of women. Given the scarcity of sympathetic women politicians in the National Assembly, the MDF chose a pragmatic strategy: unable to rely on women politicians to raise, defend and fight for women's rights in Parliament, they exerted pressure on sympathetic men. They took stands on all the controversial issues of the day: they were against part-time work for women), in favour of legal contraception; they rejected the 1965 marriage law as enshrining inequality. They worked with women in the Communist Party and in the trade unions, with the MFPF and with Jeunes Femmes. The MDF was never a mass movement, but was probably limited to a couple of hundred women at the most, and was Paris-based.[11] Even so, as Roudy noted in her autobiography, it had an unprecedented role as an 'ideas laboratory'.[12] The group's magazine, *La femme du XXe siècle* (Twentieth-century woman), written mostly by Roudy and Audry, took up campaigns and issues fearlessly. It wanted to:

> raise public consciousness by informing people about those questions called 'women's' questions which in fact concern the couple, the child and the whole of society.... This magazine is not a women's magazine like so many others. It is an organ of information and struggle, objectively analysing problems which are increasingly on the agenda today and proposing solutions linked to progressive politics.[13]

The MDF took the credit for bringing contraception to the attention of François Mitterrand who then made it part of his electoral campaign.[14] As a women's political avant-garde, the MDF was crucial in developing a feminist consciousness within the non-Communist Left; when the new Parti Socialiste (PS) was formed in 1969 and François Mitterrand became its leader in 1971, Eyquem and many other MDF women joined. Believing perhaps that women's rights issues would be incorporated into new PS programmes, MDF women put their energy into the new party and the MDF as a distinct club lost its momentum. Born at a time when women's political representation was at a low, when de Gaulle seemed immoveable and hostile to notions of women's emancipation (let alone liberation), the MDF provided a women's space for discussion and was an influential pressure group calling for action.

ASSOCIATION MATERNITÉ HEUREUSE: THE HAPPY MOTHERHOOD ASSOCIATION

The organisation which led the fight to reform the 1920 law on birth control did not describe itself as a women's rights group, or a feminist group, and presented the campaign as a women's health issue, not a women's rights issue. The initiative to found the Association came from sociologist Evelyne Sullerot who had written to Marie-Andrée Weill-Hallé after hearing of her speech to the Académie des Sciences Morales[15] and suggested that they take some action. In 1956, together with the lawyer and Freemason Maître Dourlen-Rollier, Madeleine Tric from Jeunes Femmes, Andrée Marty-Capgras, other women doctors, Mme Domenach from the left-wing Christian review *Esprit*, writer Clara Malraux and sixteen other women, Sullerot and Weill-Hallé founded the movement which was to become the Mouvement Français pour le Planning Familial (MFPF, French Family Planning Movement) in the 1960s.[16]

In 1956, however, the forming of such a group had to be done carefully both in order to stay within the law and to distinguish itself from earlier neo-Malthusian movements. The only way in which family planning could exist at all was in the form of a private non-profit-making association, dedicated to research and circulating information to its members only. The 1920 law banned propaganda concerning methods of birth control: propaganda addresses an anonymous audience, they argued, whereas an association could address its named members without suffering accusations of spreading propaganda. Nor could research be called propaganda. Furthermore, birth control, in the sense of deliberately seeking to limit the numbers of children to be born, was never a goal of the Association, which sought, rather, to make every child born a wanted child. The Statutes of the Association showed the goals to be:

> the study of the problems associated with motherhood, and its repercussions for the family, society and the nation; research and information, both in France and abroad, about these problems, the study of all questions which could improve the conditions surrounding motherhood and birth.[17]

The Association's founders always rejected the label 'feminist', claiming that what they were doing was done on behalf of women's health and the happiness of the family. According to Bouchardeau, this was little more than a strategy which allowed them to hide their radicalism under the guise of convention; according to Weill-Hallé, it was sincere.

The activities and development of the Association were recorded in its newsletter for members, *Maternité heureuse*. The first issue, published in 1956, points out yet again that the aims of the Association were not to spread anti-family 'propaganda' or to call for the lowering of the French birth rate: on the contrary, 'the true goal of our Association and the aim of our actions is to pursue ... the construction of the happy, harmonious family'.[18] Hence the name.

This first issue attacked the 1920 law, but did so in the name of the happy, harmonious family which, to exist, required a happy, healthy mother, not 'a woman exhausted by her husband's selfish demands who will bring up her children without strength, without joy and sometimes abandoned by her husband who finds a family atmosphere unappealing'. Then the focus turned from the family to the woman: 'It is in particular for women that we seek the revision of articles 3 and 4 of the 1920 law, and it is women whom we want to educate, so that they know about contraceptives for women's use'.[19]

By the mid-1960s, the Association now called the Mouvement Français pour le Planning Familial and had become a mixed group, composed of health-care professionals and others; it was not a women's group. And yet the campaign to overthrow the 1920 law undoubtedly held profound implications for women and therefore for gender relations in general. 'Freedom begins in the womb'[20] expressed the understanding that birth control was more than the issue of women's health that was claimed as Weill-Hallé's primary goal. During the 1960s, the MFPF increasingly placed its activities in the broader context of encouraging a society that, in their words, was *sexualisée* – in which sexuality was considered to be a healthy and normal part of people's lives.

WOMEN'S RIGHTS CAMPAIGNS

What did women's rights groups accomplish for women in the pre-'68 period? In very different ways, the two major women's rights reforms of the 1960s sought to increase a woman's autonomy – control of her assets, control of her body – implying an upheaval in both private and professional life that was not immediately perceptible but was to have immense consequences for the generation reaching adulthood in the late 1960s.

In the 1960s, the earlier discussions and protests over inequalities within marriage reached a more sympathetic audience than before, reflecting the changes that had taken place and the choices that women were making. This shifted the terrain of women's rights debates from small, marginal groups to the political, parliamentary domain. In the case of both the reform of the marriage law and the law legalising contraception, the passing of the new laws represented less the heralding of new beliefs than the sanctioning of already commonly held attitudes and common practices. It represented the end of a long struggle and, indeed, displacement of that struggle. The end result of protracted campaigns on behalf of women did not fulfil the hopes of those who initiated them. Nonetheless, the changes in legislation confirmed changes in socially acceptable behaviour, set out revised norms and limits and marked consolidation of the fact that women's lives were less circumscribed than before, their destiny less predictable.

Women's rights activists had been protesting against the inequality written into the Civil Code since the mid-nineteenth century, but serious revision of the law only became a parliamentary affair after the Second World War. After 1946, women's rights activists contested the law on the grounds that women's equality with men was written into the Constitution; they argued that it made no legal or practical sense to maintain the imbalance in private life. However, when the law was finally changed, it was not with women's 'inalienable' rights in mind, or with the equality of the sexes in view. The law needed to be amended in line with the changing position of women in the economy and the changing nature of family assets, which were less and less in the form of land and property and increasingly in the form of capital, shares and other 'mobile' assets.[21] Legislators did accept that the new law ought to reflect the increasingly important role of women outside the family but this was not their primary goal.

Fifteen proposals for reforming the marriage law were put forward between 1945 and 1959 without ever reaching the stage of being formally brought before Parliament (to be discussed in the National Assembly and in the Senate and put to the vote). This stage was reached in 1959, when a Bill was put to the Senate by the Minister of Justice on behalf of the government. Parliamentarians were unexcited by this issue at that stage, with at most only fifty of them ever present during the discussions.[22] The initial proposal sought to modify the 'régime légal' ('default' system) by making it the 'communauté réduite aux acquêts', that is by making the law apply to assets and possessions acquired during the marriage, not to those that each spouse brought to the marriage. The proposal was accepted by the Senate and sent to the National Assembly. The Senate had maintained the clauses of the law in which the husband administered the wife's assets as well as the jointly owned assets, thus keeping the wife manifestly in a subordinate position in relation to her husband.

The debate in the National Assembly opened on 16 November 1960. Jacqueline Thome-Patenôtre, who had moved from the Senate to the National Assembly in 1958, proposed that the system adopted when couples married without a contract should be that known as the 'séparation des biens', meaning that each spouse should be responsible for and have the right to his or her own property and other assets that each already possessed prior to marriage. She proposed that they share responsibility for commonly owned assets. The National Assembly, primarily thanks to the efforts of Thome-Patenôtre, Marcelle Devaud and Paul Coste-Floret, decided in December 1960 in favour of giving women control over their own assets ('biens propres'). Devaud said quite plainly: 'What ought we to expect after the modifications made to the law in 1907, 1938 and 1942, except a law guaranteeing the complete equality of the spouses in marriage?'[23]

She was disappointed. The Bill, somewhat amended in favour of wives, was sent back to the Senate for a second reading. The Senate, however, decided that the amendment voted by the National Assembly was incompatible with the 'harmony of the family'. The prime argument in favour of keeping the husband's privileges and control of family assets was that it was 'dans nos moeurs françaises' – ingrained in French cultural habits. Furthermore, it was argued, the population at large did not particularly want to see women have a more formal power within the family. The notion of 'family' was clearly an important factor in the Senate's view, and 'family' meant a hierarchy with the husband at the top. The Parliamentary Committee on Constitutional Law (in which there were no women) agreed with the Senate: 'Your Committee believes that ... M. Coste-Floret's amendment ... will inevitably lead to conflict between the spouses and that the unity and cohesion of the family, to which this Committee is passionately attached, may well be destroyed.'[24]

The Minister of Justice withdrew the Bill on 12 July 1961 because of the conflict revealed between the two Chambers. The whole project had to be recast.[25] He took the unusual step of commissioning a survey to be carried out by IFOP in 1963, to gauge the levels of interest and understanding of the French public where this law was concerned. It was found that 76 per cent of the French married without any specific contract and that nine out of ten of them did not try to find out their rights within marriage according to the law prior to their marriage. However, it was also found that few of them approved of the privileges given to the husband and most believed that the wife should control her own assets. Finally, 40 per cent were in favour of reforming the law, 39 per cent believed reform unnecessary and 21 per cent did not comment.[26]

A new Bill, much resembling the former one, was unanimously approved in the Senate in a vote on 11 May 1965. The major change was that the new law did give the wife control over her own assets. The discussion in the National Assembly was less smooth. There were protests from women's groups outside Parliament (the Ligue Française pour le Droit des Femmes, the Mouvement Démocratique Féminin, women lawyers – who had not been consulted on the proposed reforms) which were voiced inside Parliament by Jacqueline Thome-Patenôtre. In the proposed reform, the women's groups objected to the following provisions: the husband remained the head of the household; he retained the right to choose the family's domicile; he could oppose his wife's choice of employment 'in the interests of the family' (a right which was not reciprocal); and the wife shared responsibility for family debts while she had no control over the administration of family assets.[27]

Jacqueline Thome-Patenôtre fought to introduce major amendments to these clauses. She tried to change the power balance as it appeared in the Bill, suggesting that instead of the husband being head of household, 'both spouses are responsible for running the family'; and instead of the wife being obliged to live at a residence chosen by the husband, 'the family residence shall be chosen by the two spouses together'. Both these amendments, and others, were rejected.[28] It was broadly felt by the overwhelmingly male Assembly that 'someone' ought to be in charge of the family and that that person ought to be the man – no reason other than this view of the sexes was put forward and it was so widely shared that any questioning of it seemed unacceptable.

Not all women Deputies supported Thome-Pâtenotre. The Gaullist Deputy Odette Launay, presenting the Bill to the National Assembly, agreed with her male colleagues and spoke in favour of the man as head of household:

> The man is still the head of the family. It is desirable that there should be one person at the head of this human society that is the conjugal home. Why should the man – whom we have considered worthy enough to share our lives with – not be the one on whom we confer the honour of directing our household?[29]

This time around, there was significant interest in the issues at hand, with arguments in Parliament reflecting the fact that assumptions about male and female nature and roles were still firm. Women have real power in the home, some argued, so why take the trouble to contest the merely formal power of the husband? Women were likely to tire of this enormous responsibility, said another, and were probably going to give it over to their husband anyway. Families usually proceed by agreements reached between the parties involved, but in case of a difference of opinion, it is better to let the man decide rather than go to court; after all, they said, the woman chose her husband and he is the father of her children.[30] The new law was passed on 13 July 1965 with no opposition.

What then changed after the law was changed? Most of the French remained unconcerned; women's groups were angry and claimed that the new law was contrary to the Constitution of the Republic as the inequality of the sexes within marriage was maintained. As Odile Dhavernas noted, the new law was trying to increase women's rights without reducing men's power, to make family relations more equal while retaining the supremacy of the husband: a task that was obviously impossible.[31]

The ambiguity surrounding husband–wife relations and relative power within the family clearly responded to an ambiguity of feeling within French society as a whole. Women – who only ever appear in the Civil Code as wives, never as autonomous beings – are treated in an inconsistent and capricious way, as either dependent or responsible, seemingly at random. However, the new law did challenge the husband's supremacy in the family for the first time, albeit in a minor way. It provided a chink in the patriarchal armour that was later to lead to further erosions of the husband's power, such as the law which replaced paternal authority by parental authority in 1970, and the 1974 divorce law. The timid, frustrating reform of the marriage law had taken nearly a century to achieve, but it paved the way for far speedier changes in the 1970s.

'FREEDOM BEGINS IN THE WOMB'

The second women's rights campaign of the postwar pre-'68 period was the fight to revoke articles 3 and 4 of the 1920 and 1923 laws concerning information on birth control and the availability of contraceptives, culminating in the Loi Neuwirth, passed on 28 December 1967. This struggle to overturn at least part of the 1920 law was the most controversial issue concerning private life in the 1950s. Battle was engaged from the outset. Support came from the non-Communist Left, from the Left press (*L'Express, Libération. L'Observateur, Combat*), from *Elle* and later *Marie-Claire*, from associations such as the League of Women's Rights, the League of Human Rights, the Association of French Women University Graduates, the Women's Education League, from women's Free-masonry and Jeunes Femmes.[32] Opposition came above all from the Catholic Church, the MRP, the medical establishment and the Communist Party.

In the 1950s, debate outside Parliament was within limited circles, with the Association Maternité Heureuse acting as meeting-point for sympathetic parties, but carefully defining its objectives and activities in other terms, as described earlier.

Parliamentary support for revising the law came from the Left and Centre-Left, but not everyone wanted the same reform. In Parliament, three proposals for reform were made during 1956 by different political groups. First, in February 1956, was a proposal brought by a group of 'progressive' Deputies, including Emmanuel d'Astier de la Vigerie, who wanted to revoke articles 3 and 4 of the 1920 law. Second, there was a proposal brought by Radical Deputies, repeated two months later by Socialist Deputies, which followed similar lines. Third, in May 1956, there was a Communist proposal seeking to revise the law in order to authorise therapeutic abortion. The proposal, which restated the party's opposition to birth control, believed that:

when a married woman, who already has three children, is in poor health or is cause for social concern, when a single woman find herself in a situation which causes social concern, she may have recourse to a therapeutic abortion to interrupt her pregnancy.[33]

None of these proposals was ever discussed in Parliament. The momentum achieved through the parliamentary interest, through Weill-Hallé's actions and through the press seemed to die during the late 1950s, partly through intense opposition to it from powerful quarters and lack of support within Parliament.

Opponents of law reform also varied in their political affiliation and in their main reasons for opposing any change. The Catholic Church and the Communist Party were unlikely allies in their hostility to birth control and to Weill-Hallé's Association, and indeed approached the issue from very different angles. For Catholics, the papal encyclical *Casti Connubii* in 1931 set the tone, reiterating that only abstinence and natural methods of avoiding pregnancy were acceptable. The rhythm method of birth control, known in France as the Ogino-Knaus method (after its Japanese and Austrian originators), was accepted but none other. This was restated in 1957 during the assembly of cardinals and archbishops of France: 'All measures which, whether by contraceptive procedures or sterilising products, intend artificially to prevent children from coming into the world must be condemned.'[34]

It has been pointed out that while the Hierarchy was unequivocal on this point and the opposition of the Church was instrumental in holding back acceptance of birth control and the changing of the law, many Catholics were less clear in their own minds about how to behave. The Church could and did speak about the beauty of abstinence within marriage, or about male self-control born of respect for his wife, but this was not the experience of the vast majority of couples.

The medical establishment supported the Church on moral grounds and also opposed birth control on professional grounds: the doctor's function was to treat sick people, not healthy ones – birth control was, in the eyes of the governing body (the Conseil de l'Ordre des Médecins), not a medical question. Again, not all doctors were in agreement with the establishment, as became clear when more and more doctors sought information about birth control and then joined the Association and practised within it.

Most public attention was given to the opposition to birth control that came from the Communist Party. Claiming to have contributed to the liberation of women which would eventually take place through Communism, Jacques Derogy had dedicated his book to party leader Maurice Thorez. Thorez disputed Derogy's claim and responded publicly in an article in the party newspaper *L'Humanité* on 2 May 1956, in which he invoked Lenin, assimilated the Association Maternité Heureuse with neo-Malthusianism and denounced the campaign to legalise contraception:

> While we oppose the repressive bourgeois laws which affect the poor more than anyone else and we demand their abolition, Communists condemn the reactionary notions of those who seek to limit births and seek thereby to turn the working class away from its struggle for bread and socialism. 'Birth control' will not provide young couples with decent accommodation; it will not give a mother the means with which to raise her children. . . .
>
> We are struggling so that all women may experience the joys of motherhood, in the best possible conditions, and we oppose the regime which condemns them to hunger, which crowds them into slums, which pushes them to abort. . . .
>
> As your book contributes to the perpetuation of the illusions that our Communist Party has ceaselessly fought and will ceaselessly fight . . . it seems necessary to restate that the path for women's liberation is through social reforms, through social revolution and not through abortion clinics.

This letter sparked off a debate within the party – and women left the party because of its dogmatism on this issue – and between Thorez and Vermeersch on the one hand and Weill-Hallé on the other.[35] *France-Observateur* published both sides of the debate, as did *Le Monde*. Jeannette Vermeersch condemned birth control as a 'bourgeois vice', saying that working-class women wanted to have nothing to do with it. She also saw it as a way of keeping down the numbers of working-class babies and reducing the revolutionary potential of the working class. Vermeersch is reported to have said that contraception took the poetry out of love.[36] A point of view with which it may be easier to have sympathy, however, was the argument that a change of the law could be used by the ruling class to argue against other social reforms such as improved housing and higher levels of benefits: governments could argue that it was up to individuals to live according to their means, and not the government's duty to provide better facilities. The Communists condemned contraception as an individualistic solution to social problems and claimed that as such it was no solution at all.

The 1960s saw a change of pace in public awareness of birth control. This was the result of increased media coverage of the MFPF's radical actions and the excitement generated by the development of the contraceptive pill, first introduced to France in 1961.

In June 1961, Dr Henri Fabre, one of the earliest members of the Association Maternité Heureuse, opened a family planning centre in Grenoble. Insisting that the 1920 law outlawed propaganda about contraception, but not its use or its prescription to named individuals, the centre's founders were prepared to test the law. Its supporters were astonished at the favourable reception it won from all political colours and at the local worthies who turned out for its inauguration. There were no police raids on the centre. The press too, apart from the Catholic press, was positive in its appraisal of the centre.

In December 1961, a centre was opened in Paris, after which interest in, membership of and activities by the MFPF snowballed. In 1963, lectures in the Paris area on family planning had been given to a wide range of groups, from the Mouvement Démocratique Féminin, to the Grand Orient de France (Freemasons), a group of HLM dwellers and students at the Ecole Normale Supérieure. Also in 1963, a colloquium about family planning attracted over 300 participants. By January 1964, there were 32,000 members of the MFPF, whereas a year previously there had only been 16,000.[37]

Support for law reform became more overt. *Marie-Claire*'s agony aunt Marcelle Auclair wrote a book in 1962 following a survey in the magazine on birth control, in which she no longer advised women to 'trust life', as she had in the mid-1950s. Clearly favouring law reform, she wrote: 'Say it out loud to all the theologians and all the politicians: it is not by forcing women to have children that they will exalt maternal instinct in future generations.' And to lend medical weight to her arguments, she quotes the doctor who wrote regular columns for the magazine: 'Thirty-five years of medical practice ... have proved to me that no law, no interdict, no ukase, no conviction will stop a woman from aborting, even if she knows that she is risking death.'[38]

THE PARLIAMENTARY DEBATE

By the mid-1960s, there was widespread popular support for reform of the 1920 law, but the government's response was to do nothing.

The year 1965 was crucial in shifting the debate on contraception to the political arena. The Communist Party changed its position, although it was still clearly uncomfortable with the shape of the debate. Still emphasising the fact that motherhood was only a burden because of poor social and economic conditions, Vermeersch and other speakers accepted the validity of the MFPF's work: during the 'Semaine de la pensée marxiste' (Week of Marxist thought) in January 1965, Jeannette Vermeersch called for the Left to 'struggle together for the right to be mothers' in the best possible conditions, which included choice.[39]

In December 1965 presidential elections were held. The main candidate of the Left was François Mitterrand, who put birth control and revision of the law on his electoral programme, following discussion with Jacques Derogy, women in the Mouvement Démocratique Féminin and others.[40] His campaign speech at Nevers in October 1965 was the first time that the issue had played a part in an electoral campaign. Mitterrand was given full coverage in the press. The journalist Mariella Righini noted in November 1965 that in October of that year alone, there had been 250 articles on contraception in the French press.[41] The other presidential candidates were forced by Mitterrand's action to pronounce on the subject and from far Right to Left, all agreed that something should be done, even if this was expressed evasively by some, such as the Centrist Jean Lecanuet who said merely, 'I am in favour of freedom.'[42] General de Gaulle said nothing.

In October 1965, under pressure, the Minister of Health M. Jeanneney agreed to set up a committee which would study the consequences of the oral contraceptive for women. Hardly satisfactory, it was nonetheless a start. The committee did not include any women and the one member who was not a doctor – the sociologist Paul-Henri Chombart de Lauwe – withdrew in protest. The committee reported in December 1965 that, in their view, the Pill was acceptable as far as women's health was concerned. However, as an essentially medical report, its findings were not widely available until *Paris-Match* published a report on them in March 1966, under the headline 'Green light for the Pill'. Following that, television programmes, newspapers, everyone discussed the Pill to the point that Evelyne Sullerot wrote in *Réforme* in April 1966, 'All we hear is Pill Pill Pill', while the 1920 law remained unchanged.

In 1966, the Pill was being prescribed for thousands of French women, usually under the pretext of regulating periods or controlling period pain, or other 'special gynaecological treatments'.

In 1966 a Gaullist Deputy, Lucien Neuwirth, brought forward a proposal to abolish the two articles of the 1920 law dealing with contraception (articles 3 and 4). The government decided to support the proposal, but first waited to hear a report from yet another committee, this time the Committee on Population and the Family. The committee reported in January 1967 that it accepted the need for contraception, but only in order to avoid illegal abortion. They specifically stated that they did not accept birth control as a principle, a woman's right, and did not intend to dwell on – let alone encourage – the reassessment of sexual and social roles that some, for instance Chombart de Lauwe, seemed to think was an integral part of the question. Chombart de Lauwe understood the fullest implications of voluntary motherhood and had written in *Le Monde* on 13 April 1966:

> Through contraception, it is the image of the couple, of marriage, of the family, of male and female roles that is questioned, and thereby the image of society both today and tomorrow. Giving a woman the freedom to choose when to have children is to modify relations between the sexes and to permit a true equality which everyone talks about but few men really want.

By the beginning of 1967, reform of the 1920 law was inevitable. Prior to the legislative elections that year, *Elle* asked all political leaders to state their position on the proposed law: Mitterrand was opposed to it on the grounds that it did not go far enough; the Communist leader Waldeck-Rochet explained the party's apparent reversal of position, claiming that it had always been against the 1920 law (true) and that what they had opposed was the presentation of contraception as the answer to the economic difficulty of families; Centrist Jean Lecanuet called it a personal affair of conscience; Pierre Mendès France hoped that by reforming the law, women would have the chance to increase their participation in public life. General de Gaulle said nothing.[43]

During the parliamentary discussion of the law, it became obvious that the principle of a woman's right to choose was far from generally accepted. All the weary old arguments were rehearsed, although they had mostly lost the religious content which was now replaced by moral concerns: a woman certain of avoiding pregnancy might easily 'seek adventure'; the Pill might lead women into prostitution; one parliamentarian even understood that much of the opposition to the change of the law was to do with loss of male authority and control, which for him was unacceptable:

Have husbands realised that from now on it is the woman who holds the absolute power of having or not having a child, by taking the Pill, maybe against the husband's wishes? Men will lose the proud consciousness of their virility and women will be no more than objects of sterile voluptuousness.[44]

Other opponents of the Bill concentrated on the need to improve family benefits so that motherhood could become a desirable state and so that high moral standards would be maintained.

The law that was eventually passed in December 1967 was a disappointment to the MFPF. Contraception, via prescription only, was to be available from pharmacies; minors would have to have written consent of a parent if they wished to receive contraceptive advice and treatment; all publicity for contraception remained against the law. De Gaulle, furthermore, refused to consider reimbursement of the cost of contraception by social security, saying at the end of a well-publicised Cabinet meeting that there was no more justification for reimbursing contraception than there was for reimbursing the cost of a car: 'The Pill is for pleasure [*la distraction*]', he said.[45]

The reform of the 1920 law did not happen in the manner so hoped for by many of the activists. Weill-Hallé herself was not disappointed. She had become unhappy with the politicisation of the question which she had always seen in terms of women's health. She thought that ideas that were floated within the MFPF such as the 'right to pleasure' were silly and should not be part of the contraception issue at all. Nor did she share the view that abortion and contraception were part of the same struggle, namely a woman's right to choose. In 1967, even before the law was passed, she withdrew from the movement she had launched.

What changed as a result of the campaigns and the law? Changing the law was one step; overcoming medical hostility was another, and the acceptance of family planning was not helped by Prime Minister Georges Pompidou's apparent reluctance to countersign the Bill and in fact make it law. The number of abortions remained constant; Catholics still faced the same drama; according to Weill-Hallé, the Loi Neuwirth changed nothing. Seen as part of long-term transformation, it is hard to agree with her: the climate had changed, and with it women's perceptions of their own future. There was a diffuse awareness that more was at stake than solving individual cases of unwanted pregnancy. Women could grow up without the assumption of a destiny that either involved multiple abortions, multiple births or both. While many women still knew little of their own bodies or of contraception, sex education was on the agenda and young women realised that they were gaining control over their fertility. This control was the first step to notions of control over their destiny.

THEORISING WOMEN'S OPPRESSION

In her book on the 1960s in the United Kingdom, Sara Maitland asks how women moved from the 'passive femininity of the 1950s . . . to the feminism of the 1970s'.[46] The picture of women's rights in France only partially conforms to this vision of linear progress on behalf of women. A confusing picture of women's rights emerges, due largely to the problem of naming, to the way 'feminist' as a term was constructed and understood, and to the political gulf between different women's groups.

What becomes clear as we try to untangle changing solidarities and positions adopted on specific issues is that women's rights campaigns were fought as separate campaigns rather than as part of a challenge to 'women's condition'. The activism of the time was clearly issue-oriented, focusing on changing the law, without a theoretical framework, except where Communism or the Bible provided it. Huguette Bouchardeau, writing in 1977, remembered her experience of the feminism of the 1950s and early 1960s:[47]

> When I try to remember what our feminism was, fifteen or twenty years ago, I find it very legalistic, based on concrete demands, too pragmatic and frankly reformist, to say the least. There were some of us in trade unions, political parties, various associations, the family planning movement, etc. who identified a few areas where we could really make a difference . . . we wanted to be able to have children when we wanted them. . . . We thought that controlling our own bodies would bring down the final obstacles in the world of work: it was said that women were guilty of absenteeism, and had no continuity or ambition in their careers; all that was going to change when they no longer gave up their work when they became pregnant, willingly or not.[48]

The only feminist theory produced in France that could have informed activism was Simone de Beauvoir's *Le deuxième sexe* and this held a problematic place in discussions over womanhood and women's rights in the postwar decades. Simone de Beauvoir, so often called the 'mother' of contemporary feminism, stated that she was not a feminist at the time of writing *Le deuxième sexe*, and refused to participate in so-called feminist groups, which she found too bourgeois, too conformist. The groups mentioned above, such as the Association des Françaises Diplômées des Universités, or the Ligue Française pour le Droit des Femmes – in other words, groups of women with similar social and educational profiles to her own – were not for her: her self-definition as a feminist came later. Her denial that she was a feminist at the time of writing *Le deuxième sexe* must therefore be understood as her rejection of what feminism was thought to be at that time: 'several groups of very "nice" women [*bien sages*] who fought for political advancement, for women in government. I couldn't feel any solidarity with these groups.'[49]

In a much-quoted interview in 1972, Beauvoir was dismissive of the work of women's rights groups and said that in her view, nothing, fundamentally, had changed for women in the previous twenty years:

> Women have won a few little things, legally, concerning marriage and divorce. Contraception is more widespread than before but is still insufficient, seeing that only 7 per cent of Frenchwomen are now using the Pill. In the workplace, they haven't made major achievements. There are more women working than before, but not many.[50]

Beauvoir was too controversial a personality for the women's rights groups. Her prominent position within the group of left-wing intellectuals meant that her life was considered to be fair game for public comment, of which there was plenty. Existentialism was mocked (for instance in the article 'I exist, therefore I am not' in *Marie-France*), and as principal woman in the St Germain des Prés group of left-wing bohemian intellectuals, she was attacked.[51] Apparently without 'womanly' desires for the security of marriage and a home or for the fulfilment of motherhood, she was reviled as not being a 'real' woman. As a teacher, her influence over young girls was said to cause concern to parents (*Marie-Claire*, January 1955). As an intellectual woman, she was threatening, and as Toril Moi has pointed out, much Beauvoir criticism probably had the (unconscious) goal of denying women the right to intellectual activity.[52]

In her memoirs, she describes the writing of the book as provoking what we would think of as a feminist consciousness: 'I started to look at women with new eyes and I went from one surprise to another. It is strange and it is stimulating to discover, suddenly, at 40 years old, an aspect of the world which is so obvious and which I never saw before.'[53] For Beauvoir, it was her own research that sparked a new understanding of what it meant to be a woman. She later said that she did see *Le deuxième sexe* as a political tool: 'I wrote this book out of interest in the whole of women's condition, not just to understand women's situation, but also to fight, to help other women understand themselves.'[54]

When dipping into *Le deuxième sexe* today, the feminist reader may be critical of it in a number of ways. Beauvoir has been accused of many things: homophobia, racism and classism, élitism, excessive identification with men. The work has undoubtedly dated. However, in taking key ideas out of *Le deuxième sexe*, it is striking that we still find basic radical feminist notions that have not become outdated: oppression within marriage; women's lack of control over their own bodies; analysis of domestic labour; the social construction of gender. The central statement that 'women are made, not born' has not become outdated. Given these ideas, it is not surprising that she found 'feminist' groups somewhat tame. The radical ideas of her radical feminism were light years away from the demands for greater equality that constituted the feminism of the day. Beauvoir made the first radical attack on the oppression of private life – marriage, the family, housework – to be aired in postwar France. Instead of demanding a married woman's right to control her own property, Beauvoir launched into an attack on the institution of marriage itself. Instead of demanding increased benefits for working mothers, she suggested that women's liberation depended on the abolition of the family. Instead of seeking extension of ownership of household equipment, she rejected flatly the notion of women's fulfilment in the home.

Given that these ideas were completely new and very threatening, it is not surprising that although it became a bestseller (22,000 copies sold in its first week), the response was primarily outrage and hostility. Subsequently, many women have pointed to the book as the turning-point for their own awareness of women's oppression and their own questioning of their lives. Colette Audry said that for her, the publication of *Le deuxième sexe* was the single most important event for feminism in the postwar years.[55] Audry also spoke of the sackloads of post that Beauvoir received in response to issues raised in her book; and to the lectures she (Audry) gave around France, trying to explain the analysis in the book. The influential broadcaster Ménie Grégoire acknowledged her debt to the book, as did Betty Friedan, Yvette Roudy and many others. On Beauvoir's death in 1986, Elisabeth Badinter wrote:

We were 15 or 16 years old, when . . . we discovered *Le deuxième sexe*. I don't think that there was any other book that we talked about or admired as much as that one. By telling the history of women's oppression, by shooting down the concept of women's nature, Simone de Beauvoir liberated us from an age-old strait-jacket. I remember that while I was reading it, I felt as though I had wings. The message, so clear and so just, was heard by my entire generation.[56]

Beauvoir's influence on feminism seems to be primarily a post-'68 phenomenon. Marie-Jo Dhavernas wrote that *Le deuxième sexe* was 'certainly the book that had most affected the generation of feminists who experienced the events of May '68'.[57] The women involved in the women's rights groups described in this chapter were suspicious of her. References to *Le deuxième sexe* are absent from almost all the publications of the women's rights groups, except from Jeunes Femmes. The gap between her views on women's oppression and their desire for equality was too wide for dialogue, let alone common action. Her book challenged them, called their work unimportant, trivial. Beauvoir's writing set out an analysis of women's situation that required more than equality legislation to change it. In Beauvoir's work, women's oppression was analysed and men were identified as oppressors: but this was not a message that found echoes in women's rights activism until the 1970s.

7 May '68

This final chapter will consider the suggestion that May '68 brought an end to one particular era and opened another as far as feminism was concerned. Nobody predicted the events that rocked France, disturbed its superficial tranquillity; the France of the 1960s was not the location of 'the sixties' as they are commonly remembered. The 1960s constituted a decade of violence: it opened with war in Algeria and bombings on mainland France, with the Bay of Pigs and the assassination of John Kennedy; it continued with Vietnam, the Six-Day War, the assassinations of Robert Kennedy and Martin Luther King, student unrest throughout the developed world and Russian tanks in Prague. The 1960s, when evoked by individuals remembering their own experience, are remembered differently: a decade of excitement, the Beatles, miniskirts, followed by flower power, love and peace, Woodstock, and the moon landing.

In France, war with Algeria ended in 1962, marking the first time that France had not been at war since 1939. De Gaulle was confirmed in power and the subsequent years were, apparently, unexciting. Simone de Beauvoir wrote in the last volume of her memoirs that she did not pay much attention to events in France during the 1960s; in March 1968, Pierre Viansson-Ponté wrote, famously, in *Le Monde*, that 'la France s'ennuie': France was bored.

The decade of the 1960s in France was one of prosperity and growth, of technological progress and practically full employment. The 1960s are remembered and represented as the heyday of consumerism, a time of increased opportunity for all. Average spending power had doubled between 1949 and 1968 and households were better equipped with basic amenities such as electricity, running water and inside toilets. Georges Perec's novel *Les choses* builds an ironic picture of the consumerism and the alienation of the time, in the story of a young couple aspiring to wealth, trying to find meaning in their lives via objects:

> From shop to shop, antique shops, bookshops, record shops, restaurant menus, travel agencies, shirts, suits, cheeseshops, shoemakers, confectioners, luxury delicatessen shops, stationers, their real universe was to be found in this itinerary: *there* were to be found their ambitions, their hopes. *There* was real life, the life they wanted to experience, they wanted to lead: it was for these salmon, these carpets, this crystal, that, twenty-five years earlier an office worker and a hairdresser had brought them into the world.[1]

It was above all a period which witnessed the growing importance of youth. The new emphasis on youth was linked to numbers. Overall numbers of children in schools shot up as the baby boom reached school age. By the late 1960s, the full effect of the 1959 law raising the school-leaving age could be felt. The number of pupils in secondary schools rose from 775,000 in 1949 to 2.4 million in 1963,[2] and 3.8 million in 1968.[3] The baby-boom generation reached its midteens, did the twist, read the new teenage magazine *Salut les copains*, stayed on at school (in 1963, 11.5 per cent of them passed the Baccalauréat[4]), and then went to college. This was the generation that had not lived through the war, and that was benefiting from postwar economic prosperity and social mobility. It was also the generation that would express its disaffection from the world in which it was growing up.

For women, the 1960s had obviously brought changes, improvements. The diverse struggles begun in the 1950s to improve living conditions and working conditions, and the campaigns to change the law on key issues of private life, all bore fruit in the 1960s. The range of strategies adopted by the women's associations discussed earlier might be judged as successful; the images of womanhood – cautiously feminist, definitely feminine – promoted in *Elle* or *Marie-Claire* were probably responses to women's desire for change but their apprehension too. The 'new woman' (operating in male territory but retaining her femininity) of the late 1960s was represented as the new version of the successful woman in postwar France, and satisfied women of a certain generation and class.

Beneath the apparent calm, the 1960s witnessed new forms of political dissent: the stagnation of French political life, plus rejection of the Communist Party as the main form of opposition to Gaullism, had led many young people to seek alternative political activity.

They went to help the new revolutionary governments in Algeria or Cuba; they were attracted to Maoism or to anarchism. The women who took this route were not interested in the women's groups or in the issues raised by the women's rights activists of the previous decade. They did not, then, want to organise in women-only groups or discuss their private lives. They did not consider gender to be an issue at all. The revolutionary politics of the 1960s sought an end to capitalism, perceived as the root of all exploitation and misery. The newer generation of political activists was nothing if not ambitious for global change.

MAY '68: THE EVENTS

What was May all about? What was its impact on the women involved, on women's rights, on visions of womanhood? Trying to find the words to synthesise the meaning of the events is notoriously difficult although many have tried.[5] Commentators have spoken of the overlapping of different meanings: the student revolt, the workers' demands, the political, social and cultural crisis. Analysts have spoken of the May events in terms of different stages: first the students, then the workers and finally on to the political stage for elections in June. As the events have receded into history, the way they are remembered has evolved. As two decades passed, the political crisis and even the workers' revolt have faded in the collective memory while the students and the 'crisis of civilisation' have gained in significance.[6] As May was depoliticised in memory, so it was increasingly considered as a 'stage in the modernisation of France.'[7]

The 'May Movement' participated in a culture of protest, opposed to both the Gaullist state and organised channels of opposition. Alfred Willener called the movement an 'intersectional, politico-cultural anarcho-Marxist current':[8] this captures its diversity and reflects its disorganisation. While the first signs of student revolt dated from the mid-1960s, the period of the 1968 'events' began at the University of Nanterre, and quickly spread to other Paris universities and then to the rest of urban France. It involved students, schoolchildren, workers. It took the form of strikes and later a general strike, occupations, marches, meetings, discussions. It involved challenging the constraints of the university, of bourgeois society, of western capitalism. It contained political, social and cultural elements; it prized spontaneity and disorder over routine and planning, disdained the comforts of the nuclear family for the adventure of the community, spurned the PCF for Maoism, self-criticism, Trotskyism or anarchism, preferred the small group to the large organisation.

The Canadian writer and journalist Mavis Gallant wrote a Paris notebook during the events, in which the confusion, the personal edge to the mass movement and the various responses of onlookers are beautifully evoked.[9] The mood that she described was a mixture of euphoria and alarm, solidarity and fear, desire to protect the children (for she stresses the youth of the demonstrators) from the police and distress at the way trees on the Boulevard St Michel were cut down to strengthen a barricade. Normal daily life came to a standstill: just as in wartime, people began to stockpile goods, buying staple goods in panic, when this time there was no real need. Services stopped as strikes spread – no newspapers, no transport, no banks, no garbage collection. People lived with the radio and the telephone, trying to find out what was going on – although nobody really knew.

What did the participants want to achieve in May? It is not possible to reduce the impact of May to the reform of industrial relations contained in the Grenelle agreements signed by the government, employers and the trades unions, or to the eventual reform of the university system, although they were undeniably a result of the events. The changes that the participants sought were as qualitative as quantitative: they wanted to replace the alienation of capitalist society with a new way of interacting, new forms of work, new forms of community. They wanted to change the world. The importance of May, as I have said elsewhere, was in its effect on those who experienced it, in the way it changed lives and perceptions.[10]

WHERE WERE THE WOMEN?

There is no doubt that May '68 was a pivotal moment in the history of feminism: the women who were involved in women's rights in the 1950s and 1960s, and in the women's liberation movement (MLF, Mouvement de Libération des Femmes) in the 1970s, all speak of the impact of the events, describe May as a point of no return or a moment of heightened awareness that was to change the way they perceived themselves and the society they lived in. More generally in French society, May '68 is held responsible for changing attitudes towards women and towards sexuality, with 'women's liberation' heading the list of 'values' considered to exemplify the events.[11] Yet, as we read most accounts of the May events, we may be forgiven for thinking that there were no women there; we may also wonder why May is pinpointed as the beginning of contemporary feminism in France, as there was practically no discussion of gender relations on the revolutionary agenda.

In 1988, a flood of books about May '68 poured out, marking the twenty-year anniversary of the events. The difficulty of synthesising the meaning of the events, and the recognition of the plurality of meanings, led authors frequently to choose the biographical rather than the analytical approach. Hervé Hamon and Patrick Rotman's much-publicised books and TV programmes called *Génération*, for instance, followed the life-story of some of the prominent personal-ities of the May Movement from the early 1960s through to the post-'68 years: it is not until volume 2 – dealing primarily with the post-'68 period – that a woman appears in her own right. Elisab-eth Salvaresi's *Mai en héritage* pays more attention to the trajectory of individual women through those years, but most of the women she mentions are names on a now historical list, rather than names become familiar through public prominence. Some of the male mili-tants have become household names, through their involvement in the media or the government. The women have not been propelled – or have not propelled themselves – into the limelight.

During the events, some newspapers commented on women's presence:

> Strikes, demonstrations, barricades, they were everywhere. At the factory at Sochaux, 20-year-old women workers and 40-year-old mothers brought supplies to the strikers (food and things to throw ...). In the Latin Quarter, the women students, studious and frivolous alike, have been transformed into guerrilla fighters.[12]

> There were millions of women on strike. ... In huge numbers, they occupied factories, picketed, attended meetings, took respon-sibility while looking after their children, their homes, their kitch-ens at the same time.[13]

Women ran a 24-hour crèche and the cafeteria at the Sorbonne; women students, schoolgirls, were 'side by side with their comrades' on the barricades, in strike committees, in the huge meetings held in the lecture theatres of the Sorbonne. Women participated in all the political groups, trade unions, occupations. Piecing together women's activities during the events reminded me of women in the Resistance: women were everywhere, occupied in the full range of activity (including being tear-gassed and beaten up by the riot police) but there was a sexual division of revolutionary labour, which either trivialised their efforts or kept them silent.

Ten years later, the feminist newspaper *Histoires d'elles* parodied May '68, in the form of a play synopsis: in one scene, a woman is chastised for typing a militant tract and livening up the text by drawing a little flower at the end; another cries as her boyfriend is criticised by the group; a third, about to throw some paving stones, is offered help ('They're a bit heavy aren't they? Can I help you?'); a fourth woman arrives at an occupied factory to deliver sandwiches; a fifth tries to speak at a meeting in the Odéon theatre but can never make herself heard; a sixth addresses a meeting of 5,000 metal-workers and is told by a union representative to calm down and not get hysterical; a seventh speaks on the telephone to a friend: 'I wanted to go to the meeting but the kids ... Jean-Pierre has been there three nights in a row, I wanted to talk to him about it but he's got too much to do, anyway I'm sure he'll tell me about it.'[14] By the end of this ironic but still angry page of parody, the women activists are meeting together and laughing about the men's pretensions. Even so, the substance of the women's complaints was serious and revealed, later, how women had felt marginalised and patronised, treated as auxiliaries and secretaries, left with the traditionally female tasks or left at home.

Accounts of the events tended to represent women activists as the silent wives or girlfriends of the male militants. One male participant told Salvaresi: 'the few women who were there ... weren't there in order to represent any group or anything, but they were following their man.'[15] A woman signing herself only 'J.K.' wrote in a special issue of the journal *Partisans* in 1970 about her own political trajectory, and her account agrees with this: 'I must say that at the beginning at least, I didn't care at all about politics, but I was more or less obliged to pretend to be interested so that my boyfriend wouldn't think I was an idiot.'[16] She confirmed that it was not unusual to see a woman change her political sympathies when she changed her man. Accounts such as these reveal how women, at first anyway, accepted a secondary role, more concerned with their sexual relationship than with politics and not, at that time, making links between the two.

SEXUAL LIBERATION?

In May, sexual liberation was assumed to be part of the revolution. Sex, sexuality and sex education were not new topics for discussion in 1968. What had changed was the context and the content of the discussion. Female sexuality, in the 1950s, was not discussed in public, except on the pages of a few women's magazines and then only in relation to natural childbirth or birth control. By the early 1960s, as it was progressively dissociated from procreation, attention was also paid to sexuality as opposed to reproduction, most notably to the right to sexual pleasure. Women's magazines played a major part in this, keeping sex (married sex) on the agenda. *Elle* played a leading role in breaking the taboo surrounding sex. Françoise Giroud in interview, replying to a question about *Elle*'s role, said:

> [*Elle* was liberating for women in] bringing a certain vision, a modern vision, of women's place in society, by saying and by telling women certain truths... I myself was subversive... I think I was the first person to talk about frigidity in a non-specialist journal... [17]

Female sexuality outside marriage was shocking: the early to mid-1960s witnessed an eroticisation of marriage, but complete absence of any joyful, fulfilled sexual relationships outside it – and certainly no homosexual relations. Sexual pleasure was discussed in articles medicalised to give them legitimacy: 'Doctor, why are there unsatisfied wives?' (*Marie-Claire*, November 1960); the magazine's resident medical adviser was asked 'Are there really women who are frigid?' (*Marie-Claire*, August 1962); the magazine's educational function was emphasised when matters of sex were discussed: 'The school of conjugal happiness' (*Elle*, March 1962), and so on. The other more traditional magazines did not yet follow suit.

By the time of the Loi Neuwirth in December 1967, all the progressive magazines were discussing sex education and sexuality. Even the cautious *Marie-France* in May 1967 included an article on sex that would have been unthinkable five years previously:

> for centuries, the man was the only sexual person in the couple and everything was quite simple. Nowadays, it is accepted that women have the right to find as much happiness in carnal love as men, and it is one of the conditions of women's fulfilment. Men know that this fulfilment depends on them and that the man is guilty if the woman is frigid.[18]

Writing in *Elle* in 1967, Ménie Grégoire expressed horror at women's ignorance of sex: 'For 90 per cent of you, it is the same story. You reach marriage and love [i.e. sex] at the same time, in a

state of unbelievable ignorance.'[19] Also in 1967, *Elle* journalist Françoise Tournier summed up the contents of the magazine's postbag:

> Since we have won the right to have contraception, your letters
> have become vehement. You write straight out what you used to
> suggest between the lines. . . . You are saying 'We have won the
> right to love without fear. Now we want the right to make love
> with pleasure.'[20]

This article, which claimed that 12 million Frenchwomen experienced no pleasure from sex, took what was then a progressive view
about lovemaking:

> in the sexual act, anything that contributes to pleasure is good. . . .
> Nothing is abnormal, there are no norms in love. The only norm
> is a frank and open discovery of the sexual self of a man and a
> woman who are profoundly complicit – emotionally, physically,
> psychologically, intellectually and morally.[21]

Far from being non-normative, the conditions of a successful sexual
partnership were rather strict. Sexuality was a wonderful thing as
long as it was heterosexual and monogamous, and as long as the
couple was 'really in love'. The frequent use of the word *amour*
coyly referring to sex reinforces the insistence that love and sex
(and preferably marriage) go together like a horse and carriage.

It was not until the run-up to the events of May '68 that discussion
about sexuality and sex education was removed from a very cautious
context and given a 'revolutionary' content.[22] 'Sexual politics' as a
term had not yet been invented. 'Sexual liberation', on the other
hand, was very much part of the French students' movement. In
1966, students at Strasbourg University published a pamphlet called
*De la misère en milieu étudiant considéré sous ses aspects écono-
miques, politiques, psychologiques, sexuels et notamment intellectuels,
et de quelques moyens pour y rémédier* ('On the poverty of student
life considered in its economic, political, psychological, sexual and
notably its intellectual aspects, and on some ways of improving it').
This, plus other texts written and distributed by students influenced
by the Situationist International,[23] suggested that sex was subversive
when it undermined married monogamy (nobody mentioned
heterosexuality). Sexual liberation was not about improved conjugal
relations, nor about female sexuality. It involved the notions of
pleasure and freedom, understood as a rejection of celibacy and
monogamy.

In the early days of the May Movement, sex was present as a

metaphor for freedom: student leader Daniel Cohn-Bendit questioned François Missoffe, Minister of Youth and Sport, in January 1968, asking him why his report on youth contained no reference to sexuality; the girls' dormitory at the University of Nanterre was stormed in February 1968, provoking reactions and arrests; a lecture on 'Sexuality and repression' was held in March 1968, also at Nanterre.

Sexual activity was equated with revolution as was obvious from the graffiti of '68. One slogan on a wall in the Sorbonne was: 'The more I make love, the more I want to make a revolution. The more I make the revolution, the more I want to make love.' Another at the Odéon theatre: 'Make love and start again', and another at the Sorbonne: 'Fuck each other or they'll fuck you.'[24]

Press attention also focused on supposed student sexual promiscuity, writing about the love-ins and orgies that were allegedly taking place at the Sorbonne and in the occupied Odéon theatre. In Louis Malle's film *Milou en mai*, the sex-obsessed truck driver says 'They say that the Sorbonne floor is slippery with sperm . . . '

Sexual liberation did not seem to have had much to do with women: it seems mainly to have meant men's right to have women available to them. Accounts of the 1968 events at Nanterre do not tell about the women: did the girls actually want the boys in their dormitory? Were women demanding sexual liberation? Whose sexuality was under discussion? Whose pleasure? Whose repression? Male–female relations at the time seemed as male-dominant as before.[25] Henri Weber defends the notion of the sexual revolution as it was perceived at the time:

> It couldn't be reduced to the simple demand to have multiple partners and experiences as a revolt against the teachings of the holy mother Church. It contained the Utopia of new relations between the sexes, a new – non-possessive – idea of the couple, stripped of frustration, of hypocrisy, of jealousy, of bourgeois lies.[26]

When women began to write about their experiences, however, the reality of the sexual revolution from their perspective was seen to be less than satisfying.

SEXUAL POLITICS?

Gender relations were not collectively questioned by the May Movement. Attention to issues such as domestic labour, childcare, birth control and motherhood, formulated either in terms familiar to pre-'68 groups as separate issues or as they were later to be elaborated as part of a global challenge, were not part of the May revolt. Alain Schnapp and Pierre Vidal-Naquet's detailed account of the student events mentions in the introduction that in April 1968, at Columbia University's occupation of the campus, a male leader asked for women to volunteer for cooking duty. He was met with jeers and with the cry: 'Liberated women are not cooks.' The cooking duty was shared. The authors comment: 'It wasn't like that at the Sorbonne.'[27] Women activists could accept a 'feminine' role or could imitate men. One writer remembers that the more prominent militant women were often antiwomen: 'proud to have been accepted into a male milieu, they were wounded by the thought of women's oppression because they liked to believe that they were free.'[28] They did not want to analyse 'women's issues', did not want the label 'feminist' and denied that they were subject to any discrimination.

Some women did take exception to the lack of attention to gender relations, in particular to the sexual division of labour and to women's position in the revolutionary movement. Anne Zelensky and Jacqueline Feldman, members of the MDF, tried to do something about it. They had a stand in the courtyard of the Sorbonne and distributed leaflets pointing out women's invisibility and the absence of discussion about gender relations. Addressing women students, the leaflet read:

> You were on the barricades, the police charged you and beat you, just like the men, your comrades.
>
> You are participating in the discussions, in the committees, in the demonstrations.
>
> Girls' schools are involved, women's colleges have sometimes led the way for others, and among the 10 million strikers, women workers have had a strong role to play.
>
> Yet during these decisive days, no woman has appeared as spokesperson in the general meetings, on the radio, on the television.
>
> In the negotiations between trades unions, management and government, nobody has formally demanded equal pay for women and men workers, nobody has thought about collective services, crèches to help women in their double workday.
>
> In the immense debate that has now begun across the country, in the major reassessment of structures and values, no voice has

been raised to declare that changing relations between men also means changing relations between men and women.

Students and young people want a moral code that is the same for girls and boys. It is an aspect of change. It is only one aspect of change.

Other taboos must be overturned. The society that will be built must be the work of women as well as men, it must give all women equality of opportunity with men.

If you agree with all this, what are you ready to do about it? Come and discuss it with us.[29]

They proposed holding a meeting on 'Women and revolution' on 4 June, and this was welcomed by the male militants, one of whom confided: 'We've been holding seminars on everything for two weeks now and suddenly we realised that, oh God, we've forgotten women!'[30]

Zelensky and Feldman put up posters in the Sorbonne, inviting women to the meeting on 'Women and revolution':

[Men] students, as you rethink everything, the relation of pupil to teacher, have you also thought about questioning the relation of men to women? [Women] students, as you participate in the revolution don't be fooled any more. Don't just follow others, define your own demands. You were on the barricades, but are you really among the leaders? You go to the discussions, but can you really say what you are thinking? You want to work, but what can you do with the children?[31]

Zelensky describes that first meeting:

I was trembling with emotion. Paralysed at the idea of talking in front of so many people ... an hour later the room was full ... the atmosphere was joyful, I've never seen a meeting like it. When it was time to leave, nobody wanted to go.[32]

These were drops in the ocean but nonetheless marked a new kind of collective questioning by women of women's 'condition', which was slowly to emerge over the next two or three years. The influences were both positive and negative. Feminists took ideas and some practices from the May Movement, for instance the rejection of hierarchy and leadership that for quite a while was an integral part of the MLF, and the strategy of provocation and the style of rebellion. The May activists had their intellectual heroes – Louis Althusser, Wilhelm Reich, Mao and the Situationist writers Guy

Debord, Raoul Vaneigem and Henri Lefebvre; women militants shared these interests and influences and were not, then, interested in Beauvoir or Friedan.[33] The politicisation of the personal, the 'revolution of daily life' – ideas associated with the Situationists which came to the foreground in May – were instrumental in giving theory to a feminist revolt born of personal experience, and in contributing to the fact that women could claim value for personal experience in the elaboration of any theory.

It was not the theory behind the actions (or rather the wide variety of theories) that alienated the women who were later to form the MLF from the 'revolutionary' Left of the May Movement. It was the practice of the groups, and in particular the disparity between the two. Françoise Picq wrote later: 'the MLF only really appeared ... as women realised that their hopes would not be fulfilled in the May Movement and that the anti-hierarchy discourse of the men was contradicted by their political practice.'[34]

Many of the women were conscious of being kept in secondary roles, even if they did not complain about it at the time. J. K. wrote that in her political group:

> the option for women was either to play at being secretaries or to imitate men. In the 'gauchiste' [alternative Left] organisations, like everywhere else, the ability to think or to speak was almost exclusively reserved for men.... For example, for months and months, I didn't dare speak at a meeting for fear of looking stupid, because I thought that more attention would be paid to the fact that it was a girl speaking than to what I was saying. So I settled for working as best I could, saying to myself that although I wasn't capable of thinking and taking part in discussions, at least I would be the one who made the best photocopies.[35]

Elisabeth Salvaresi wrote of her own disappointment with the alternative Left: 'I know about revolutions: first they say we're equal to men in everything, when it is about being sacrificed for the cause. Then they decide we're "different" and send us back to the kitchen.'[36] J.K.'s gradual disillusionment with alternative left-wing politics was based not only on practice but also on the feeling that what went on inside the group meetings had little or nothing to do with anything outside the meeting: an enclosed world of its own was created within the group, with its own vocabulary and codes, which had no connection with the concerns and realities of people's lives, especially women's lives.

The split between public and private, political and personal, was still acute during the events; the women militants discovered the hard way that 'the revolution' was unlikely to make any personal difference to them, and that – in spite of rhetoric about the revolution of daily life – the substance of their lives was of no interest to their male comrades. A poem published in *Partisans* emphasised this split between women and men, personal and political:

Where are the women

While you march in formation
on Sunday mornings
alongside the disinherited?

they are shopping
doing the dishes from Saturday night
cleaning the house
watching the children
while you are marching in the street
on Sunday mornings
alongside the disinherited

where are the women
while you remake the world to your own model?
a red world, a black world
in the evening
round the table?

they are cooking
laying the table
putting the food on the table
filling the plates
while you remake the world to fit yourselves

where are the women
while you are making love to them?
far away
they are thinking about the next day
about the shopping
the dishes
the housework
the children
the cooking
the table

the food
the plates
they are thinking about the next day[37]

While women gained much that was positive from the events of May, it was their negative experience that led them to found a women-only women's liberation movement, the MLF. They had already rejected traditional political parties, primarily on ideological grounds: the PCF as too doctrinaire and Stalinist, the socialist groups in the FGDS as too unfocused and reformist, the parties of the Right – mainly the Gaullist Party – as the representatives of the bourgeois, capitalist state they wanted to oppose. The behaviour of men on the so-called alternative or revolutionary Left was, as far as women were concerned, just as bad as that of the opposition. As one woman wrote later, 'it takes just as long to cook a steak for a revolutionary man as it does for a bourgeois'.[38]

A SENSE OF AN ENDING?

It is easy to understand May as the beginning of something new, the beginning of the 1970s rather than the end of the 1960s. However, the May events marked a major change for the women's rights activists of the previous decades. They experienced May mostly as onlookers, often as mothers: they may have sympathised with the revolt, or have participated in it in some way, but they were not an integral part of it. Women from organisations such as the MDF or the MFPF participated in the events as individuals, but the organisations themselves did not take a public stand.

All the pre-'68 women's rights groups and organisations had to have a response of some kind to the events. From *Elle* to *Antoinette*, each organisation, group or publication addressed the issues selectively, interpreted the events in the light of its own preoccupations. They all revealed sympathy but also a certain reticence in the face of the events, which were almost always interpreted as being a youth revolt which adults could not hope to understand. *L'école des parents* interviewed Gilbert Mury, director of the Office Français des Sciences Humaines in June 1968. He was clearly sympathetic with the students up to a certain point: there had been children in the Resistance, young people in the anti-Algerian war movement; it was quite correct, in his view, that young people should challenge the world of their elders; his sorrow was that his generation too had wanted to change the world – but they had failed. According to M.

Mury, the youth revolt of '68 was really simply a matter of it being their turn to try to change the world.[39]

Jeunes Femmes was more worried: the special issue of July 1968 stated, imitating the Prime Minister Georges Pompidou, that 'Our movement Jeunes Femmes will never be the same again.' The local JF groups were concerned at the disarray they witnessed. The Passy (Paris) group reported on their post-May meeting: 'We want to reaffirm our attachment to the values that we believe are essential and that are at risk of being destroyed for ever by disorder and anarchy: freedom of expression, tolerance, the protection of the family and individual spiritual beliefs.'[40] On the positive side, some members of the group reported having experienced 'moments of exaltation' during the events. Jeunes Femmes as a movement seems to have been close to the thinking of May even before the event: the Cévennes-Languedoc regional congress, held on 4–5 May 1968, took as its theme two concepts that were to be key elements in the May revolt: 'participation and challenge'. The Normandy congress, held in October 1968, picked up the theme clearly derived from May of 'Imagination in power', and members debated the nature of power, the relationship of teachers and students, the Church and authority, the lessons to be learned from May.[41] In other words, Jeunes Femmes, as a discussion group, found a way of using the May events within the structures it had chosen for itself. The dominant tone of the reports from regional congresses is anxiety rather than exhilaration. Jeunes Femmes, the movement, was not carried along by the enthusiasm of the May Movement.

The editorial team of *Antoinette* focused exclusively on the workers' involvement in the May events. The June 1968 issue barely mentions the events, the students, the challenge to bourgeois capitalist society as it took place outside the channels of party and union. Such mention as there is emphasises the strikes, the negotiations and the concrete achievements at the workplace as they appear in the Grenelle agreements. The essential achievements of May, for the CGT women's magazine, were 'higher wages, more holidays, a reduced working week, the right to hold union meetings, and, for we women in particular, lowering the age of retirement, subsidies for the crèche, special time off, better working conditions'.[42] Yet even *Antoinette* seemed infected by the joy of May: 'During the two weeks of the strike, this wonderful, extraordinary strike of spring '68, we have experienced some unforgettable moments! We haven't finished talking about it or thinking about it. . . . It was truly wonderful! There are no other words for it.'[43] *Antoinette* spoke of the dreams women workers had during May – if we had more time what would we do with it? If we had more money, how would we spend it? This was not what the Situationists or the students had in mind; but to each her revolution.

In the publications of the women's associations such as the Ligue Française pour le Droit des Femmes, the concern was expressed in their habitual fashion: the League wrote a letter to the Prime Minister, hand-delivered by a member's child on a bicycle as there was no transport operating in Paris. Their polite request that the Prime Minister do something (and their belief that this kind of approach was appropriate) was shown to be even more ineffectual and out of place than ever. *Femmes diplômées* wrote in June 1968 that the grievances of May were mainly about the deficiencies of the university system and that the students were probably right. The editors commented that in May 'everyone is talking about participation. We probably don't participate enough.' After the summer of 1968, there was no further discussion about the events; the League was once again focusing on the lack of women Deputies elected in June 1968; the Association des Françaises Diplômées des Universités carried on as before. Their own perceived role as champions of women had been overtaken by events.

The women's magazines, *Elle* and *Marie-France*, published special issues. *Elle*'s strategy was to produce:

> an issue that was both austere and full of hope. Readers must be made to believe that we in the editorial team are well placed to transmit to them, with discretion and good taste, the unforgettable nature of these few nights and a few days full of discussion and freedom.[44]

Hélène Gordon-Lazareff's editorial stresses the 'rejuvenated relationship' between *Elle* and its readers. The magazine took over the word 'freedom' and other concepts associated with May for its own purposes: be beautiful, be young, be revolutionary! The editorial of the June issue spoke of the need to show both how serious the events were and yet how life goes on:

> We have to show them that for them, their sons, their daughters, their husbands, nothing will be quite the same again. That doctors, architects, professors won't be the same again. That their way of life, their work, their way of dressing may be different ... [45]

The readers are clearly positioned as mothers, witnesses of the events, not participants: 'One of our writers experienced the nightmare of the Latin quarter from her window, with her children and their terrified cat. Another anxiously followed her medical student son's actions. . . . Another dived into the maelstrom at the Sorbonne, trying to understand.'[46]

Elle commented on the massive involvement of girls, whose courage was 'terrifying'. The pictures of the events on *Elle*'s pages however, showed the crèche at the Sorbonne, with the caption 'Women's work: meals and tenderness'.[47]

Marie-France was less positive than *Elle*. The editorial, knowing its readers, assumed their absence from and ignorance of the events:

> In this great furore, are there not those who have been forgotten? Yes, those who have not been on the front pages, those whose voice was weak and whose anguish was immense: mothers, fathers, parents. . . . You. Or us. *Marie-France* is thinking of all these people. For many parents, the shock has been enormous: suddenly they have seen their children pass from Rag Day to Molotov cocktails. Let us say it: many were afraid.[48]

Marie-France also used its special issue on the events to reassure readers that society was not crumbling around their ears. On the one hand, the events were reduced to the same level as tablecloths and dresses ('young people in revolt, parents bewildered; summer dresses in the Andalusian sun; tablecloths: elegant but inexpensive' were the cover titles in July 1968); on the other, the editorial spoke of the desire to understand. A round-table discussion which included students ('but not the *enragés*, not the firebombers. Boys and girls who are fully aware of their responsibilities') concludes, like *Elle*, by taking its vocabulary from the events and using it in an unthreatening – even meaningless – way: 'We must have the courage to reconcile imagination and love. Then everything becomes possible.'[49]

Marie-Claire ignored the events almost completely. There was no special issue, no articles on the events, no editorial, and no explanation about why this was so. In 1968, *Marie-Claire* was calling itself, 'the magazine of the couple' and was emphasising relationships in its articles ('The Pill cures jealousy', 'Can one be happy in the shadow of a man?', 'How to stay the mistress of your husband', 'Does a husband stand a chance against a Don Juan' are just some titles of articles in July and September 1968). The 'events' are mentioned only in the context of fashion: 'Autumn '68. Revolution. Everything has changed. Influence of the "events"? Why not? Obligatory change in a consumer-based economy? Possibly. The causes are unimportant.' These magazines which carried the 'new woman' message decided that May could be fruitfully tamed and incorporated into the message.

The responses to the May events by these groups and publications, which all liked to consider themselves progressive, and which were defined as such by others, are telling. Some chose aspects of the events for comment selectively; others appropriated the vocabulary but left the concepts and the politics behind; some tried to confront the issues at hand; others were simply baffled, overwhelmed. The events showed that the climate had changed, that the notion of progress had changed and that – as they all liked to say – things would never be the same again.

TURNING POINT?

Were there any connections between the women's rights campaigns and campaigners prior to May '68 and the feminism that came later? Did the one emerge from the other? Women who were to form the disparate groups in the MLF came from a range of political backgrounds, activisms and experiences, mostly from somewhere to the left of the mainstream Left. Many of the women had no prior political experience at all. They were not from the UFF, the League of Women's Rights or from the other women's rights groups of earlier decades.

The May activists were part of a different generation from the women's rights campaigners of 1944 to 1968. A recent study of the sociology of a sample of the first MLF activists in Paris reveals that they were largely of the baby-boom generation, with a significant number of them born in 1948; they came from all social classes; 40 per cent of them came from families with no sons; 75 per cent came from homes where the mother went out to work; a small proportion were married; some were lesbians; very few had children. Of those who had been active in politics prior to the MLF, this activity had mostly taken the form of participation in trade unions, in alternative Left groups and student politics, in opposition to the Algerian war.[50] The women militants of May, later to be these first post-May feminists, were younger than the feminists of the 1950s and 1960s: they had not yet discovered the oppressions of daily family life (from the mother's perspective), the tyranny of fertility, the injustices of the world of work. They were marked differently by history, achieving political awareness mainly through the Algerian war rather than the Second World War. They were more educated than their parents and had different expectations. They had different priorities and different understandings of the problems.

The May Movement was a revolt against the world into which pre-'68 feminists had been trying to fit, which they had been trying to improve, in however piecemeal a way. The May militants turned against the major influences and aspirations of their parents – whether the consumerism of the postwar period, the influence of American culture and of the Soviet Communist Party, or loyalty to the Republican tradition in France. For them, the women's rights groups, the sections of parties and trade unions, which made concrete demands for specific legislative changes, were tame compared with the global revolution they envisaged and were as much part of the established order as the government.

The achievements of the previous generation of women's rights activists were not acknowledged by the MLF. Post-'68 feminists did indeed reject everything that had gone before in the sweeping gesture of starting afresh common to 'revolutionary movements', rather than acknowledging and incorporating the struggles of the previous generation. Elisabeth Salvaresi in her book on the May militants wrote: 'who among us remembered that there had been feminist movements in the past and that they had died? Nobody.'[51]

The story of the birth of the MLF, from the perspective of individual personal involvement, shows that in some respects the new feminism had almost nothing in common with the earlier women's rights campaigns; in other respects, the political journey of individual women sometimes involved in both pre- and post-'68 feminisms becomes clear; and finally, some of the features of post-'68 feminism that were considered innovatory, or revolutionary, can be seen to have existed in other forms in the 1960s.

In *Histoires du MLF*, Anne Zelensky tells of how she saw Andrée Michel and Geneviève Texier's book *La condition de la Française d'aujourd'hui* in a bookshop window. Struck by how rare a sight it was to see a book about women, she bought it and was so excited by its radical content that she wrote a letter to Andrée Michel. Michel invited her to a seminar that she was organising with other women who had reacted in the same way to the book. At this meeting, Michel suggested that Anne and another woman, Jacqueline Feldman, go to MDF meetings if they wanted to carry on any feminist political discussions.[52] Anne went to meetings, but was not unduly impressed: 'MDF meetings were hardly wildly exciting, but they did me good, after the total desert that had been my experience of feminist encounters up till then.' Anne and Jacqueline decided that they wanted to start something more radical – and include men – but retain links with the MDF. The group Féminin-Masculin-Avenir (FMA, Feminine-Masculine-Future) was formed by the end of 1967. It was very small, with a fluctuating attendance of up to fifteen people, mostly women, at its meetings.

Christine Delphy met Jacqueline in 1968 and joined the FMA, which had four or five members at the time.[53] After May, the group gained some members, but later fell back down to six – four women, two men. The name was changed to Féminisme-Marxisme-Action (Feminism-Marxism-Action), the two men understood the need for a women-only group and left, and the four women (Christine Delphy, Emmanuelle de Lesseps, Anne Zelensky and Jacqueline Feldman) were to be involved in the actions and texts which were the first markers of a women-only, radical feminist movement in 1970.[54]

Other groups were formed in the same *ad hoc* way: there was, for instance, a group called 'Nous sommes en marche' ('We're on our way'), which met every evening at the University of Paris at Censier (5th *arrondissement*) in May '68 until the building was closed by the police. Another group called 'Les oreilles vertes' ('Green ears') was also apparently in existence. One group, formed at the University of Paris at Vincennes after the events, around Antoinette Fouque, Monique Wittig and others had a psychoanalytic focus; there was a group called the 'groupe du jeudi' (the 'Thursday group'), more of a women's consciousness-raising group. These informal discussion groups were really the foundation of the MLF, although they were not perceived as such at the time and most probably did not know of the others' existence until later. Delphy wrote:

> for these two years [1968–70] we were troubled by one thing: were we the only group of this kind in France or were there others? There may have been others but we didn't know because we couldn't make our own existence known; and the others, if they existed, couldn't get past the barrier of the press any more than we could. And so we would never meet . . . [55]

May did mark the beginning of a new way of conceptualising women's situation, replacing the vocabulary of 'condition' and 'emancipation' by 'oppression' and 'liberation'. Women's experience of May led them to reject organisation and hierarchy; to reject male participation; to defy the law; to recognise the need for developing feminist theory and to ground the theory in women's reality. And yet it should be noted that certain aspects of post-'68 feminism that were thought to be original had already existed in the 1950s: small, informally constituted women's discussion groups existed, such as Jeunes Femmes; even the more conventional women's rights groups discussed and supported action in favour of contentious issues such as birth control – little could be more grounded in the reality of women's lives than that; the MFPF had defied the law. The sense that political reform would not come about by itself, but that women had to fight for women, was also already there; after May '68, it was pushed to its extreme form of refusing (or at least claiming to refuse) to recognise the value of political reform at all.[56]

What, then, was the significance of May for women? Was it an ending, a turning point, a beginning? It marked an ending for the women's rights organisations which, although they continued to exist, lost the prerogative of speaking on behalf of women, were no longer considered progressive, let alone a vanguard of activism, and increasingly lost a focus for their activity.

It was a turning point in several ways. It contributed to altering the content of discussion and the framing of demands; it changed the thinking of women already involved in politics, whether in the clubs, the unions or the alternative Left. Individual women across the full range of women's groups were profoundly affected by May: the movement brought a new political analysis to women's rights activists just as the experience of the May events contributed to the development of feminist analysis among political activists. Some pivotal figures provided continuity between the pre- and post-'68 feminisms. Groups and individuals were active on a number of fronts simultaneously. Their own thinking was not static but evolved, influenced by May '68 and the MLF.

It was a new beginning for the women who discovered sexual politics and who created in the MLF a movement that met their needs. They sought to change the definition of 'revolution' so that it included both public and private, political and personal: in other words so that it was a revolution both for and by women: 'The revolution that allows me to be myself, to laugh and to think for myself – well I've got to do it differently and to do it myself.'[57]

It seems, then, as though May '68 was not a false beginning after all, and that, apart from a handful of individuals, there was little to connect the women of the 1950s and 1960s feminisms to the women of May '68 and of the MLF. Women's anger was not expressed as such and was not aired collectively until after May '68, hence the pinpointing of May '68 as the beginning of the second wave of feminism in France. However, May set up a division between pre- and post-'68 feminisms that tends to simplify a complex situation. There was overlap afterwards: during the abortion campaign (and what could be more concrete and reformist – as well as revolutionary – than the demand to change the abortion law?), MFPF, Socialist and Communist women joined MLF women. There was as much diversity and conflict afterwards as there had been before.

I would suggest that connections become clearer when a longer term view is taken. By concentrating on the 1944–68 period, it becomes possible to re-evaluate the achievements and difficulties of those years, and also to consider the MLF in a different light. The MLF can be seen as part of a continuum of feminist activity stretching both backwards and forwards, but that has taken different forms at different times. Pre-'68 feminism can be perceived not simply as the lull before the storm of the 1970s – the bourgeois reformism to be replaced by the revolutionary MLF – but in its own right, and the reforms of the 1960s can be acknowledged as an integral part of feminism in France. This then allows the MLF to be seen as an example, a particular manifestation of feminism, the experience of one generation of women (and not all of them), rather than as feminism itself. The current absence of a 1970s-style feminist movement cannot then be used to proclaim that feminism is dead.

As a more institutionalised feminism developed over the 1980s and the MLF's style and structures were criticised, pre-'68 women's rights activism was rehabilitated as appropriate feminist strategy, and the 'reform versus revolution' dichotomy discredited. There may not have been a vibrant and influential feminist movement between 1944 and 1968, but there were determined pioneers and individual women making their own decisions based on their own needs. There is no doubt in my mind that their efforts paved the way for a more obviously radical discourse to emerge after May. However, the contribution of women who were rejected in May as being reformist, legalistic and with no analysis of women's oppression is only now being acknowledged. If the lives of young women in France today are very different from those of previous generations, their mothers and grandmothers can take the credit; and while the 'progress' they achieved must be balanced against the inadequate childcare, professional obstacles and prescriptive view of women's place that still exist in the 1990s, the efforts of women on their own behalf must not be hidden and must not be forgotten.

Notes

All translations of French sources are my own.

INTRODUCTION

1 Jean Fourastié, *Les trente glorieuses ou la révolution invisible de 1946 à 1975* (Paris: Fayard, 1979). The term is widely used to refer to the rapid transformation of French society and the French economy between these dates.
2 See Jane Jenson, 'The liberation and new rights for women', in Margaret Randolph Higonnet, Jane Jenson, Sonya Michel and Margaret Collins Weitz (eds) *Behind the Lines: Gender and the Two World Wars* (Newhaven: Yale University Press, 1987), pp. 272–284.
3 See Martine Muller, Danielle Tucat, Sylvie Van de Casteele-Schweitzer, Dominique Veillon and Danièle Voldman, *Etre féministe en France. Contribution à l'étude des mouvements de femmes 1944–1967* (Paris: Institut d'Histoire du Temps Présent, 1985), p. 3.
4 Claire Duchen, *Feminism in France from May '68 to Mitterrand* (London: Routledge & Kegan Paul, 1986).
5 Title of an influential issue of the journal *Partisans* published in 1970 (Paris: Maspero, 1970).
6 See discussion of sources in Chapter Five.
7 The question of women in trade union organisations, the role of the Church, the experience of lesbian women, immigrant women and women in agriculture are just some of the issues that require investigation.

1 LIBERATION

1 Simone de Beauvoir, *La force des choses 1* (Paris: Gallimard, 1963 [1976 edition]) pp. 13–14.
2 Catherine Gavin, *Liberated France* (London: Jonathan Cape, 1955), p. 39.
3 Raymond Ruffin, *Journal d'un J3* (Paris: Presses de la Cité, 1979), p. 241.

4 Edith Thomas, *La Libération de Paris* (Paris: Editions Mellottée, 1945), pp. 12–13.
5 Willis Thornton, *The Liberation of Paris* (London: Rupert Hart-Davis, 1963), p. 200.
6 Benoîte and Flora Groult, *Journal à quatre mains* (Paris: Denoël, 1962), pp. 383–384.
7 Edith Thomas, op. cit., p. 12.
8 Catherine Gavin, op. cit., p. 49.
9 Hanna Diamond, 'Women's experience during and after World War Two in the Toulouse area 1939–1948: choices and constraints' (D.Phil thesis, University of Sussex, 1992), p. 138. This thesis has been an invaluable source of information for this chapter.
10 Simone de Beauvoir, op. cit., p. 14.
11 Benoîte Groult, *Les trois-quarts du temps* (Paris: Grasset, 1983), pp. 245–246.
12 Benoîte and Flora Groult, op. cit., p. 429.
13 Benoîte Groult, op. cit., p. 246.
14 Flora and Benoîte Groult, op. cit., pp. 386–387.
15 Alfred Sauvy, *La vie économique des Français de 1939 à 1945* (Paris: Flammarion, 1978), annexes pp. 238–239.
16 Alfred Sauvy, 'Démographie et économie de la France au printemps 1944', in *La Libération de la France* (Paris: CNRS, 1976), p. 291.
17 Ibid., p. 299.
18 See Henri Frenay, who was Minister of Prisoners of War, Deportees and Refugees, in ibid., pp. 739–740. See also Frenay's memoirs, *La nuit finira* (Paris: Laffont, 1973).
19 There are now many books and articles published about the role of women in the French Resistance. See, for instance, *Les femmes dans la résistance*, (Paris: Editions du Rocher, 1976); Guylaine Guidez, *Femmes dans la guerre* (Paris: Perrin, 1989); Paula Schwarz 'Redefining resistance: women's activism in wartime France', in Margaret Randolph Higonnet, Jane Jenson, Sonya Michel and Margaret Collins Weitz (eds) *Behind the Lines: Gender and the Two World Wars* (Newhaven: Yale University Press, 1987); Dominique Veillon, 'Résister au féminin', *Pénélope*, No. 12, Spring 1985. Memoirs of women active in the Resistance have recently been reprinted: Brigitte Friang, *Regarde-toi qui meurs* (Paris: Plon, 1989); Lucie Aubrac, *Ils partiront dans l'ivresse*, (Paris: Le Seuil, 1984); Marie-Madeleine Fourcarde, *L'Arche de Noé* (Paris: Plon, 1989). There is practically no solid information on women's collaborationist involvement.
20 See Joan Scott, 'Rewriting history', in Margaret Randolph Higonnet *et. al.*, op. cit., pp. 21–30.
21 See Hanna Diamond, 'The everyday experience of women during the second world war in the Toulouse region', in Michael Scriven and Peter Wagstaff (eds) *War and Society in Twentieth-century France* (Oxford: Berg, 1992), pp. 49–62.
22 See Miranda Pollard, 'Femme. Famille. France. Vichy and the politics of gender. 1940–1944', Ph.d. thesis, Trinity College, Dublin, 1990, Paula Schwarz, op. cit., and especially Hanna Diamond, 'Women's experience', op. cit.

23 As Paula Schwarz points out (op. cit.), awards were also given according to political affiliation. Gaullist Resisters were far more likely to be decorated than Communists.

24 Cited in Roger Faligot and Rémi Kauffer, *Les Résistants: de la guerre de l'ombre aux allées du pouvoir 1944–1989* (Paris: Fayard, 1989), p. 84.

25 See Peter Novick, *The Resistance versus Vichy* (New York, 1968); Jean-Pierre Rioux, 'L'épuration en France', *L'Histoire*, No. 5, October 1978; Marcel Baudot, 'L'épuration', in *La Libération de la France*, op. cit., pp. 759–783.

26 Herbert Lottman, *The People's Anger* (London: Hutchinson, 1986), p. 41.

27 Jean Goueffon, 'La Cour de Justice d'Orléans (1944–1945)', *Revue d'histoire de la deuxième guerre mondiale*, No. 130, April 1983 pp. 51–64.

28 Herbert Lottman, op. cit., p. 17. Note, however, that the account emphasises the horror of the father rather than the ordeal of the daughter.

29 Hanna Diamond, 'Women's experience', op. cit., p. 204.

30 Henri Amouroux, *La grande histoire des Français après l'Occupation*, Vol. 9, 'Le règlement de comptes' (Paris: Laffont, 1991), p. 121.

31 Margaret Randolph Higonnet and Patrice L.-R. Higonnet, 'The double helix', in Margaret Randolph Higonnet *et al.*, op. cit., p. 37.

32 Emmanuel d'Astier, *De la chute à la libération de Paris* (Paris: Gallimard, 1965).

33 Herbert Lottman, op. cit., p. 66.

34 Ibid., p. 68.

35 Ibid., p. 67.

36 Corran Laurens, in 'La femme au turban' (unpublished paper, University of Southampton 1991), has made the first attempt that I know of to theorise the shaving of women's heads at the Liberation from a woman-centred perspective. French historians are only now beginning to look at this aspect of war history. Interestingly the first book to be published on the 'femmes tondues' is by a philospher, Alain Brossat (*Les Tondues*, Levallois-Perret: Editions Manya, 1993).

37 Marie-France Brive, 'L'image des femmes à la Libération', in Rolande Trempé (ed.) *La Libération du Midi de la France* (Toulouse: Eché Editeur, 1986), pp. 389–402.

38 Ibid., p. 391.

39 Ibid.

40 Yves Durand, *La captivité* (Paris: Fédération Nationale des Combattants, Prisonniers de Guerre et Combattants d'Algérie, 1980).

41 Ibid., p. 414.

42 See Corran Laurens, op. cit.

43 Yves Durand, op. cit., p. 417.

44 Alfred Sauvy, *La vie économique*, op. cit., p. 110.

45 Simone de Beauvoir, op. cit., p. 40.

46 Henri Amouroux, op. cit., p. 683.

47 Georgette Elgey, *La république des illusions* (Paris: Fayard, 1965) p. 57.

48 Ibid.

49 Catherine Gavin, op. cit., pp. 84–85.

50 Henri Amouroux, op. cit., p. 727.
51 Fred Kupferman, *Les premiers beaux jours* (Paris: Calmann-Lévy, 1985), p. 89.
52 *Journal officiel*, Débats parlementaires, séance du 27/2/45.
53 *Journal officiel*, Débats parlementaires, séance du 12/3/45.
54 *Pour la vie*, No. 3, January 1946.
55 Henri Amouroux, op. cit., p. 699.
56 Charles-Louis Foulon, *Le pouvoir en province à la Libération* (Paris: FNSP, 1975), p. 188.
57 Ibid., p. 189.
58 Annie Lacroix-Riz, *La CGT de la Libération à la scission* (Paris: Editions Sociales, 1983), p. 39.
59 Janet Flanner, *Paris Journal 1945–1965* (London: Victor Gollancz, 1966), p. 13.
60 Ibid., pp. 5–6.
61 Annie Lacroix-Riz, op. cit., p. 64.
62 Alfred Sauvy in *La Libération de la France*, op. cit., p. 299.
63 G. Madjarian, *Conflits, pouvoir et société à la Libération* (Paris: UGE, 1980), p. 280.
64 *Journal officiel*, Débats parlementaires, séance du 27/2/45.
65 *Journal officiel*, Débats parlementaires, séance du 28/2/45.
66 *La vie des Français sous l'Occupation* (Stanford: Hoover Institute, 1958), Vol. 1, p. 337.
67 Figures from Charles-Louis Foulon, op. cit., p. 194; and from Valérie-Anne Montassier, *Les années d'après-guerre* (Paris: Fayard, 1980), p. 193. Figures vary from source to source.
68 Janet Flanner, op. cit., p. 6.
69 Raymond Ruffin, *La vie des Français au jour le jour: de la Libération à la Victoire 1944–45* (Paris: Presses de la Cité, 1986), p. 36.
70 *Pour la vie*, Nos 1 and 2, 1945.
71 R. Ruffin, op. cit., p. 234.
72 Interview, Yolande Léautey, 5 May 1988.
73 Alfred Sauvy, *La vie économique*, op. cit., p. 127.
74 R. Ruffin, op. cit., p. 233.
75 *Pour la vie*, No. 3, January 1946, p. 114.
76 Ibid., pp. 118–120.
77 See Chapter Four for details about *les travailleuses familiales*, or home helps.
78 *Pour la vie*, No. 15, 1947.
79 *Véronique*, 7 October 1945.
80 *Elle*, 2 November 1945.
81 The turban was also used to hide the fact that a woman's head had been shaved, whether as an alleged collaborator and victim of the purges or as a deportee and victim of the Nazis.
82 *Marie-France*, 5 January 1945.
83 On Pétainist family policy, see Aline Coutrot, 'La politique familiale', in *Le gouvernement de Vichy 1940–42* (Paris: FNSP, 1972); on women in Pétainist discourse, see Miranda Pollard, 'Women and the national revolution', in R. Kedward and R. Austin (eds) *Vichy France and the Resistance: Culture and Ideology* (London: Croom Helm, 1985).

84 Henri Frenay in *La Libération de la France*, op. cit. pp. 739–740. See also Jean-Pierre Rioux, *La France de la Quatrième République* (Paris: Le Seuil, 1980), pp. 26–29.

85 *Journal officiel*, Débats parlementaires, séance du 22/4/45.

86 Ibid.

87 Henri Frenay, *La nuit finira*, op. cit., p. 493.

88 Sarah Fishman, *We Will Wait. Wives of French Prisoners of War 1940–1945* (Newhaven: Yale University Press, 1991), p. 154.

89 Ibid., p. 155.

90 Raymond Ruffin, op. cit., p. 164.

91 Ibid., p. 186.

92 L'Amicale de Ravensbrück et l'Association des Déportées Internées de la Résistance, *Les Françaises à Ravensbrück* (Paris: Gallimard, 1965), p. 299.

93 Olga Wormser-Migot, *Le retour des déportés* (Brussels: Editions. Complexe, 1985), p. 195.

94 Ibid., p. 220.

95 For a profoundly moving account of waiting for a returning deportee, see Marguerite Duras, *La douleur* (Paris: P.O.L., 1985).

96 This contradiction is one of the main themes of the chapter by Sarah Fishman 'Waiting for the captive sons of France' in Margaret Randolph Higonnet *et. al.*, op. cit.

97 Sarah Fishman, *We will Wait*, op. cit., pp. 152–153.

98 Christophe Lewin, *Le retour des prisonniers de guerre français* (Paris: Publications de la Sorbonne, 1986), pp. 70–71.

99 Hanna Diamond, 'Women's experience', op. cit., pp. 220–224.

100 See oral evidence in Sarah Fishman, op cit., and Hanna Diamond, op. cit.

101 Janet Flanner, op. cit., pp. 25–26.

102 *Les Françaises à Ravensbrück*, op. cit., pp. 300–302.

103 In Guylaine Guidez, op. cit., pp. 326–327.

104 Ibid., p. 323.

105 Ibid., p. 325.

106 Sarah Fishman (op. cit., p. 163) estimates that the PoW divorce rate was about 10 per cent, that is only slightly higher than the national average.

107 Christophe Lewin, 'Retour des prisonniers de guerre français', *Guerres mondiales et conflits contemporains*, No. 147, July 1983. This article sums up many of the points made in the book-length study.

108 13 March 1946.

109 Frédérique Boucher, 'Abriter vaille que vaille, se loger coûte que coûte', *Images, discours et enjeux de la reconstruction des villes françaises après 1945* (Cahier de l'IHTP, No. 5, June 1987), p. 120.

110 Ibid., p. 122.

111 Ibid., p. 128.

112 Ibid., p. 129.

113 For postwar family policy, see Pierre Laroque (ed.) *La politique familiale française depuis 1945* (Paris: Documentation Française, 1986).

114 As in the quotation from a CNR brochure cited in ibid., p. 195.

115 *Journal officiel*, Débats parlementaires, séance du 19/7/46.

116 See Pierre Laroque, 'L'évolution de l'action sociale des caisses d'allocations familiales', in Pierre Laroque, op. cit., pp. 291–370.

117 See Chapter Four.

118 Pierre Laroque, op. cit., p. 11.

2 WOMEN IN PUBLIC LIFE: THE POLITICAL ARENA

1 Guylaine Guidez, *Femmes dans la guerre* (Paris: Perrin, 1986), p. 331.

2 See Siân Reynolds, 'Marianne's citizens? Women, the Republic and
universal suffrage in France', in S. Reynolds (ed.) *Women, the State
and Revolution* (Brighton: Wheatsheaf, 1986), p. 108.

3 See Fernand Grenier, 'La Résistance et le droit de vote aux femmes'
in *Les femmes dans la Résistance* (Paris: Editions du Rocher, 1976),
pp. 258–262.

4 The suffrage debates of the Third Republic are well documented. See
for instance S. Hause and A. Kenney, *Women's Suffrage and Social
Politics in the French Third Republic* (Princeton: Princeton University
Press, 1984); L. Klejman and F. Rochefort, *L'égalité en marche* (Paris:
des femmes, 1989); Huguette Bouchardeau, *Pas d'histoire, les femmes*
(Paris: Syros, 1977). On women's suffrage in France more generally,
see Siân Reynolds op. cit., pp. 102–122.

5 For the best accounts of the setting up of the Fourth Republic, see
Dorothy Pickles, *The First Years of the Fourth Republic* (London: Royal
Institute of International Affairs, 1953); Philip Williams, *Crisis and
Compromise: Politics in the Fourth Republic* (London: Longman, 1964);
Gordon Wright, *The Reshaping of French Democracy* (New York:
Reynall and Hitchcock, 1948); Valérie-Anne Montassier, *Les années
d'après-guerre* (Paris: Fayard, 1980).

6 *La Femme*, 31 March 1945.

7 Pamphlet produced by the Catholic women's organisation, the UFCS,
in 1945.

8 *Femmes françaises*, 7 December 1944.

9 *Elle*, 30 April 1946.

10 *Femmes françaises*, 9 November 1944.

11 *Le droit des femmes*, November–December 1946, p. 64.

12 See Pierre Barral, Claude Leleu and François Goguel, 'Pour qui votent
les femmes', in F. Goguel (ed.) *Nouvelles études de sociologie électorale*,
(Paris: Armand Colin, 1954).

13 V.-A. Montassier, op. cit., p. 112.

14 *Les femmes dans la Résistance*, op. cit., p. 281.

15 It may be forgiven to be a little sceptical about the motives for these
honours: see Renée Rousseau, *Les femmes rouges. Chronique des
années Vermeersch* (Paris: Albin Michel, 1983).

16 Leaflet produced by the MRP, 1945.

17 *Réforme*, 1951.

18 For studies on women and politics during the decade following the
Second World War, see Mattei Dogan and Jacques Narbonne, *Les
Françaises face à la politique* (Paris: Armand Colin, 1955); Maurice
Duverger, *La participation des femmes à la vie politique* (Paris:

UNESCO, 1955); and a special issue of the journal *Sondages* in 1954 on 'La psychologie politique des femmes' (Women's political psychology).

19 The first analysis of Dogan and Narbonne which questions the bases of their conclusions was by Andrée Michel in her article 'Les Françaises et la politique' in *Les temps modernes*, April 1965.

20 *Revue politique et parlementaire*, 1945.

21 *La vie heureuse*, 16 January 1946.

22 UFCS leaflet 1945.

23 'La vie politique et les femmes', in *La femme dans la vie sociale*, 1945.

24 *La femme dans la vie sociale*, February 1945.

25 MRP leaflet, 1944.

26 *Cahiers de l'UFF*, June 1945.

27 *Femmes françaises*, 7 December 1944.

28 Ibid.

29 *Cahiers de l'UFF*, December 1945.

30 See Renée Rousseau, op. cit., Chapters Two and Three.

31 Ibid., p. 86.

32 See Chapters Four and Five on motherhood and employment.

33 *Le rassemblement*, 15–22 February 1952.

34 See Chapter Six.

35 On the Comités Départementaux de la Libération (CDL), see Charles-Louis Foulon, *Le pouvoir en province à la Libération* (Paris: FNSP, 1975), and also his 'Prise et exercice du pouvoir en province à la Libération' in *La Libération de la France* (Paris: CNRS, 1976), pp. 501–527.

36 See Charles-Louis Foulon in *Les femmes dans la Résistance*, op. cit., pp. 273–275. The woman leader was Madame Mir, who went on to lead a women-only list in the local elections of 1945 and won 3 per cent of the vote.

37 See *Les femmes dans la Résistance*, op. cit.

38 Ibid., p. 274.

39 *La Libération de la France*, op. cit., p. 514.

40 The role of the CDLs and de Gaulle's patronising attitude towards them led to much bitterness after the war. For de Gaulle, the CDLs were merely local consultative bodies with no official mandate to govern. However, the former Resisters who made up the CDLs had no intention of relinquishing their political role after the new Republic had been restored. See Charles-Louis Foulon, op. cit.

41 Mattei Dogan and Jacques Narbonne, op. cit., give the figures for the three major parties as: PCF, 18 per cent women members; SFIO, 17 per cent; MRP, 16 per cent. Dogan and Narbonne estimate that of these members, 35 per cent were activists in the PCF, 15 per cent in the SFIO, and 10 per cent in the MRP. While these figures are not necessarily reliable, and the criteria of 'activism' remain undefined, we can still assume that the number of women political activists and therefore the influence that women had on party decision-making, was minimal. Figures vary according to source: in Maurice Duverger's *Partis politiques et classes sociales* (Paris: Armand Colin, 1955), contributors

put women's membership of these parties in the early 1950s as slightly lower all round.

42 Siân Reynolds used this expression to describe women in the French Revolution, but it seems highly appropriate to women in postwar politics as well.

43 Alain Gourdon, in Maurice Duverger, op. cit., p. 229.

44 See Renée Rousseau, op. cit.

45 For instance, *Nous les femmes*, *Femmes républicaines*, *La femme*, *Femmes de France*. Local UFF groups also had their own local newsletters.

46 As the women were told by the General Secretary of the party, Jean-Paul David, in *Femmes républicaines* in 1951.

47 Simply trying to find out about the life of these groups in the face of total denial by party archivists (MRP, SFIO, RPF) that they had ever existed seems to indicate the lack of seriousness with which they were considered. See also Andrée Michel, in 'Les Françaises et la politique', *Les temps modernes*, April 1965.

48 Two examples: Socialist congresses had a session devoted to a report of the activities of its women's section. The time and space allocated to this report was progressively reduced over the course of the 1950s and the spokeswoman always complained – politely – of lack of support for women within the party, whether over designation of candidates, dealing with 'women's issues' in the party press or giving money to support women's activities.

On the Radical Party, Alain Gourdon writes (in Maurice Duverger, op. cit.), that party congresses were the 'pretext for distractions of all kinds for husbands, so very few wives were ever there'.

49 In her speech 'Les femmes dans la nation' at XIth PCF Congress, 25–28 June 1947.

50 There were, however, three Radical women Senators: Mme Delabie, Mme Thome-Patenôtre and Mme Schreiber-Crémieux.

51 Duchesse de la Rochefoucauld, *Flashes* (Paris: Grasset, 1982), p. 78.

52 Simone Rollin (MRP Deputy in 1945, Senator from 1946 to 1948), for instance, said in *La revue des électrices* (No. 7, January 1946): 'My six children are aged from 14 years to 20 months. I have organised my household so that I can fulfil my task here ... some mothers have the duty to respond to their vocation and participate in the political life of their country.'

53 M. Dogan and J. Narbonne, op. cit., p. 147.

54 Ibid., p. 151. But 7 per cent is a higher figure than was seen again until the 1980s.

55 Philip Williams, op. cit., p. 323.

56 In *Le Populaire*, 5 September 1945.

57 *Nous les femmes*, journal of PRL (conservative) women, 1 November 1951.

58 *La vie heureuse*, 2 April 1947.

59 *Revue des femmes républicaines*, 1950.

60 *Femmes, face à vos responsabilités*, MRP leaflet, 1945.

61 *La revue de la femme socialiste*, 1947.

62 These examples are taken from *Le Droit des femmes*, October–December 1947, pp. 5–6.

63 *Pour l'information féminine*, 1956.

64 Mathilde Péri, *Journal officiel*, Débats parlementaires, séance du 8/5/45.

65 The three women members of government were: Andrée Vienot (SFIO) in Léon Blum's one-month-long (December 1946) Socialist government as Under-Secretary for Youth and Sport; Germaine Poinso-Chapuis (MRP) in Georges Bidault's and Robert Schuman's 1947–8 governments as Minister of Health; Nafissa Sid-Cara as Responsible for Algerian Affairs in 1959, the first government of the Fifth Republic.

66 Cited in Florence Montreynaud, *Le XXe siècle des femmes* (Paris: Nathan, 1992), p. 335.

67 M. Dogan, 'L'origine sociale du personnel parlementaire français élu en 1951', in Maurice Duverger, op cit., p. 292.

68 Ibid., p. 297.

69 They were Mathilde Péri (PCF), Marie-Claire Vaillant-Couturier (PCF), Gilberte Brossolette (SFIO).

70 As well as Péri and Vaillant-Couturier, the women who remained throughout the Fourth Republic were: Germaine Degrond (SFIO), Marie-Madeleine Dienesch (MRP), Emilienne Galicier (PCF), Rose Guérin (PCF), Francine Lefebvre (MRP), Rachel Lempereur (SFIO) and Jeannette Vermeersch (PCF). Gilberte Brossolette moved to the Council of the Republic.

71 They were: Gilberte Brossolette (SFIO), Marie-Hélène Cardot (MRP), Marcelle Delabie (RGR), Marcelle Devaud (PRL), Yvonne Dumont (PCF), Suzanne Girault (PCF), Jacqueline Thome-Patenôtre (RGR). At first, the Council of the Republic included forty-two members chosen by Deputies in the National Assembly, and many women became Senators in this way. When the electoral system changed, and Deputies were no longer designated Senators, the number of women dropped.

72 *La femme*, 14 November 1945.

73 In *Le Figaro*, 21 August 1947.

74 In *L'Epoque*, 9 July 1946.

75 By the second Legislature (1951–6), there was one woman in the committee on foreign affairs (out of a membership of forty-four) and none in the other two.

76 *Le Figaro*, 21 August 1947.

77 For a fascinating discussion of women in politics in the 1980s, which seems to confirm much of the early experience of women politicians, see Mariette Sineau, *Des femmes en politique* (Paris: Editions Economica, 1988).

78 Alain Touraine, 'Thèmes et vocabulaire d'une campagne électorale', in Maurice Duverger (ed.), *Les élections de 1956* (Paris: FNSP, 1957).

79 For the best analysis of women and politics during the Fourth Republic that does not make assumptions about women's nature, etc., see Andrée Michel and Geneviève Texier *La condition de la Française d'aujourd'hui* (Paris: Denoël-Gonthier, 1964).

80 Maurice Duverger, 'Les femmes sont-elles antiféministes?', *Le courrier de l'UNESCO*, No. 11, 1955, p. 24.

81 Gisèle Charzat, *Les Françaises sont-elles des citoyennes?* (Paris: Denoël-Gonthier, 1972), p. 28.
82 See Mariette Sineau, 'Gender and the French electorate', in Mary Katzenstein, and Hage Skjeie (eds), *Going Public. National Histories of Women's Enfranchisement and Women's Participation within State Institutions* (Oslo: Institute for Social Research, 1990), pp. 80–103.
83 Philip Williams, *The French Parliament 1958–1967* (London: Allen & Unwin, 1968), p. 29.
84 *L'Express*, 1 August 1963.
85 In the elections following the May events, there were only eight women elected – 1.6 per cent of the total.
86 Yvette Roudy, *A cause d'elles* (Paris: Albin Michel, 1983), p. 89. The women were Yvette Roudy, Colette Audry, Marie-Thérèse Eyquem, Gisèle Halimi, Cécile Goldet, Evelyne Sullerot and one other.
87 Gisèle Charzat, op. cit., p. 62.
88 Ibid., p. 92.
89 These issues are fully discussed in Chapter Six.
90 Mariette Sineau, 'Gender and the French electorate', op. cit., pp. 91–2.
91 See Chapter Six.

3 HOUSE AND HOME

1 Mme E. Compain, *La science de la maison* (Paris: Fouches, 1959, new edn), p. 7.
2 Judy Giles, 'A home of one's own: women and domesticity in England, 1918–1950', *Women's Studies International Forum*, Vol. 16, No. 3, 1993, p. 244.
3 Robert Prigent in *Renouveau des idées sur la famille*, Cahier de l'INED 18 (Paris: PUF, 1953), p. 309.
4 G. D'Arcy in *La femme dans la vie sociale*, May 1948, p. 39.
5 Paul-Henri and Marie-Jo Chombart de Lauwe, *La femme dans la société* (Paris: CNRS, 1963), pp. 342–343.
6 Evelyne Sullerot, *La vie des femmes* (Paris: Gonthier, 1965), p. 93.
7 Mme Foulon-Lefranc, *La femme au foyer* (Paris: Editions de l'école, 1953, 11th edn), pp. 9–10.
8 Ibid., pp. 11–12.
9 Robert Prigent, op. cit., p. 309.
10 Ginette Mathiot, *Comment enseigner l'éducation ménagère* (no publisher, 1957), p. 14.
11 'L'aide aux mères de famille', *Pour la vie*, No. 34, 1950.
12 Dominique Ceccaldi, *Politique française de la famille* (Paris: Privat, 1957), p. 91.
13 Mme Foulon-Lefranc, op. cit., p. 7.
14 Ginette Mathiot, op. cit., pp. 32, 53.
15 Dena Attar, *Wasting Girls' Time* (London: Virago, 1990), p. 22.
16 For the work of the CAFs, see Chapter Four.
17 M.-J. Durupt, *Les mouvements d'action catholique rurale, facteur d'évolution du milieu rural* (IEP, thèse de 3e cycle, 1963), p. 30.
18 JACF *Une aide semblable à lui* (pamphlet, no publisher, 1960), p. 34.

19 *Informations sociales*, March 1948, p. 313.
20 Ibid., pp. 314–315.
21 Paulette Bernège, *De la méthode ménagère* (no publisher, 1928), p. 62.
22 M.-L. Lemonnier, in *Education ménagère*, September–October 1960, p. 17.
23 M. Romien, 'L'information des ménagères', *Informations sociales*, October 1957.
24 Hélène Strohl, 'Inside and outside the home: how our lives have changed through domestic automation', in Anne Showstack Sassoon (ed.) *Women and the State* (London: Hutchinson, 1987), pp. 288–9.
25 J. and F. Fourastié, *Les arts ménagers* (Paris: PUF, 1950), p. 101.
26 *Femmes d'aujourd'hui*, 23 February 1956.
27 *Femmes d'aujourd'hui*, 11 October 1956.
28 *Nouveau fémina*, May 1955.
29 *Marie-Claire*, No. 1, October 1954.
30 P.-H. Chombart de Lauwe (ed.) *La vie quotidienne des familles ouvrières* (Paris: CNRS, 1956), p. 45.
31 These groups and initiatives are described in 'Les mouvements familiaux populaires et ruraux – naissance, développement, mutations 1939–1955', *Les cahiers du Groupement pour la Recherche sur les Mouvements Familiaux*, No. 2, 1984, pp. 188–214.
32 *La maison française*, No. 1, 1958.
33 P.-H. Chombart de Lauwe, op. cit., p. 46.
34 A. Girard and H. Bastide, 'Le budget-temps de la femme mariée à la campagne', *Population*, No. 2, 1959, p. 263.
35 *Arts ménagers et culinaires*, 22 February 1956.
36 Not forgetting, of course, that *Maison et jardin* was the French version of the American magazine, *House and Garden*.
37 *La revue des travailleuses*, No. 31, 1955, p. 3.
38 Definition provided by the Ministère de la Reconstruction et de l'Urbanisme, quoted in 'Nos maisons et nos villes', *Esprit*, 1953, p. 451.
39 Ibid.
40 Louis Henry and Maurice Febvay, 'La situation du logement dans la région parisienne', *Population*, No. 1, 1957.
41 E. Preteceille, *La production des grands ensembles* (The Hague: Mouton, 1973), p. 277.
42 Andrée Vieille 'Les hôtels meublés dans la région parisienne', *Esprit*, 1953, p. 470.
43 Michel Gervais, Marcel Jollivet and Yves Tavernier, *Histoire de la France rurale de 1914 à nos jours*, Vol. 4 (Paris: Le Seuil, 1976), p. 277.
44 Louis Crombez, 'Le mouvement squatter', *Esprit*, 1953, p. 505.
45 Geneviève Dermenjian, 'L'action des femmes dans la LOC-MPF pendant la seconde guerre mondiale et l'après-guerre', *Les cahiers du Groupement pour la Recherche sur les Mouvements Familiaux*, No. 3, 1985, p. 253.
46 *La maison française*, No. 3, 1947.
47 P.-H. Chombart de Lauwe, op. cit., p. 83.
48 'Conditions, attitudes et aspirations des ouvriers', *Sondages*, No. 2, 1956, p. 18.
49 *L'école des parents*, 1951.

50 Jean Stoetzel, 'Le budget-temps de la femme mariée dans les agglomérations urbaines', *Population*, No. 1, 1948, p. 57.
51 Ibid., pp. 54–55.
52 See Chapter Four.
53 A. Girard, 'Le budget-temps de la femme mariée dans les agglomérations urbaines', *Population*, No. 4, 1958, p. 618.
54 Alison Ravetz, 'A view from the interior', in Judy Attfield and Patricia Kirkham (eds), *A View from the Interior. Feminism, Women and Design* (London: Virago, 1989), p. 189.
55 The situation of women involved in agriculture was even more difficult, as lines between 'home' and 'work' were blurred to say the least. Most women saw their activity not as work, but as helping their husband.
56 P.-H. Chombart de Lauwe, op. cit., p. 49.
57 M. Allauzen, *Le paysanne française aujourd'hui* (Paris: Gonthier, 1967), p. 16.
58 L. Bouvet, 'JAC et JACF dans l'Orne du début des anneés 1950 au début des anneés 1960' (thèse de 3e cycle, IEP, Paris, 1986), p. 41.
59 *Pour la vie*, No. 13, July–August 1947. Domestic work was often an undeclared activity and so real figures cannot be known.
60 *Maison et jardin*, No. 2, 1950.
61 From the *Annuaire de la presse*, 1956.
62 See Chapter Four.
63 P.-H. Chombart de Lauwe, op. cit., p. 59.
64 *Marie-France*, 29 January 1947.
65 P.-H. Chombart de Lauwe, op. cit., p. 204.
66 Simone de Beauvoir, 'La femme mariée', *Le deuxième sexe* (Paris: Gallimard, 1949, 1976 edn), Vol. 2, pp. 221–329.
67 Jeannette Vermeersch, 'Françaises, le PCF vous parle', speech at the Vel d'Hiv', 11 April 1945.
68 Ibid.
69 Michel Garbez, 'La question féminine et le Parti Communiste Français', in Jacques Chevallier *et al.*, *Discours et idéologie* (Paris: 1980), pp. 301–393.
70 André Barjonet, contribution to discussion of 'La femme et le travail' in *Femmes du XXe siècle* (Paris: PUF, 1965), p. 6.
71 See Chapter Six.
72 All these quotations come from *Arts ménagers et culinaires*, 6 February 1956.
73 Simone de Beauvoir, op. cit., p. 279.
74 Dr G. Montreuil-Strauss, 'Le surménage de la mère de famille française', *Informations sociales*, October 1953, p. 1014.
75 Ibid., p. 1022.
76 'Conditions de vie des ménages, 1967', in *Données statistiques sur l'évolution de l'équipement des ménages jusqu'à la fin de l'année 1968*, Collections de l'INSEE, Série M (Paris: Documentation Française, 1969), p. 54.
77 R. Kaës, *Vivre dans les grands ensembles* (Paris: Editions Ouvrières, 1963), p. 63.
78 Ibid., p. 39.
79 Ibid., p. 59.

80 Ibid., p. 60.
81 Ibid., p. 77.
82 Maryse Huet, *Les femmes dans les grands ensembles* (Paris: CNRS, 1971), p. 110.
83 Christiane Rochefort, *Les petits enfants du siècle* (Paris: Grasset, 1961), pp. 19–20.
84 Ibid., pp. 10–11.
85 Geneviève Chauveau, 'Logement et habitat populaire de la fin de deuxième guerre mondiale aux années 1960', in Annie Fourcaut (ed.) *Un siècle de banlieue parisienne* (Paris: L'Harmattan, 1988), p. 139.
86 Michèle Huguet, 'Les femmes dans les grands ensembles', *Revue française de sociologie*, VI, 1965, pp. 215–227.
87 Brigitte Gros, *Les paradisiennes* (Paris: Laffont, 1973), pp. 134–154.
88 Ibid., p. 111.
89 Ibid., p. 219.
90 *Marie-France*, March 1960, p. 44.
91 Ibid., p. 45.
92 *Le Monde*, 4 April 1953.
93 Paulette Bernège, op. cit., p. 158.
94 Yvette Roudy, *A cause d'elles* (Paris: Albin Michel, 1983), pp. 76–77.
95 'Situation de la femme d'aujourd'hui', lecture given in Japan, September 1966, in C. Francis and F. Gonthier, *Les écrits de Simone de Beauvoir* (Paris: Gallimard, 1976), pp. 422–438.
96 See Chapter Five.
97 Ménie Grégoire, *Le métier de femme* (Paris: Plon, 1965), p. 23.
98 *Elle*, 11 April 1968.
99 *Bulletin mensuel*, CAF, No. 10, October 1968, p. 676.
100 'L'évolution du rôle du père et de la mère' in *L'école des parents*, July–August 1966, p. 7.
101 Andrée Michel, *Statut professionnel féminin et structure du couple français urbain* (Paris: CNRS, 1972), p. 3.
102 M. Guilbert, N. Lowit and J. Creusen, 'Enquête comparative de budget-temps (II)', *Revue française de sociologie*, VI, 1965, p. 510.
103 'Les jeunes', *Sondages*, No. 2, 1968, p. 70.
104 Evelyne Sullerot, op. cit., p. 95.

4 MARRIAGE AND MOTHERHOOD

1 In a speech of 17 June 1940.
2 Marshal Pétain, 'Message aux mères françaises', 25 May 1941.
3 See A. Armengaud, *La population française, XXe siècle* (Paris: PUF, 1973); C. Dyer, *Population and Society in Twentieth-century France* (London: Hodder & Stoughton, 1978).
4 Figures from the national statistics office INSEE, quoted in J. Brémond and M.-M. Salort, *La famille en question* (Paris: Hatier, 1986) p. 40.
5 Ibid., p. 34
6 *Daily Mail*, 3 September 1946.
7 Age on marriage rose; numbers who married fell; couples living together and having children outside marriage rose; the birth rate fell

– hence the continued existence of a population crisis mentality in France.

8 See Chapter Six.

9 *Marie-France*, 19 July 1945.

10 Simone de Beauvoir, *Le deuxième sexe*, Vol. 2 (Paris: Gallimard, 1949; new edn 1976), p. 221.

11 *Elle*, 19 March 1946.

12 *Marie-Claire*, August 1955.

13 Ibid.

14 Institut Français d'Opinion Publique, *La Française et l'amour* (Paris: Laffont, 1960) p. 227.

15 Mme Foulon-Lefranc, *La femme au foyer* (Paris: Editions de l'école, 1953), pp. 12–13.

16 Christiane Rochefort, *Les stances à Sophie* (Paris: Grasset 1963), pp. 99–100.

17 *Marie-Claire*, May 1960.

18 *Intimité du foyer*, March 1960.

19 Ibid.

20 Cited in Pierre Waline, 'Les conditions d'existence des familles françaises' (mimeograph, 1946), p. 170.

21 *Forces nouvelles*, 2 June 1945.

22 Circular of 17 March 1947, cited in *Population*, No. 4, 1948.

23 *Marie-France*, 31 May 1945.

24 *L'école des parents*, No. 27, 1951.

25 Ibid.

26 Andrée Butillard, 'La crise de la maison', in *La femme dans la vie sociale*, May 1948, p. 5.

27 Cited in Nicole Questiaux and Jacques Fournier, 'France', in S. B. Kammerman and A. J. Khan (eds), *Family Policy: Government and Families in Fourteen Countries* (New York: Columbia University Press, 1978), p. 128.

28 Pierre Laroque, *La politique familiale en France depuis 1945* (Paris: Documentation Française, 1986), p. 217.

29 'Logement des jeunes ménages dans le département de la Seine', *Population*, No. 2, 1952.

30 Pierre Laroque, op. cit., p. 211.

31 'La femme au travail', *Esprit*, No. 5, May 1961, p. 886.

32 MRP Congress 1950. Report on family policy by Germaine Poinso-Chapuis.

33 'Enquête sur l'information du public en matière démographique', *Population*, No. 4, 1947. Most of those asked why they wanted an increased birth rate cited the prestige of France and the need to increase production without being dependent on immigrant labour. The 1950s, in fact, saw, large numbers of immigrants coming to work in France, which could not have completed its postwar recovery and embarked on its expansion without their contribution.

34 Nicole Questiaux and Jacques Fournier, op. cit., pp. 128–149.

35 Louis Henry, 'La reprise de la natalité', in *Cahiers français d'information*, March 1952.

36 Cf. C. Dyer, op. cit., p. 173.

37 Christiane Rochefort, *Les petits enfants du siècle* (Paris: Grasset, 1961), pp. 110–111.
38 *Pour la vie*, No. 9, March 1947, p. 13.
39 *Pour la vie*, No. 34, February–March 1950, p. 13.
40 *Elle*, 30 April 1956.
41 *Bonnes soirées*, 9 September 1956.
42 *Cahiers du GRMF* No. 2, 1984, p. 170.
43 *Pour l'information féminine*, August 1957, pp. 20–21.
44 See Yvonne Knibiehler and Catherine Fouquet, *L'histoire des mères du moyen âge à nos jours* (Paris: Editions Montalba, 1977); Karen Offen, 'Body politics: women, work and the politics of motherhood in France 1920–1950', in Gisela Bock and Pat Thane (eds) *Maternity and Gender Politics* (London: Routledge, 1991).
45 *Forces nouvelles*, 27 October 1945.
46 *Forces nouvelles*, December 1946.
47 *Marie-France*, 23 January 1946.
48 Jeannette Laot, *Stratégie pour les femmes* (Paris: Stock, 1977), p. 60.
49 In *La femme dans la vie sociale*, January–March 1948.
50 *Femmes françaises*, 7 June 1947.
51 This attention to natural childbirth allowed motherhood to be perceived as positive and joyful, whereas the PCF usually stressed the difficulties of the double shift and the financial burdens of motherhood.
52 *Femmes françaises*, 5 July 1945.
53 Resolution presented by Marie Couette of the CGT Women's Committee to the 1948 Congress, in *La question féminine dans les congrès confédéraux et les conférences nationales de la CGT: choix de textes* (Paris: Institut CGT, no date), p. 35.
54 'Annexe du projet de programme de la CGT, 1959', in ibid., p. 51.
55 'Protégeons la mère et l'enfant' in 'Tribune de la femme', *La revue socialiste*, No. 2, June 1946.
56 *La vie heureuse*, No. 34, 14 August 1946.
57 *Revue de la femme socialiste*, No. 5, April 1947.
58 'Programme du RFR', in RFR publication *Femmes*, no date.
59 UFCS, *La femme dans la vie sociale*, October 1955.
60 Jeannette Vermeersch, 'Les femmes dans la nation', speech at the 11th PCF Congress, 1947.
61 *Pouponnières* took children in full-time, not just during the day; *garderies* took children aged between 3 and 6.
62 Marie-Louise Tournier, 'L'aide aux mères qui travaillent', *Esprit*, No. 5, 1961, pp. 848–849.
63 Ibid.
64 Survey carried out by INED and reported in *Population*, No. 3, 1948.
65 See 'L'évolution de l'action sociale des Caisses d'Allocations Familiales', *Informations sociales*, No. 11, 1966, p. 143.
66 Cf. Bernadette Bonamy, 'Pour une histoire des TF rurales et populaires', *Cahiers du GRMF*, No. 3, 1985.
67 *Marie-France*, 31 May 1946.
68 *Informations sociales*, February 1949.
69 *Informations sociales*, December 1947, p. 644.
70 Among the reasons why this proposal failed were some that had

nothing to do with the fact that it represented exploitation of the young woman in question or that young women did not want to do it: it failed because it would have been impossible to organise without setting up a massive network for training and referrals; and with voluntary work, it would have been difficult to verify the young woman's credentials and qualifications.

71 *Travailleuse familiale*, No. 2, 1960.
72 A. Girard and H. Bastide, 'Une enquête sur l'efficacité de l'action sociale des CAF', *Population*, No. 1, 1958, pp. 49–50.
73 *Données statistiques sur les familles*, No. 175, Collections de l'INSEE (Paris: Documentation Française, 1975) p. 13.
74 *Année politique*, 1966, p. 378.
75 *Données statistiques sur les familles*, op. cit., p. 15.
76 *L'école des parents*, July–August 1966, p. 7.
77 UFCS survey on 'Mothers and work', cited in *L'école des parents*, November 1965, p. 38.
78 *Elle*, 22 July 1968.
79 *Elle*, 11 May 1968.
80 *Marie-France*, February 1967.
81 Y. Roudy and L. Pechadre, *La réussite de la femme* (Paris: CEPC, 1970), p. 86.
82 Ménie Grégoire, *Le métier de femme* (Paris: Plon, 1965), p. 8.
83 Ibid., p. 51.
84 Judy Giles, 'A home of her own: women and domesticity in Britain, 1918–1950', *Women's Studies International Forum*, Vol. 16, No. 3, 1993. Her analysis of women and domesticity in Britain between the wars seems quite appropriate as a description of women in postwar France.
85 Antoine Prost, 'La politique familiale de 1938 à 1981', *Le mouvement social*, No. 129, 1984, p. 15.
86 *Bulletin mensuel des CAF*, Nos 5–6, May–June 1968, p. 257.
87 Edgar Andréani, 'La famille', in 'La protection sociale', *Cahiers français*, No. 214, March–April 1984, p. 54.
88 Pierre Laroque, op. cit., p. 225.
89 Ibid., pp. 218–221.
90 Henri Bastide and Alain Girard, 'Attitudes et opinions des Français à l'égard de la fécondité et de la famille', *Population*, Nos 4–5, July–October 1975, p. 698.
91 Ibid., pp. 716–720.
92 C. Dyer, op. cit., p. 156.
93 Quoted in *La Française et l'amour*, op. cit., p. 235.
94 Ibid., pp. 234–236. All the above quotations are taken from this survey.
95 All the above quotations are taken from P. and M. Lambert, *3,000 foyers parlent* (Paris: Editions Ouvrières, 1966).
96 Marie-Andrée Lagroua Weill-Hallé, *La grand'peur d'aimer* (Paris: Julliard, 1961; Gonthier, 1964), pp. 135–6 (Gonthier edn).
97 Ibid., pp. 148–149.
98 Brussels: Editions Select, 1946.
99 Simone de Beauvoir 'La mère', in op. cit., 1976 edn, Vol. 2, p. 387.
100 Ibid., p. 388.
101 Ibid., p. 389.

102 In interview with author, December 1988.

103 Jacques Derogy, *Des enfants malgré nous* (Paris: Editions de Minuit, 1956), p. 171.

104 Ibid., p. 17.

105 Ibid., p. 40.

106 Ibid., pp. 200–210. It is not surprising that most of those in favour of birth control were Protestant.

107 According to Evelyne Sullerot addressing the General Assembly of the Association Maternité Heureuse on 19 October 1957, reported in the Association's newsletter *Maternité heureuse*, No. 4, 1958.

5 PERSISTENT INEQUALITIES: WOMEN AND EMPLOYMENT

1 Jean Fourastié, *Les trente glorieuses ou la révolution invisible de 1946 à 1975* (Paris: Fayard, 1979).

2 Hanna Diamond, 'The everyday experience of women in the Second World War in the Toulouse region', in Michael Scriven and Peter Wagstaff (eds), *War and Society in Twentieth-Century France* (Oxford: Berg, 1992), pp. 229–247.

3 Geneviève Texier, 'Les enquêtes sociologiques servent-elles à mystifier les femmes?', *Les temps modernes*, No. 235, 1965.

4 J.-J. Carré, P. Dubois and E. Malinvaud, *La croissance française* (Paris: Le Seuil, 1972), pp. 59–63.

5 The liberal professions originally meant those where the practitioners were remunerated by a fee rather than a salary and were independent rather than employed.

6 G. Vincent, *Les Français 1945–1975. Chronologie et structure d'une société* (Paris: Masson, 1977), p. 274, and *Données statistiques sur les familles* (Paris: Documentation Française, 1975), p. 53.

7 *Données statistiques sur les familles*, op. cit., p. 19.

8 Marie Allauzen, *La paysanne française aujourd'hui* (Paris: Gonthier, 1967), p. 12.

9 Viviane Isambert-Jamati, 'Le choix du métier', *Esprit*, special issue 'La femme au travail' ('Women at work'), No. 5, May 1961, p. 893.

10 Maurice Parodi, *L'économie et la société française depuis 1945* (Paris: Armand Colin, 1981), p. 240.

11 E. Morel and A. Zegel, *Tous les métiers féminins* (Paris: UGE, 1964), p. 174.

12 Special issue 'Carrières féminines en milieu rural' ('Rural careers for women'), *Avenirs*, January 1968, p. 15.

13 Ibid., p. 74.

14 Discussed in *La Croix*, 13 June 1956.

15 Françoise Guelaud-Leridon, *Le travail des femmes*, Cahier de l'INED No. 42 (Paris: PUF, 1964) p. 53.

16 Paul-Henri Chombart de Lauwe (ed.) *La vie quotidienne des familles ouvrières* (Paris: CNRS, 1956), p. 49. Of the women in the survey 49 per cent said that they would prefer to stay at home.

17 Claire Etcherelli, *Elise ou la vraie vie* (Paris: Denoël, 1967); Christiane Peyre, *Une société anonyme* (Paris: Julliard, 1962).

18 Michèle Aumont, *Femmes en usine* (Paris: Spès, 1953), p. 36.

19 Ibid., p. 53.

20 Report to the 'Conférence sur la réduction du temps de travail des femmes', 6–7 March 1965.

21 Madeleine Guilbert, *Les fonctions des femmes dans l'industrie* (The Hague: Mouton, 1966), pp. 132–135.

22 Ibid., pp. 213–214.

23 Ibid., p. 208.

24 E. Morel and A. Zegel, op. cit., pp. 26–29.

25 Maurice Parodi, op. cit., p. 241.

26 But she was not allowed to practise at the Bar until 1900. M. Albistur and D. Armogathe, *Histoire du féminisme français*, Vol 2 (Paris: des femmes, 1977), p. 582.

27 *Le Monde*, 21 March 1957.

28 S. Pauthier-Camier in *Femmes diplômées*, No. 50, 1964, pp. 59–63.

29 *Le Monde*, 21 March 1957.

30 *Le Monde*, 23 March 1957.

31 Guy Thuillier, *Les femmes dans l'administration depuis 1900.* (Paris: PUF, 1988), p. 82.

32 Michel Cézard 'Les cadres et leurs diplômes', *Economie et statistique*, No. 42, February 1973, pp. 25–40.

33 E. Morel and A. Zegel, op, cit., p. 31.

34 Cited in *La femme du XXe siècle*, No. 5, April 1966, p. 9.

35 M. Guilbert and V. Isambert-Jamati, 'La répartition par sexe', in Georges Friedmann and Pierre Naville (eds) *Traité de sociologie du travail* (Paris: Armand Colin, 1962), p. 271.

36 Ibid.

37 *Etudes et conjonctures*, December 1964, Annexe 2, pp. 69–70.

38 *Pour la vie*, No. 15, November 1947, p. 6.

39 Marie-Thérèse Renard, *La participation des femmes à la vie civique* (Paris: Editions Sociales, 1965), p. 32. This must be qualified by taking account of the age factor, the salary received, whether or not a woman was able to afford or find childcare. Even so, the nature of the job itself and the woman's personal investment in it affected whether or not she would stay in it.

40 Viviane Isambert-Jamati, 'L'absentéisme féminin', *Revue française de sociologie*, No. 1, 1959.

41 M. Guilbert, and M. Colin, 'Les femmes actives en France, bilan 1978', in *La condition féminine*, ouvrage collectif sous la direction du CERM (Paris: Editions Sociales, 1978), p. 87.

42 Claude Roux, 'Aspects professionnels de la reprise d'activité des femmes mariées', *Revue française des affaires sociales*, No. 3, July–September 1969, pp. 31–75.

43 Nicole Dubrulle and Geneviève Gontier, 'Les désirs d'activité professionnelle des femmes mariées chargées de famille', *Population*, No. 3, 1969, pp. 60–83.

44 Viviane Isambert-Jamati, in *Femmes du XXe siècle, Semaine de la pensée marxiste* (Paris: PUF, 1965), p. 12.

45 L. Bernot and R. Blancard, *Nouville, un village français* (Paris: Institut d'Ethnologie, 1953), p. 144.
46 Christiane Rochefort, *Les petits enfants du siècle* (Paris: Grasset, 1961), pp. 122–124.
47 Survey by M. Reuchlin and F. Bacher, cited in *Vivre au féminin*, Cahiers Français, No. 171, 1975, p. 33.
48 Linda Clark, *Schooling the Daughters of Marianne* (Albany, NY: SUNY, 1984), p. 137.
49 The above quotations are from M. 'Ballot' and R. Aveillé, *Education morale et civique* (Paris: Charles-Lavauzelle & Cie, 1952), pp. 85–86.
50 Viviane Isambert-Jamati, 'Le choix du métier', in *Esprit*, 'La femme au travail', No. 5, May 1961, pp. 892–903.
51 A. Michel, and G. Texier, *La condition de la Française d'aujourd'hui* (Paris: Denoël-Gonthier, 1987), p. 145.
52 Françoise Guelaud-Leridon, *Recherches sur la condition féminine* (Paris: PUF, 1967), p. 66.
53 A. Michel and G. Texier, op. cit., p. 147.
54 Ibid.
55 Figures from the Ministry of Education, cited in F. Guelaud-Leridon, *Recherches*, op. cit.
56 Ibid., p. 71.
57 A secretarial role for women could in fact be seen as a perfect 'feminine' job: the wife's supportive and organisational role transposed to the world of work.
58 F. Guelaud-Leridon, *Recherches*, op. cit., p. 75.
59 Ibid., p. 74.
60 Ibid.
61 Ibid., pp. 101–103.
62 As Odile Dhavernas says, this amounted to saying that there was no discrimination except where there was discrimination. See Odile Dhavernas, *Droits des femmes, pouvoir des hommes* (Paris: Le Seuil, 1979), p. 291.
63 Report to the Plan of the 'Groupe emploi féminin,' no title, 1957, p. 3.
64 Ibid., p. 17.
65 UNESCO, 1 December 1962, cited in Françoise Lantier, *Le travail et la formation des femmes en Europe* (Paris: Documentation Française, 1972), p. 8.
66 'Problèmes du travail féminin', *Revue française des affaires sociales*, No. 3, July–September 1969, p. 5 (no author).
67 Ibid., p. 21.
68 Maurice Parodi, op. cit., p. 253.
69 'Problèmes du travail féminin', p. 29.
70 Supplément to 'Vivre au féminin', *Cahiers français*, No. 171, May–August 1975, p. 3 (no author).
71 'Problèmes du travail féminin', p. 43.
72 Françoise Giroud, *La nouvelle vague: portraits de la jeunesse* (Paris: Gallimard, 1958), p. 224.
73 These quotations are all from ibid., pp. 268–286.
74 *Heures claires*, February 1956, pp. 24–25.
75 Françoise Giroud, op. cit., p. 322.

76 *Esprit* 'La femme au travail', No. 5, May 1961, p. 783.
77 Madeleine Colin, *Ce n'est pas d'aujourd'hui* (Paris: Editions Sociales, 1965), p. 35.
78 Cf. Odile Dhavernas, op. cit., pp. 259–261.
79 There were still only 608 crèches in France at the end of the decade. Although half of these were in the Paris region, over 10,000 requests for crèche places in Paris were turned down in 1967. Seventeen departments had only one crèche and another sixteen had none at all. Relatively few women had paid help in the home: few received salaries permitting them to pay for it. Gisèle Charzat, *Les femmes sont-elles des citoyennes?* (Paris: Denoël-Gonthier, 1972), p. 147.
80 Andrée Michel, 'Le statut de la travailleuse française', in *Esprit*, 'La femme au travail', No. 5, May 1961, p. 879.
81 Evelyne Sullerot, *Histoire et sociologie du travail féminin* (Paris: Gonthier, 1968), p. 315.
82 Ibid.
83 A. Michel and G. Texier, op. cit., Vol. 2, p. 157.
84 Geneviève Becane-Pascaud, *Les femmes dans la fonction publique*, Notes et Etudes Documentaires No. 4 056–4 057 (Paris: Documentation Française, 1974), pp. 44–45.
85 These examples (and there are plenty more) are from Odile Dhavernas, op. cit., pp. 293–299.
86 The Fédération de l'Education Nationale (FEN).
87 See A. Michel and G. Texier, op. cit., Vol. 2, pp. 61–65; see also *La question féminine dans les congrès confédéraux et les conférences nationales de la CGT 1948–1982 (Choix de textes)*, Supplement to 'Cahiers de l'institut CGT d'histoire sociale', no date.
88 See Madeleine Colin, op. cit.; see also Margaret Maruani and Marie-Noëlle Thibault, 'Féminisme et syndicalisme de la Libération aux années soixante-dix', in FEN (ed.), *Le féminisme et ses enjeux* (Paris: FEN-Edilig, 1988), pp. 88–113.
89 A minority of the CFTC decided to keep the name and the identity and the CFTC has been recognised as a legitimate trade union organisation.
90 Margaret Maruani, *Le syndicalisme face à l'épreuve du féminisme* (Paris: Syros, 1979), p. 36.
91 Colette Audry in 'Féminisme et syndicalisme de la Libération aux années soixante-dix' in FEN, ed., op. cit., pp. 102–103.
92 See Chapter Six.
93 Jacqueline Sellier, 'Dans toutes les professions des femmes responsables', *Avenirs*, April–June 1967, speaking of a Mme M, Doctor of Law and head of the Centre of Documentation in the Institut Français du Pétrole.
94 'Problèmes du travail féminin', p. 15.
95 *Antoinette*, February 1968.
96 Rose-Marie Lagrave, 'Une émancipation sous tutelle', in Georges Duby and Michelle Perrot (eds) *Histoire des Femmes*, Vol. 5, *Le XXe siècle* (Paris: Plon, 1992), p. 459.
97 Evelyne Sullerot, op. cit., p. 366.

6 WOMEN'S RIGHTS

1 The information about these groups comes from a number of sources: the publications of each group; the report by Martine Muller, Danielle Tucat, Sylvie Van de Casteele-Schweitzer, Dominique Veillon and Danièle Voldman, *Etre feministe en France. Contribution à l'étude des mouvements de femmes, 1944–1967* (Paris: Institut d'Histoire du Temps Présent, 1985); Andrée Michel and Geneviève Texier *La condition de la Française d'aujourd'hui* (Paris: Denoël-Gonthier, 1964); Marie-Thérèse Renard *La participation des femmes à la vie civique* (Paris: Editions Sociales, 1965).

2 Andrée Michel and Geneviève Texier, op. cit., Vol. 2. p. 92.

3 Martine Muller *et al.*, op. cit., p. 10.

4 Marie-Thérèse Renard, op. cit., p. 45. The Catholic women's magazine available to the general public (and in no sense feminist), *L'echo des Françaises*, had over 2 million subscriptions in 1961.

5 During the Third Republic, women's groups associated with the Radical Party and with the Radical-Socialists had been at the forefront of the avant-garde. After the Second World War, the decline of those parties and the rise of the Communist and non-Communist Left which appropriated the progressive ground, the groups seemed more staid. After May '68, they seemed positively out of date. See Chapter Seven.

6 The work of these women is mentioned throughout the book and so will not be given special attention here.

7 *Jeunes femmes*, Bulletin No. 1, 1953, p. 3.

8 Explained to me by Simone Iff and Colette Audry, interviews June 1988 and December 1988.

9 *La femme au XXe siècle*, No. 1, no date, p. 1.

10 After 1968, the MDF and MLF continued to disagree about tactics as well as analysis – the MLF tending to greater degrees of revolt and rejection of French society as it was, the MDF continuing to believe in pressure and parliamentary reform as a means of improving women's lives. This type of conflict was generally expressed in a possibly erroneous reform versus revolution opposition.

11 An article in *Le Monde* in 1967 claims 10,000 members or sympathisers and 7,000 copies of *La femme au XXe siècle* printed. Colette Audry estimated that far fewer women were involved.

12 Yvette Roudy, *A cause d'elles* (Paris: Albin Michel, 1983), p. 84.

13 *La femme au XXe siècle*, No. 1.

14 It should be noted that other people also took this credit – Jacques Derogy and Pierre Simon among them.

15 See Chapter Four, p. 124.

16 Much of the detail that follows comes from: MFPF, *D'une révolte à une lutte. 25 ans d'histoire du planning familial* (Paris: Tierce, 1982).

17 Ibid., p. 84.

18 *Maternité heureuse*, No. 1, 1956.

19 Ibid., p. 5.

20 Quoted by Simone de Beauvoir in her introduction to Weill-Hallé's book *La grand'peur d'aimer* (Paris: Julliard, 1961; republished in 1964 in Colette Audry's series with Denoël-Gonthier).

21 See Odile Dhavernas, *Droits des femmes, pouvoir des hommes* (Paris: Le Seuil, 1979), pp. 98–106.
22 According to François Terré, 'La signification sociologique de la réforme des régimes matrimoniaux', *Année sociologique*, Vol. 16, 1965, pp. 3–83.
23 *Journal officiel*, Débats parlementaires, 1960–1, 1ere session.
24 M. Sammarcelli, on behalf of the Committee on Constitutional Law, in the report dated 7 July 1961.
25 Jean Foyer, Minister of Justice, in 1965 upon presenting the new government project to the Senate. Projet de loi No. 131, brought before the Senate on 17 March 1965, p. 2.
26 'La réforme des régimes matrimoniaux', *Sondages*, No. 1, 1967, pp. 19–41.
27 Reported in *Le Monde* in various articles in June 1965.
28 *Le Monde*, 29 June 1965.
29 Odette Launay in *Journal officiel* Débats parlementaires, séance du 26 June 1965.
30 These examples are from the Débats parlementaires, in the *Journal officiel*, séance du 29 June 1965.
31 Odile Dhavernas, op. cit., p. 104.
32 Jeunes Femmes' involvement with the Association Maternité Heureuse was the first of their public commitments. They first discussed birth control in 1956 and their involvement with the Association began with its foundation. Women from Jeunes Femmes were most visible as *hôtesses* – non-medical women who welcomed clients – when the first family planning centres opened in France in 1961.
33 Proposition de loi No. 1945, 25 May 1956. Cited in Janine Mossuz, 'La régulation des naissances. Les aspects politiques du débat', *Revue française de science politique*, Vol. XVI, No. 5, 1966, p. 924.
34 Ibid., p. 926.
35 According to Derogy, the controversy over birth control was a tactic used by the party leadership in 1956 to divert attention away from the very thorny questions that were creating tensions within the party at that time, notably the PCF's support of government special powers to deal with the Algerian war, and the revelation of Stalin's crimes in Khrushchev's speech of 1956. The debate on birth control was described as light relief in comparison with these other issues. Cf. Michel Garbez, 'La question féminine et le Parti Communiste Français', in Jacques Chevallier *et. al.*, *Discours et idéologie* (Paris: 1980), p. 341.
36 Colette Audry, interview with the author, December 1988.
37 All this information is from the bulletin *Maternité heureuse*, which changed its name in March 1964 to become *Planning familial*.
38 Marcelle Auclair, *Le livre noir de l'avortement* (Paris: Fayard, 1962), p. 239.
39 See her contribution to *Femmes du XXe siècle* (Paris: PUF, 1965), pp. 209–219. See also the contribution by Yvonne Dumont of the PCF's Central Committee, pp. 143–145.
40 Janine Mossuz, op. cit., p. 932.
41 Mariella Righini, 'La loi du silence', *Le Nouvel Observateur*, 10 November 1965.

42 Janine Mossuz, op. cit., p. 933.
43 *Elle*, articles of 23 February 1967 and 2 March 1967.
44 Cited in Lucien Neuwirth, *Que la vie soit* (Paris: Grasset, 1979), p. 68.
45 At a Cabinet meeting on 8 June 1967.
46 Sara Maitland (ed.), *Very Heaven. Looking Back at the 1960s* (London: Virago, 1988), p. 10.
47 Until 1993 Huguette Bouchardeau was a Deputy affiliated to the Socialist Party. She was presidential candidate of the marginal PSU in 1981 on a feminist platform, and was supported by the feminist group in the PS. She was Minister for the Environment in Laurent Fabius's government until the elections of March 1986. Before becoming a politician, Bouchardeau taught law at Lyon University and wrote a number of books, including the influential *Pas d'histoire, les femmes...* (Paris: Syros, 1977).
48 Huguette Bouchardeau, op. cit., p. 183.
49 '*Le deuxième sexe* 25 ans après', interview with John Gerassi in *Society*, January–February 1976, pp. 79–85.
50 Simone de Beauvoir, interview with Alice Schwarzer in *Le Nouvel Observateur*, 14 February 1972, pp. 47–54.
51 *Marie-France*, 13 March 1946. A caricature of the existentialist lifestyle was given in Guillaume Hanoteau's book, *L'Age d'Or de St Germain des Près*, in which the female existentialist is described as having 'straight hair, down to the chest; a few tame white mice in the pocket of her trousers' (Paris: Denoël, 1965, pp. 79–80). Existentialists were said to lounge about all morning in the Café de Flore, eat on credit in a local bistro, return to the Flore for the afternoon, work for half an hour between 6 and 6.30, spend the evening in bars and dance all night in the *Tabou* club.
52 Toril Moi, 'Politics and the intellectual woman: clichés in the reception of Simone de Beauvoir's work', in *Feminist Theory and Simone de Beauvoir* (Oxford: Blackwell, 1990), p. 22.
53 Simone de Beauvoir, *La force des choses 1* (Paris: Gallimard, 1963), p. 259.
54 'La femme révoltée', in *Le Nouvel Observateur*, 14 February 1972.
55 In FEN (ed.), *Le féminisne et ses enjeux* (Paris: FEN-Edilig, 1988), p. 100.
56 Elisabeth Badinter, *Le Nouvel Observateur*, 18–26 April 1986, p. 39.
57 Marie-Jo Dhavernas in *Libération*, 15 April 1986.

7 MAY '68

1 Georges Perec, *Les choses* (Paris: Julliard, 1965), p. 85.
2 Michèle Tournier, 'L'accès des femmes aux études universitaires en Allemagne et en France 1861–1967', Thèse de 3e cycle, Paris, 1972, p. 103.
3 M. Goubert and J.-L. Roucolle, *Population et société françaises 1945–1988* (Paris: Editions Sirey, 1988), p. 104.
4 Michel Winock, *Chronique des années soixante* (Paris: Le Seuil, 1987), p. 101.

5 The best attempts to date are, in my view, Michel Winock, *La fièvre hexagonale* (Paris: Le Seuil, 1986); Henri Weber, *Vingt ans plus tard, que reste-t-il de mai?* (Paris: Le Seuil, 1988). Accounts which take individual trajectories through the 1960s include Hervé Hamon and Patrick Rotman, *Génération* (Paris: Le Seuil, 1988, 1989). Other accounts which I found particularly interesting: Alfred Willener, *The Action-Image of Society* (London: Tavistock, 1970); Daniel Cohn-Bendit, *Obsolete Communism: The Left Wing Alternative* (Harmondsworth: Penguin, 1969); Mouvement du 22 mars, *Ce n'est qu'un début, continuons le combat* (Paris: Maspero, 1968); Mavis Gallant, *Paris Notebooks* (London: Bloomsbury, 1988).

6 François Cornut-Gentille and Philippe Méchet, 'Mai 68 dans la mémoire collective', in SOFRES, *L'état de l'opinion. Clés pour 1989* (Paris: Le Seuil, 1989), p. 53.

7 Ibid., p. 57.

8 Alfred Willener, op. cit., p. xiv.

9 Mavis Gallant, *Paris Notebooks* (London: Bloomsbury, 1988), pp. 1–95.

10 Claire Duchen, *Feminism in France from May '68 to Mitterrand* (London: Routledge & Kegan Paul, 1986), pp. 4–8.

11 François Cornut-Gentille and Philippe Méchet, op. cit., p. 58.

12 Nicole Bernheim, *Le Monde*, 28 June 1968.

13 *Antoinette*, June 1968, p. 26.

14 Nancy Huston and Dominique Meunier, 'Le mai des saints malgré lui (scénario-agenda)', in *Histoires d'elles*, April/May 1978, p. 11.

15 Elisabeth Salvaresi, *Mai en héritage* (Paris: Syros, 1988), p. 114.

16 *Partisans*, special issue: 'Libération des femmes: année zéro' (Paris: Maspero, 1970), pp. 145–146.

17 Françoise Giroud, *Si je mens . . .* (Paris: Stock, 1972), p. 127.

18 *Marie-France*, May 1967.

19 *Elle*, 22 June 1967.

20 Françoise Tournier, 'La vérité médicale sur la frigidité', *Elle*, 21 December 1967.

21 Ibid.

22 See Janine Mossuz-Lavau, *Les lois de l'amour. Les politiques de la sexualité en France, 1950–1990* (Paris: Payot, 1991), pp. 137–185.

23 A group of surrealist artists and writers promoting political subversion. Cf. René Vienet, *Enragés et situationnistes dans le mouvement des occupations* (Paris: Gallimard, 1968); Raoul Vaneigem, *Traité de savoir-vivre à l'usage des jeunes générations* (Paris: Gallimard, 1967).

24 *Les murs ont la parole* (Paris: Tchou éditeur, 1968).

25 See Robert Merle's novel *Derrière la vitre* (Paris: Gallimard, 1970) for a fictionalised account of the student events of May '68 at the University of Nanterre. The relationships described in the book show the full range of men and women students' attitudes towards each other. Also worth noting is the fact that homosexuality was not discussed in May '68 and, just as the MLF was formed as a response to the absence of attention paid to women's needs and desires, so the Front Homosexuel d'Action Révolutionnaire (FHAR, Homosexual Front for Revolutionary Action) was formed by homosexual men and women.

26 Henri Weber, op. cit., p. 180.

27 Alain Schnapp and Pierre Vidal-Naquet, *Journal de la commune étudiante. Textes et documents. Novembre 1967–juin 1968* Paris: (Le Seuil, 1969), p. 57.
28 Ibid., p. 193.
29 Ibid., pp. 604–605.
30 *Partisans*, op. cit., p. 193.
31 Sylvie Coquille, *Naissance du mouvement de libération des femmes en France 1970–1973*, (Mémoire de maîtrise, Université de Paris X, 1982), p. 28.
32 Anne Tristan and Annie de Pisan, *Histoires du MLF* (Paris: Calmann-Lévy, 1977), p. 39.
33 Given that Simone de Beauvoir was considered the 'mother' of contemporary feminism and that May '68 was given as the starting point of feminism in France, it is curious to note the almost complete absence of attention to *Le deuxième sexe* either during or immediately after the May events as feminists in France began to theorise women's oppression. It seems as though Beauvoir's importance to women in France was less through her written theory than through her continued presence on the feminist frontline. She was a prestigious figure who was nonetheless prepared to put herself at risk for women and to commit herself to the women's liberation movement. Beauvoir's name at the top of a petition, her participation in the Bobigny trial of 1972, her public support and her financial support of feminist projects meant that she played a role very different from that of symbol or historical precedent.
34 Françoise Picq, 'The MLF; run for your life', in *French Connections: Voices from the Women's Movement in France*, ed and trans. by Claire Duchen (London: Hutchinson, 1987), p. 24.
35 *Partisans*, op. cit., p. 147.
36 Elisabeth Salvaresi, op. cit., p. 133.
37 Poem published in *Partisans*, special issue 'Libération des femmes: année zéro' (Paris: Maspero, 1970), p. 153.
38 La Griffonne, *Douze ans de lutte au quotidien* (Paris: La Griffonne, 1981).
39 *L'école des parents*, June 1968, pp. 5–15.
40 *Jeunes femmes*, No. 108, July 1968, n.p.
41 Themes announced in July 1968.
42 *Antoinette*, June 1968, p. 32.
43 Ibid.
44 Denise Dubois-Jallais, *La tzarine. Hélène Lazareff et l'aventure de 'Elle'* (Paris: Laffont, 1984), p. 199.
45 *Elle*, spécial, June 1968, p. 6.
46 Ibid., p. 7.
47 Ibid.
48 *Marie-France*, July 1968, p. 80.
49 Ibid., p. 134.
50 Françoise Picq, with Liliane Kandel, Nadja Ringart and Françoise Barret-Ducrocq, 'Quand ce n'était qu'un début... Itinéraires de femmes à Paris', in GEF (ed.), *Crise de société, féminisme et changement* (Paris: Tierce, 1991).

51 Elisabeth Salvaresi, op. cit., p. 135.
52 Anne Tristan and Annie de Pisan, op. cit., p. 34.
53 Christine Delphy, 'Les origines du mouvement de libération des femmes en France,' in *Nouvelles questions féministes*, Nos 16–17–18, 1991, p. 139.
54 The placing of a wreath on the tomb of the unknown soldier dedicated to his wife; the preparation of the special issue of *Partisans* 'Libération des femmes: année zéro'. See Claire Duchen, *Feminism in France*, op. cit.; Cathy Bernheim, *Perturbation, ma soeur* (Paris: Le Seuil, 1983).
55 Christine Delphy, op. cit., p. 139.
56 As Françoise Picq has said, the MLF maintained a 'revolutionary' posture while having in many ways a reformist practice. While they claimed to reject legislative reform, there was no larger mobilising force than the fight for the abortion law in the early 1970s. Françoise Picq, 'The MLF; run for your life', op. cit.
57 From *Le torchon brûle*, No. 0, 1970, p. 3.

Sources and further reading

Primary sources for this study ranged from the publications produced internally by the organisations studied and women's magazines produced for the general market, to sociological research and surveys carried out in the 1950s and 1960s. The daily and weekly press was useful, as were party political newspapers (*Forces nouvelles* and *L'Aube* for the MRP, *Le Populaire* for the SFIO, *L'Humanité* for the PCF, *L'Etincelle* and *Le Rassemblement* for the RPF).

These publications were consulted mainly at the Bibliothèque Nationale's annexe at Versailles and at the Bibliothèque Marguerite Durand in Paris. Complete collections of publications produced by women's organisations were not always available. I also consulted documentation published by political parties held at the Office Universitaire de Recherche Socialiste, at the Institut Charles de Gaulle and at the Archives Nationales (Fonds MRP). The library of the Institut d'Etudes Politiques in Paris has an invaluable press cuttings collection. I consulted the dossiers marked *Femmes/France, Main d'oeuvre féminine/France, Famille/France, Contrôle des naissances/ France, Jeunesse/France*.

WOMEN'S MAGAZINES

Elle, Marie-Claire, Marie-France, Femmes d'aujourd'hui, Bonnes soirées, Nouveau fémina, Intimité du foyer, Véronique. I read the entire collection when feasible. For weekly titles which continued publication throughout the period, I sampled as follows: 1944–9; 1956–8; 1962–8.

Useful for analysing the content and the function of women's magazines:

Ballaster, Rosalind, Beetham, Margaret, Frazer, Elizabeth and Heron, Sandra. *Women's Worlds. Ideology, Femininity and the Woman's Magazine.* Basingstoke: Macmillan, 1991.
Sullerot, Evelyne. *La presse féminine.* Paris: Armand Colin, Editions Kiosque, 1963.
White, Cynthia. *Women's Magazines 1693–1968.* London: Michael Joseph, 1970.
Winship, Janice. *Inside Women's Magazines.* London: Pandora, 1987.

PUBLICATIONS OF SPECIFIC GROUPS

Political parties: *Femmes françaises, Heures claires, Cahiers de l'UFF, Nous les femmes, Femmes républicaines, Le devoir national, La vie heureuse, La revue des électrices, Pour l'information féminine, La revue de la femme socialiste.* Many of these did not have numbers or dates: I have given the most complete information about each that I could find. Most parties produced leaflets and occasional pamphlets on specific themes (the vote, motherhood) at irregular intervals; I read those that were available.

Women's organisations: *Antoinette, Bulletins du CNFF, Le droit des femmes, Femmes chefs d'entreprise, La femme dans la vie sociale, Femmes diplômées, La femme du XXe siècle, Jeunes femmes, La revue des travailleuses, Union professionnelle féminine.*

Mixed organisations: *Bulletin du planning familial, Cahiers du Groupe de Recherches sur les Mouvements Populaires Familiaux, L'école des parents, Maternité heureuse, Pour la vie.*

Other: *Arts ménagers et culinaires, Education ménagère, La maison française, Maison et jardin, Travailleuse familiale.*

Many organisations (JACF, UFCS) also put out occasional pamphlets. Finding copies of them seems to be a matter of chance and, again, I read those that were available.

SCHOLARLY JOURNALS AND OFFICIAL PUBLICATIONS

The following publications were of constant interest: *Année politique, Avenirs, Bulletin mensuel des CAF, Cahiers de l'INED, Collections de l'INSEE (Série M), Etudes et conjonctures, Informations sociales, INSEE notes et documents, Journal officiel, Population, Revue française des affaires sociales, Revue française de sociologie, Sondages.*

BOOKS, CHAPTERS, SPECIAL ISSUES OF JOURNALS, ARTICLES

Women in France

Indispensable reading:

Beauvoir, Simone de. *Le deuxième sexe.* Paris: Gallimard, 1949.

Charzat, Gisèle. *Les femmes sont-elles des citoyennes?* Paris: Denoël-Gonthier, 1972.

Dhavernas, Odile. *Droits des femmes, pouvoir des hommes.* Paris: Le Seuil, 1979.

Guelaud-Leridon, Françoise. *Recherches sur la condition féminine.* Paris: PUF, 1967.

Lehmann, Andrée. *Le rôle de la femme française au milieu du vingtième siècle.* Paris: Ligue Française pour le Droit des Femmes, 1965.

Michel, Andrée and Texier, Geneviève. *La condition de la Française d'aujourd'hui*. Paris: Denoël-Gonthier, 1964.

Muller, Martine, Tucat, Danielle, Van de Casteele-Schweitzer, Sylvie, Veillon, Dominique and Voldman, Danièle. *Etre féministe en France. Contribution à l'étude des mouvements de femmes, 1944–1967*. Paris: Institut d'Histoire du Temps Présent, 1985.

Renard, Marie-Thérèse. *La participation des femmes à la vie civique*. Paris: Editions Sociales, 1965.

Other relevant works:

Allauzen, Marie. *La paysanne française aujourd'hui*. Paris: Gonthier, 1967.

Benoît, Nicole, Morin, Edgar and Paillard, Bernard. *La femme majeure*. Paris: Club de l'Obs/Editions du Seuil, 1973.

Bouchardeau, Huguette. *Pas d'histoire, les femmes...* Paris: Syros, 1977.

Chombart de Lauwe, Paul-Henri and Marie-Jo. *La femme dans la société*. Paris: CNRS, 1963.

Duby, Georges and Perrot, Michelle (eds). *Histoire des femmes*, Vol. 5 *Le XXe siècle'*. Paris: Plon, 1992.

Femmes du XXe siècle. Semaine de la pensée marxiste. Paris: PUF, 1965.

Grégoire, Ménie. *Le métier de femme*. Paris: Plon, 1965.

Laubier, Claire. *The Condition of Women in France. 1945 to the Present. A Documentary Anthology*. London: Routledge, 1990.

Montreynaud, Florence. *Le 20e siècle des femmes*. Paris: Nathan, 1992.

Roudy, Yvette and Pechadre, Lydie. *La réussite de la femme*. Paris: CEPC, 1970.

Sartin, Pierrette. *La femme libérée*. Paris: Stock, 1968.

Sullerot, Evelyne. *La vie des femmes*. Paris: Gonthier, 1965.

Victor, Eliane. *Les femmes... aussi*. Paris: Mercure de France, 1973.

The postwar period in France

Fourastié, Jean. *Les trente glorieuses ou la révolution invisible de 1946 à 1975*. Paris: Fayard, 1979.

Goubert, Michel and Roucolle, Jean-Louis. *Population et société françaises depuis 1945*. Paris: Sirey, 1992.

Hanley, David, Kerr, Pat and Waites, Neville. *Contemporary France*. London: Routledge & Kegan Paul, 1984.

Mendras, Henri. *La seconde révolution française, 1965–1984*. Paris: Gallimard, 1988.

Parodi, Maurice. *L'économie et la société française depuis 1945*. Paris: Armand Colin, 1981.

Vincent, Gérard. *Les Français 1945–1975. Chronologie et structure d'une société*. Paris: Masson, 1977.

Wright, Vincent. *The government and politics of France*. London: Unwin Hyman, 1989.

The Liberation

Amouroux, Henri. *La grande histoire des Français après l'Occupation*, Vol. 9 *Le règlement de comptes*. Paris: Laffont, 1991.

Brive, Marie-France. 'L'image des femmes à la Libération' in Rolande Trempé (ed.) *La Libération du Midi de la France*. Toulouse: Eché Editeur, 1986.

Brossat, Alain. *Les Tondues*. Levallois-Perret; Editions Manya, 1993.

Cahiers de l'IHTP. No. 5, June 1987. 'Images, discours et enjeux de la reconstruction des villes françaises après 1945'.

Diamond, Hanna. 'Women's experiences during and after World War Two in the Toulouse area 1939–1948. Choices and constraints.' D.Phil thesis, University of Sussex, 1992.

Les femmes dans la Résistance. Actes du colloque. Paris: Editions du Rocher, 1976.

Foulon, Charles-Louis. *Le pouvoir en province à la Libération*. Paris: FNSP, 1975.

Higonnet, M. and Higonnet, P. 'The double helix', in Margaret Randolph Higonnet, Jane Jenson, Sonya Michel, and Margaret Collins Weitz (eds). *Behind the Lines. Gender and the Two World Wars*. Newhaven: Yale University Press, 1987.

Jenson, Jane. 'The Liberation and new rights for women', in Margaret Randolph Higonnet *et al.* (eds). *Behind the Lines. Gender and the Two World Wars*. Newhaven: Yale University Press, 1987.

Kupferman, Fred. *Les premiers beaux jours*. Paris: Calmann-Lévy, 1985.

Lewin, Christophe. *Le retour des prisonniers de guerre français*. Paris: Publications de la Sorbonne, 1986.

La Libération de la France (colloque). Paris: CNRS, 1976.

Madjarian, Grégoire. *Conflits, pouvoir et société à la Libération*. Paris: UGE, 1980.

Montassier, Valérie-Anne. *Les années d'après-guerre*. Paris: Fayard, 1980.

Pickles, Dorothy. *The First Years of the Fourth Republic*. London: Royal Institute of International Affairs, 1953.

Ruffin, Raymond. *La vie des Français au jour le jour: de la Libération à la Victoire*. Paris: Presses de la Cité, 1986.

Wormser-Migot, Olga. *Le retour des déportés*. Brussels: Editions Complexe, 1985.

Wright, G. *The Reshaping of French Democracy*. New York: Reynal & Hitchcock, 1948.

Politics

Barral, Pierre, Leleu, Claude and Goguel, François. 'Pour qui votent les femmes', in François Goguel (ed.). *Nouvelles études de sociologie électorale*. Paris: FNSP, 1954.

Dogan, Mattei and Narbonne, Jacques. *Les Françaises face à la politique*. Paris: Armand Colin, 1955.

Duverger, Maurice. *La participation des femmes à la vie politique*. Paris: UNESCO, 1955.

Duverger, Maurice (ed.). *Partis politiques et classes sociales*. Paris: Armand Colin, 1955.

Garbez, Michel. 'La question féminine et le Parti Communiste Français', in Chevallier, Jacques (ed.). *Discours et idéologie*. Paris: PUF, 1980.

Michel, Andrée. 'Les Françaises et la politique', in *Les temps modernes*, April 1965.

Pascal, Jean. *Les femmes députés de 1945 à 1988*. Published by the author, 1990.

Rousseau, Renée. *Les femmes rouges. Chronique des années Vermeersch*. Paris: Albin Michel, 1983.

Reynolds, Siân. 'Marianne's citizens? Women, the Republic and universal suffrage in France' in Siân Reynolds (ed.). *Women, the State and Revolution*. Brighton: Wheatsheaf, 1986.

Sineau, Mariette. 'Gender and the French electorate', in Mary Katzenstein and Hage Skeie (eds). *Going Public. National Histories of Women's Enfranchisement and Women's Participation within State Institutions*. Oslo: Institute for Social Research, 1990, pp. 80–103.

Williams, Philip. *Crisis and Compromise*. London: Longman, 1964.

Williams, Philip. *The French Parliament 1958–1967*. London: Allen & Unwin, 1968.

Family and the home

Bernège, Paulette. *De la méthode ménagère*. No publisher, 1928.

Brémond, Janine and Salort, Marie-Martine. *La famille en question*. Paris: Hatier, 1986.

Ceccaldi, Dominique. *Politique française de la famille*. Paris: Privat, 1957.

Chombart de Lauwe, Paul-Henri (ed.). *La vie quotidienne des familles ouvrières*. Paris: CNRS, 1956.

Collange, Christiane. *Madame et le management*. Paris: Tchou, 1969.

Compain, Mme E. *La science de la maison*. Paris: Fouches, 1959.

Données statistiques sur l'évolution de l'équipement des ménages jusqu'à la fin de l'année 1968. Paris: INSEE, 1969.

Données statistiques sur les familles. Paris: INSEE, 1975.

L'enseignement ménager français face au monde en évolution. Paris: Ministère de l'Education Nationale, 1964.

Esprit: 'Nos maisons et nos villes'. 1953.

Foulon-Lefranc, Mme. *La femme au foyer*. Paris: Editions de l'école, 1953.

Galant, Henri. *Histoire politique de la sécurité sociale française*. Paris: FNSP, 1955.

Gros, Brigitte. *Les Paradisiennes*. Paris: Laffont, 1973.

Huet, Maryse. *Les femmes dans les grands ensembles*. Paris: CNRS, 1971.

Kaës, R. *Vivre dans les grands ensembles*. Paris: Editions Ouvrières, 1963.

Laroque, Pierre. *La politique familiale en France depuis 1945*. Paris: Documentation Française, 1986.

Mathiot, Ginette and Lamaze, Nicole de. *Manuel d'éducation ménagère*. Paris: ESE/Istria, 1959.

Michel, Andrée. *Statut professionnel féminin et structure du couple français urbain*. Paris: CNRS, 1972.

Peterson, W. *The Welfare State in France*. Nebraska: University of Nebraska Press, 1960.

Pitrou, Agnès. *La famille dans la vie de tous les jours*. Paris: Privat, 1972.

Prost, Antoine. 'La politique familiale de 1938 à 1984', *Le mouvement social*, No. 129, 1984.

Questiaux, Nicole and Fournier, Jacques. 'France', in S. B. Kammerman and A. J. Kahn (eds). *Family Policy: Government and Families in Fourteen Countries*. New York: Columbia University Press, 1978.

Renouveau des idées sur la famille (Cahier de l'INED 18). Paris: PUF, 1953.

Motherhood and family planning

Auclair, Marcelle. *Le livre noir de l'avortement*. Paris: Fayard, 1962.

Derogy, Jacques. *Des enfants malgré nous*. Paris: Editions de Minuit, 1956.

Dumas, André. *Le contrôle des naissances. Opinions protestantes*. Paris: Les Bergers et les Mages, 1965.

Iff, Simone. *Demain, la société sexualisée. Le combat du MFPF*. Paris: Calmann-Lévy, 1975.

Knibiehler, Y. and Fouquet, C. *L'histoire des mères du moyen age à nos jours*. Paris: Montalba, 1977.

Lambert, P. and M. *3000 foyers parlent*. Paris: Editions Ouvrières, 1966.

Leclercq, J. *Le contrôle des naissances et le malaise conjugal*. Brussels: Editions Select, 1946.

Mossuz-Lavau, Janine. *Les lois de l'amour. Les politiques de la sexualité en France, 1950–1990*. Paris: Payot, 1991.

MFPF. *Planning familial: colloque à Royaumont, 1963*. Paris: Maloine, 1965.

MFPF. *D'une révolte à une lutte: 25 ans du planning familial*. Paris: Tierce, 1982.

Pernoud, Laurence. *J'élève mon enfant*. Paris: Pierre Horay, 1965.

Weill-Hallé, Marie-Andrée Lagroua. *La grand'peur d'aimer*. Paris: Julliard, 1961.

Weill-Hallé, Marie-Andrée Lagroua. *Les Français et la contraception*. Paris: Maloine, 1967.

Employment

Becane-Pascaud, Geneviève. *Les femmes dans la fonction publique*. Notes et Etudes Documentaires No. 4 056–4 057. Paris: Documentation Française, 1974.

Cézard, Michel. 'Les cadres et leurs diplômes', *Economie et statistiques*, No. 42, February 1973.

Colin, Madeleine. *Ce n'est pas d'aujourd'hui*. Paris: Editions Sociales, 1965.

CGT. *La question féminine dans les congrès confédéraux et les conférences nationales de la CGT: choix de textes*. Institut CGT, no date.

Daric, J. *L'activité professionnelle des femmes en France*. (Cahiers de l'INED No. 5). Paris: PUF, 1947.

Droulers, M.-F. *Le travail à temps partiel*. Valenciennes: published by the author, 1972.

Esprit. 'La femme au travail', May 1961.

Guelaud-Leridon, Françoise. *Le travail des femmes* (Cahiers de l'INED No. 42). Paris: PUF, 1964.

Guilbert, Madeleine and Isambert-Jamati, Viviane. 'La répartition par sexe', in G. Friedmann, and P. Naville (eds). *Traité de sociologie du travail*. Paris: Armand Colin, 1962.

Guilbert, Madeleine. *Les fonctions des femmes dans l'industrie*. The Hague: Mouton, 1966.

Guilbert, Madeleine and Colin, Madeleine. 'Les femmes actives en France. Bilan, 1978', in *La condition féminine*. Ouvrage collectif sous la direction du CERM. Paris: Editions Sociales, 1978.

Lantier, Françoise. *Le travail et la formation des femmes en Europe*. Paris: Documentation Française, 1972.

Laot, Jeanette. *Stratégie pour les femmes*. Paris: Stock, 1977.

Lazard, Françoise. *Le travail de la femme est-il un progrès? Est-il nuisible à l'enfant?* Paris: Cahiers du CERM, 1963.

Maruani, Margaret. *Le syndicalisme face à l'épreuve du féminisme*. Paris: Syros, 1979.

Simon, Catherine. 'Syndicalisme au féminin', in *Questions clefs*. Paris: EDI, 1981.

Sullerot, Evelyne. *Histoire et sociologie du travail féminin*. Paris: Gonthier, 1968.

Thibault, Marie-Noëlle and Maruani, Margaret. 'Féminisme et syndicalisme de la Libération aux années soixante-dix', in FEN (ed.). *Le féminisme et ses enjeux. Vingt-sept femmes parlent*. Paris: FEN-Edilig, 1988.

Thuillier, Guy. *Les femmes dans l'administration depuis 1900*. Paris: PUF, 1988.

May '68 and feminism

Bernheim, Cathy. *Perturbation ma soeur*. Paris: Le Seuil, 1983.

Cohn-Bendit, Daniel. *Obsolete Communism: the Left-wing Alternative*. Harmondsworth: Penguin, 1969.

Coquille, Sylvie. *Naissance du mouvement de libération des femmes en France. 1970–1973*. Mémoire de maîtrise, Université de Paris X, no date.

Delphy, Christine. 'Les origines du mouvement de libération des femmes en France', *Nouvelles questions féministes*, Nos 16–17–18, 1991.

Duchen, Claire. *Feminism in France from May '68 to Mitterrand*. London: Routledge & Kegan Paul, 1986.

Hamon, Hervé and Rotman, Patrick. *Génération*, 2 vols. Paris: Le Seuil, 1988, 1989.

Partisans, 'Libération des femmes: année zéro'. Paris: Maspero, 1970.

Picq, Françoise. 'Sauve qui peut, le MLF', *La revue d'en face*, No. 11, 1981.

Picq, Françoise with Kandel, Liliane, Ringart, Nadja and Barret-Ducrocq, Françoise. 'Quand ce n'était qu'un début. Itinéraires de femmes à Paris' in GEF (ed.). *Crise de société, féminisme et changement*. Paris: Tierce, 1991.

Picq, Françoise. *Libération des femmes: les années-mouvement*. Paris: Le Seuil, 1993.

Salvaresi, Elisabeth. *Mai en héritage*. Paris: Syros, 1988.

Schnapp, Alain and Vidal-Naquet, Pierre. *Journal de la commune étudiante. Textes et documents, novembre 1967–juin 1968*. Paris: Le Seuil, 1969.

Tristan, Anne and Pisan, Annie de. *Histoires du MLF*. Paris: Calmann-Lévy, 1977.

Weber, Henri. *Vingt ans après que reste-t-il de mai?* Paris: Le Seuil, 1988.

Memoirs, essays and novels

d'Astier, Emmanuel. *De la chute à la Libération de Paris*. Paris: Gallimard, 1965.

Beauvoir, Simone de. *La force des choses*. 2 vols. Paris: Gallimard, 1963.

Duras, Marguerite. *La douleur*. Paris: P.O.L., 1985.

Flanner, Janet. *Paris Journal 1945–1965*. London: Victor Gollancz, 1966.

Francis, Claude and Gonthier, Fernand. *Les écrits de Simone de Beauvoir*. Paris: Gallimard, 1976.

Gallant, Mavis. *Paris Notebooks*. London: Bloomsbury, 1988 (re-edition).

Giroud, Françoise. *Si je mens*. Paris: Stock, 1972.

Grégoire, Ménie. *Telle que je suis*. Paris: Laffont, 1976.

Groult, Benoîte. *Les trois-quarts du temps*. Paris: Grasset, 1983.

Groult, Benoîte and Flora. *Journal à quatre mains*. Paris: Denoël, 1962.

Merle, Robert. *Derrière la vitre*. Paris: Gallimard, 1970.

Neuwirth, Lucien. *Que la vie soit*. Paris: Grasset, 1979.

Perec, Georges. *Les choses*. Paris: Julliard, 1965.

Peyre, Christiane. *Une société anonyme*. Paris: Julliard, 1962.

Rochefort, Christiane. *Les petits enfants du siècle*. Paris: Grasset, 1961.

Rochefort, Christiane. *Les stances à Sophie*. Paris: Grasset, 1963.

Roudy, Yvette. *A cause d'elles*. Paris: Albin Michel, 1983.

Simon, Pierre. *De la vie avant toute chose*. Paris: Mazarine, 1979.

Miscellaneous

Bouvet, L. 'JAC et JACF dans l'Orne du début des années 1950 au début des années 1960'. Thèse de 3e cycle, Institut d'Etudes Politiques, Paris, 1986.

Durupt, M.-J. 'Les mouvements d'action catholique, facteur d'évolution du milieu rural.' Thèse de 3e cycle, Institut d'Etudes Politiques, Paris, 1963.

Giroud, Françoise. *La nouvelle vague. Portraits de jeunesse*. Paris: Gallimard, 1958.

Heron, Liz (ed.) *Truth, Dare or Promise. Girls Growing up in the Fifties*. London: Virago, 1985.

Institut Français de l'Opinion Publique. *La Française et l'amour*. Paris: Laffont, 1960.

Lesselier, C. 'Aspects de l'expérience lesbienne en France 1930–1968.' Paris: Mémoire de maîtrise, 1987.

Martin, M. 'Femmes et société: le travail ménager.' Thèse de 3e cycle, Paris VII, 1984.

Maitland, Sara (ed.). *Very Heaven. Looking Back at the 1960s*. London: Virago, 1988.

Morin, Edgar. *L'esprit du temps*. Paris: Grasset, 1962.

Texier, Geneviève. 'Les enquêtes sociologiques servent-elles à mystifier les femmes?', *Les temps modernes*, No. 235, 1965.

Tournier, M. 'L'accès des femmes aux études universitaires en France et en Allemagne 1861–1967.' Thèse de 3e cycle, Paris X, 1972.

Wilson, Elizabeth. *Only Halfway to Paradise. Women in Postwar Britain. 1945–1968*. London: Tavistock, 1980.

Winock, Michel. *Chronique des années soixante*. Paris: Le Seuil, 1987.

Index